Mass Informed Consent

Mass Informed Consent

Evidence on Upgrading Democracy with Polls and New Media

Adam F. Simon

ROWMAN & LITTLEFIELD PUBLISHERS, INC.
Lanham • New York • Toronto • Plymouth, UK

Published by Rowman & Littlefield Publishers, Inc.
A wholly owned subsidary of The Rowman & Littlefield Publishing Group, Inc.
4501 Forbes Boulevard, Suite 200, Lanham, Maryland 20706
http://www.rowmanlittlefield.com

Estover Road, Plymouth PL6 7PY, United Kingdom

British Library Cataloguing in Publication Information Available

Library of Congress Cataloging-in-Publication Data

Simon, Adam F., 1965–
  Mass informed consent : evidence on upgrading democracy with polls and new media /
Adam F. Simon.
    p. cm.
  Includes bibliographical references and index.
  ISBN 978-0-7425-6255-4 (cloth : alk. paper) — ISBN 978-1-4422-0934-3 (electronic)
  1. Public opinion—United States.   2. Public opinion polls—United
States.   3. Mass media and public opinion—United States.   4. Democracy—
United States.   5. United States—Politics and government—2001–2009—Public
opinion.   6. United States—Politics and government—2009—Public opinion.   I. Title.
  HN90.P8S53 2011
    303.3'80973—dc22   2010042442

Printed in the United States of America

Table of Contents

Chapter 1

Who Deserves the Blame for Invading Iraq (and Other Mistakes)?

This book concerns democracy and public education, focusing on the role polls and public opinion play in politics. At the outset, let me say that I think these four concepts go together; we will discuss some observers who disagree. I also will not hide my faith in polls and the public they represent. This book represents my best effort to demonstrate that sample surveys are the finest democratic technology yet devised (though I concede that polling is imperfect and can be abused). Too many citizens, as well as some politicians and members of the media, fundamentally misunderstand polling—a lack of familiarity that leads them to belittle polling's value. In truth, using polls to channel mass informed consent—my label for the conditions surrounding valid poll results—is the best step we can take to address our country's problems. In the following pages, we will detail polling in its entirety to understand and appreciate its value. In addition, we will learn something about how to gather and analyze public opinion data. This evidence will allow us to address criticisms related to the public's competence (or lack thereof) and the connection between poll results and the news.

To see the import of polling and the reason for this book, consider how democracy's central questions nearly always concern the relationship between the public and government action. Take these three:

- Why do people support misguided wars or vote against their own interests?
- Should legislators obey citizens reflexively, or use their own judgment?
- How can presidents and ordinary citizens alike make a difference in politics?

All of these items bring in public opinion: when anyone votes for a candidate or supports a policy, they express public opinion; legislators must know public opinion—specifically, what the public wants—before they can decide whether to agree; democratic change demands transforming public opinion.

The next chapter argues that sample surveys (often called scientific surveys), the proper name for polls, supply the best measure of public opinion. Before going into these details, we need to motivate ourselves by discussing the importance of investigating what lay behind poll results. Look at how the answers to our three democratic questions depend on the grade we give the public's "ability." One could say, for instance, that people support misguided wars because people are stupid. Likewise, a good answer to the second question could be that representatives ought to listen whenever the public's wants are reasonable. Finally, proposing that individuals should respond to good arguments seems close to the mark. In short, a lesser-known twin shadows our faith in democracy—namely, our perception of the public's competence. The most democratic among us believe wholeheartedly in the public's wisdom and intelligence, while those who doubt the common folk's good judgment lean toward restricting self-governance.

Beliefs like our faith in democracy survive in some realm beyond proof, meaning that they are not firmly bound to the evidence we collect. Worse, the amazing complexity of humans' political activities can produce some evidence that contradicts the rest. For these reasons, we (read: every citizen), should learn a bit about the science of public opinion research—how to systematically collect and analyze observations regarding sample surveys. My brief lessons may not make us "experts," but they are a good start. We will cover enough to grasp the fundamentals of American political behavior. In addition, many of this book's chapters contain a complete scientific study that is designed to confirm the chapter's central point. Some may find the technical aspects difficult; but I promise to do my best to make them clear. I hope these studies will increase your faith in fellow citizens and prompt you to embark on a deeper analysis of other poll results you encounter. This scientific background will also help you assess future claims made about the public.

The ultimate goal of this book is to improve democracy and our political system. Learning about polling and social science will help us tackle some tough questions. Take one of the toughest from the chapter's title: who should we blame when the government makes a mistake? The right answer is deceptively simple. According to democracy's definition, we deserve the blame. Some might believe our government is not democratic—the next section discusses democracy. Conspiracy theorists, for example, believe powerful groups collude to control the government and cause fiascos. Others master the obvious and blame presidents; if going to war was a mistake, for instance, it is the president's fault. This view, of course, neglects the fact that we elect the president. What's more, if we knew what they were doing, we condoned it; if we didn't, we were ignorant. Possibly, presidents exaggerate to win our support. This sounds better, but that answer is incomplete. If so, then we should add the media and other politicians to the list of culprits, if only because they failed to contest his messages. Oddly enough, reflection leads me to side with the so-called nuts—no that I believe in aliens or some unseen boss; rather, I mean that government's mistakes implicate many wrongdoers: the president, the media, special interests . . . and us.

Instead of a conspiracy, however, we should think of this constellation of actors as our political system. Thus, I believe our political system produces mistakes accompanied by perceptions of widespread public support. You probably don't find this statement very perceptive; indeed, it is merely a point to start. We need to dig deeply into this system to produce a satisfying answer—the kind of investigation that characterizes political science. On the other hand, we cannot cover everything. We shall leave Congress, the judiciary, and the rest of our institutions for others to explore, mentioning them only as needed. We are going to concentrate on public opinion, as you now know, and on its relationship to the information the public receives. This scope offers a very rough guess (read: hypotheses): blame for mistakes lies with the public, with the public's education, with neither, or with both. Moreover, if we fault the education, we can look into its provision and how it can be fixed; thus, all we need to do is sort out these four possibilities!

THE PROTAGONISTS:
WALTER LIPPMANN AND JOHN DEWEY

Our investigation of democracy and public education begins in 1922—long before Iraq or Afghanistan were on Americans' radar. At that time, everyone's concern also centered on the public's support for a tragic war. The question then (as now) was how we blundered into war, and, more important, what changes would avoid similar mistakes. Walter Lippmann and John Dewey provide the most relevant answers to these questions. Besides being smart, they—conveniently enough—ably personify the two sides in the ongoing dispute over democracy's potential. Though hardly anyone remembers their stances, they were once celebrities. Each was a public intellectual, a thinker who wrote about deep issues for general audiences. It may surprise you to hear that their work was popular. We can think of them as mixing Stephen

Hawking with Oprah. More relevantly, they held diametrically opposed views about the public and democracy.

Lippmann essentially claims (his ideas live, if he does not) that distractions prevent citizens from getting the information they need to make good decisions. He also suggests that their lack of sophistication (read: stupidity), keeps citizens from using whatever good information they get properly. Dewey responds that if we could educate people sufficiently, they would do fine. Thus, Lippmann recommends curtailing democracy by turning governance over to experts, even as Dewey proposes more democracy, by increasing citizens' role in governance. Diehard populists will want to dismiss Lippmann, possibly thinking that he was a closeted fascist. Likewise, the elitists among us (and everyone has this tendency) will want to ignore Dewey; they could argue that Dewey's vision sounds like a fairy tale. I trust you to not dismiss either view so quickly.

These arguments, to build some more motivation, list the obstacles that anyone who hopes to reform democracy faces. At the same time, their debate occurred just before the invention of sample surveys. Thus, while they share our conceptions of democracy and public opinion, not to mention our awareness of key players like the news media and interest groups, they do not let polling's minutiae (read: the little things that can go wrong), bog them down, unlike some polling critics today. The best reason for paying attention to Lippmann and Dewey is that many pundits repeat their points when talking about current events. This repetition would seem incredible, except it has been going on for a long time. The ancient Greeks, which any serious political book must mention, disagreed over the average person's ability. Plato, perhaps the first political philosopher, snobbishly advocates elitism just like Lippmann. A rigorously nurtured set of guardians rule the Republic, his ideal state. On the other hand, Aristotle's *Politics* offers a view any populist could adopt:

> A man may not be able to make a poem, but he can tell when a poem pleases him. He may not be able to make a house, but he can tell when the roof leaks. He may not be able to cook, but he can tell whether he likes what is prepared for him.

Were he alive today, Aristotle could easily substitute any issue, saying that citizens "may not know all the details but know what should be done" to express democratic faith.

Scanning Amazon's current offerings uncovers elitists who still want to rid us of democracy. Brian Caplan, for instance, proposes that citizens do not know enough about economics; in *The Myth of the Rational Voter* he argues that we should revere economists much like Plato's guardians. Elitist undercurrents also run through works that claim to deconstruct political messages in order to explain how to win public support. The linguistics professor George Lakoff—*Moral Politics*—asserts that the right language (he calls it metaphor) makes political appeals successful. Similarly, psychologist Drew Westen's *The Political Brain* concludes that pressing the right emotional button generates political support. Though these authors claim to be democrats, their works actually supply recipes for manipulation (to foreshadow chapter 6).

Leaving aside the fact that our investigation will suggest that these "experts" are wrong, I have little sympathy for works that glorify political tricks, for such techniques do not enhance democracy. Manipulation transfers control away from citizens. Furthermore, political questions rarely have right and wrong answers; rather, justice turns on the public's informed consent. Nevertheless, we should be aware of elitism's attractiveness. It's natural—some say psychologically healthy—for us to think of ourselves better than average, as elite. In Garrison Keillor's Lake Wobegon, "all the women are strong, all the men are good-looking, and all the children are above average." Simple mathematics, of course, uncovers his humor, showing that not everyone can be above the average. Our inclination to think we are special often hides elitist implications. For example, if you are not an economist, Caplan expects you to maintain a respectful silence in public debate.

I do, however, sympathize with Lippmann; he does his best to solve a serious problem, and one that he helped create. Lippmann was 33 in 1922, the year he published *Public Opinion*, the book that lays out his views on citizens and governance. *Public Opinion* was so well received that a sequel, *The Phantom Public*, appeared a few years later. Everyone recognized that Lippmann was a great journalist, the Anderson Cooper of his day. Before becoming a journalist, however, Lippmann advised Woodrow Wilson's victorious presidential campaigns. Critically, this job led him to aid in drafting Wilson's Fourteen Points, which spelled out Wilson's argument for the United States' entry into World War I. Dewey, in contrast, never worked within the political system. And he was also older: he wrote *The Public and its Problems*, his response to Lippmann, in 1925, aged 63. A phenomenal academic, Dewey contributed ideas to philosophy, psychology, and education that we still use.

WORLD WAR I, IRAQ, AND PUBLIC COMPETENCE

Though they did no fighting, Lippmann and Dewey witnessed World War I's horror. Many of us are unacquainted with this mess. To us, it was the war preceding the better-known World War II. To Lippmann and Dewey, it was the Great War—the War to End all Wars—and it was bad. Fighting was mostly a bloody stalemate. Soldiers faced each other from trenches filled with mud, poison gas, and corpses. Every so often, officers ordered them to charge into "no man's land"—and enemy machine-gun fire. They died in shocking numbers. Canadian soldier John McCrae wrote: "in Flanders fields the poppies blow / between the crosses row on row," in his poem describing just one of the cemeteries filled with men killed in their youth.

Authors try to convey war's horror in many ways. Anyone who has read Hemingway, a World War I ambulance driver, or the rest of the heart-wrenching World War I literature finds the carnage repulsive. Still, I want to introduce statistics. Consider that this literature also contains glamorous works. If you have time, watch the movie *Wings*, 1929's Best Picture, or *The Blue Max*—both about gallant fighter pilots. And *Peanuts* fans know that Snoopy fights the Red Baron—a World War I German ace pilot. Cold and dry statistics, in contrast, give us a concrete comparison that affirms the shock and belies the glamour.

One statistic emphasizes the Great War's ferocity. According to Wikipedia, World War II caused 407,300 military deaths, compared to World War I's 116,708. However, although more Americans died in World War II, it lasted longer. The United States' combat in World War II lasted roughly four years, 1941 to 1945; its combat in World War I lasted just six months: 1,460 and 180 days, respectively. Division tells how many soldiers died on an average day. That number (read: stat) for World War II is 279. For World War I, it is 648—over twice as much. It may seem callous to subject these unfortunate deaths to analysis, but this simple comparison brings home the relative impact of each war. It underscores the carnage of the so-called Great War.

After the war, hindsight made the catastrophic losses more appalling. Lippmann, Dewey, and almost every other serious observer concluded that America's involvement in the struggle was a mistake. Lippmann assisted in drafting the Fourteen Points—the war aims Woodrow Wilson set out in 1917. These goals sound entirely reasonable to our ears: open covenants of peace, freedom of navigation and the like (you can google the rest). Wilson also wanted to be merciful with Germany. Though we lack good evidence—sample surveys had yet to be invented—Americans embraced these goals. The public cheered as troops paraded on to the ships that took them to Europe, for instance. Yet, Britain and France, America's allies, forced a harsh peace on Germany and ignored the substance of Wilson's goals. Many suspect that punishment laid the ground for World War II.

The horror prompted numerous inquires—people demanded to know how America got itself involved in the tragedy. None of the investigators, including Lippmann and Dewey, failed to acknowledge the decisive role of propaganda. Propaganda (again, see chapter 6) is a kind of persuasion—communicative attempts to get people to think or do what they otherwise would not. Many sources testify to British propaganda's effectiveness at mobilizing citizens' support—and bringing the United States into conflict. In 1914, Britain's first hostile act was to cut transatlantic cables, impairing German communication with the United States. From then on, "the British worked diligently to involve the United States as an active belligerent on its side while Germany sought vainly to maintain a precarious American neutrality," according to Stewart Ross in *Propaganda for War* (2). Charles Beard's *The Rise of American Civilization* recounts Britain's message:

> The Germans had hacked their way through Belgium, a small and helpless country whose neutrality had been guaranteed by all the powers in their fond desire to safeguard the rights of little countries; and in cutting their way through this defenseless kingdom, the Germans had committed shocking deeds, crimes against humanity.... To crown their infamy, so ran the Entente articles of faith, the Germans did what no other Christian people would do, namely, employ the submarine, a new instrument of warfare, sending cargo, crew, and passengers alike to the bottom of the sea. (616)

Lippmann and Dewey, among others, saw this propagandistic message as a total success.

The word *propaganda* fits this campaign well. While everyone heard the British message, few citizens heard the German response, Ross concludes (2):

> This struggle was unequal, for Americans were inextricably bound to their former mother country by both language and unspoken tradition. Moreover, this nation's print media overwhelmingly sided with England and her allies.

Postwar investigations confirmed that the atrocity stories were fabrications, and exposed secret agreements allying Belgium and France. The passenger liner sinkings that dominated the news, and that served as Wilson's primary war rationale, may have been justified; Britain had blockaded Germany, causing widespread starvation, even as a neutral United States traded in contraband materials with the Entente powers, including ammunition carried by the *Lusitania* (for details, see James Hayward's *Myths and Legends of the First World War*). Britain stopped attempts to ship food to Germany. In short, the claim that the British, with the Wilson administration's acquiescence, tricked us into going to war is only a slight exaggeration.

By this point, I expect we see the parallels between 1917's First World War and 2003's Iraq. First, the ideas that brought us into conflict originated with the president. Second, propaganda led to public support for the war. In Iraq, Saddam Hussein, terrorism, and weapons of mass destruction replaced the Kaiser, atrocities, and sunken ships. Third, costly fighting failed to bring about the president's stated goal. In sum, both episodes feature the president relying on propaganda to mobilize support for a fiasco (Thomas Ricks's title). It would be nice if these were the only wars caused by presidential fiat and propaganda, but my review of American history suggests at least five more conflicts adhere to this pattern—including the Spanish American War and the Viet Nam conflict, which we will detail later on in this book.

LIPPMANN'S RECOMMENDATION AND DEWEY'S RESPONSE

Lippmann sought to explain what happened in the Great War, and then to use this story as a cautionary tale to support his advice that we curtail democracy. He starts by questioning why Britain's propaganda worked so well. His answer comes in the form of a theory of citizens' political choices. As we shall discover, his answer is a theory because it specifies how certain factors, known as variables, come together to cause an outcome. You already know of his theory's foundational concept, the idea of a stereotype. *Public Opinion* introduces this term because humans "never see, touch, smell, hear or remember" vast portions of the world, so they rely on "picture inside [their] heads" to guide abstract judgments (18). Lippmann observes that citizens depend on the news media for knowledge about the world; as a journalist, however, he did not think much of the media. In his words, the media fails to "bring to light hidden facts, to set them into relation with each other and make a picture of reality on which men can act"; he says the media "signalizes" events, presenting them in a haphazard and episodic fashion (358). Lippmann thinks that the media deserves the blame for those of citizens' pictures that offer unreliable guides to reality.

Lippmann singles out oversimplification as the main contributor to the discrepancy between reality and citizens' mental representations. He gives the example of John Bull, "who is jovial and fat, not too clever, but well able to take care of himself," as a stereotype that represents the whole of the people and history of England (160). Stereotypes explain Britain's propaganda success, as well. The public was told of Belgium, an innocent country invaded by evil "Huns" who attacked nuns and killed babies. These same Huns sneaked beneath the ocean in fiendish submarines that blew up passenger liners, killing innocent men, women, and children. Hence, Germany morphs into the Kaiser, with his diabolical mustache and pickelhaube—spiked helmet—abusing innocent Belgium and sending monsters to sea. Then brave England steps up to defend Belgium and put the evil Kaiser in his place. And now, John Bull needs our help! No wonder people cheered Wilson's call for war.

Before thinking that Wilson's supporters were fools, recall more recent history. Just before the first Gulf War, one prominent story had Iraqi soldiers taking Kuwaiti babies from incubators and leaving them to die on hospital floors. As the HBO documentary *Live from Baghdad* recounts, the story sourced to "Nayirah," a 15-year-old Kuwaiti girl, who testified to this Iraqi crime in 1991's Congressional hearings. Long after the war authorization vote, reporters discovered that she was actually the daughter of the Kuwaiti Ambassador to the United States and that in all probability, she was nowhere near Kuwait during the invasion. The moral: myths continue to influence public opinion as well as government actions.

Remarkably, little separates Lippmann's theory from theories about political judgments used by political science today. When we substitute the term "heuristic" for *stereotype* (which it matches well enough), the overwhelming majority of empirical evidence supports his idea that citizens use mental shortcuts. Heuristics are simple rules that people employ to evade the work that complex decisions demand. Take buying a car; lots of types, brands, and models present too many choices. We cannot investigate them all practically, so we use one imperfect but satisfactory criterion. My safety-conscious wife reads some crash test ratings and chooses the car at the top of that list. Someone else might care about fuel efficiency, picking the car with the best gas mileage. You might be concerned with speed, style, price, or so on. In any case, having a criterion simplifies the choice; in addition, using heuristics does not make these decisions idiotic. Given the goal, such decisions seem reasonable, even satisfactory.

Nearly all political scientists believe that nearly all political decisions work the same way. When we vote, instead of laboriously examining candidates and choosing the absolute greatest, we use shortcuts. In fact, reality compels this practice. Politics consumes time and energy that most citizens cannot spare. Think of the word *junky*, the disparaging term for people who spend too much time on politics. In 1960, *The American Voter* (chapter 4) reports that barely anyone qualifies as a junky—we tend to have little political information. Yet we vote, often using the simple rules heuristics describe. With partisanship, for instance, people often vote according to whether they consider themselves to be Democrats or Republicans. Other votes come from a straightforward examination of the economic situation. Perhaps we think things are going poorly, so we vote against incumbents. Likewise, when the economy booms, we vote for incumbents, or may not vote at all.

Unlike Lippmann, however, most political scientists generally see political heuristics as relatively benign. They believe that heuristics compensate for the lack of information. So long as there is a reason to be a Republican, then why not vote for the Republican candidate? When recessions arise, why not punish the incumbent? The threat of punishment will at least push incumbents to do their best to keep the economy humming. I think citizens can do more, but we will save that conversation until later. Lippmann, at the other extreme, thinks simplistic thinking is a serious threat. Specifically, he presents a prognosis that brings him into conflict with John Dewey: citizens are more than just ill-informed, they lack the ability to competently use what little information they acquire. He writes in a letter published later:

> I do not frankly believe it's possible to educate the people on all the factors that are relevant to all the wise decisions that have got to be made . . . The matters are too intricate, prejudices are too deep and complex, the technical knowledge is too lacking. (*Public Philosopher: Selected Letters of Walter Lippmann*, John Morton Blum 1985, 305)

A closer look at heuristics bolsters Lippmann's perception. Observe how much structure surrounds the partisanship and economic voting heuristics. When voters and candidates belong to a party, partisan voting merely demands matching the two. Other political decisions, like going to war, have less structure; more accurately, it is harder to find a good criterion for choice. When we have many choices, we—average citizens—lack the ability to choose the best. Faced with complex problems, we could be left grasping for clues and end up basing decisions on the obvious. As the tale of World War I shows, sometimes the obvious is wrong.

This premise that people use unreliable pictures of reality to make political decisions brings us to Lippmann's finale. He recommends that we cut back on democracy and adopt technocratic governance. In the *Phantom Public* Lippmann categorizes citizens as "insiders and outsiders," arguing that "only the insider can make decisions, not because he is inherently a better man but because he is so placed that he can understand." The outsider is "necessarily ignorant, usually irrelevant and often meddlesome, because he is trying to navigate the ship from dry land" (150). Lippmann urges us to leave decisions to insiders. He advocates creating "an independent, expert organization for making the unseen facts intelligible." These experts would let citizens "escape from the intolerable and unworkable fiction that each of us must acquire a competent opinion about all public affairs" (*Public Opinion*, 31).

Many instinctively reject Lippmann's argument for reining in democracy. Our taste for freedom prevents us from cheerfully relinquishing control over our destiny. I do not doubt that this impulse serves us well. But I do still value Lippmann's points. To state the obvious, some independent board of experts could have improved our Iraq plans. Perhaps experts might solve other national problems, too. To take some real examples, the Federal

Reserve Board and the Supreme Court govern the money supply and protect the Constitution, supposedly without regard for public opinion. Moreover, the majority of evidence on American citizens' political behavior, which we will review throughout this book, supports Lippmann's points. Still, I do not want us to be too pessimistic; after all, if we took Lippmann's advice we would not need sample surveys.

Dewey's response to Lippmann shows the same indignation you may feel. Despite this emotion, Dewey agrees with most of Lippmann's observations. Dewey renounces the Great War's waste, and he admits that propaganda was behind the public's support. He breaks with Lippmann solely over the changes our political system needs to forestall future mistakes. Basically, he sides with Lippmann when it comes to the diagnosis of our political ills, but then he advocates a different cure. Above all, Dewey blames faulty education for the public's perceived incompetence. His book *The Public and Its Problems* asserts that better education would "render nugatory the indictment of democracy drawn on the basis of the ignorance, bias, and levity of the masses" (218). Nugatory, a legal term, translates as having no strength. Here and throughout our investigation, education has two levels—a foundation in the use of language and analysis, as well as information relevant to the situation. Thus, education refers to the general schooling citizens need to function in a democracy as well as the facts the public needs to make choices in particular cases.

Thus Dewey agrees with Lippmann on the need for reform, first suggesting that the press would play a central role in his scheme. However, Dewey would not let experts act independently; "no government by experts in which the masses do not have the chance to inform the experts as to their needs can be anything but an oligarchy managed in the interest of the few" (207). Instead, Dewey proposes that "the enlightenment of the public by experts have priority over the enlightenment of the administrators" (*New Republic* December 2, 1925, 52). Dewey's system would use experts as educators and not as decision makers; hence instead of leaving policy to expert squabbling, Dewey would have citizens chart the course of government. With this enhanced information, Dewey imagines citizens would live up to their potential, and as a result, wisdom would flow from the fountain of public opinion.

The scientific term "hypothesis" pinpoints the crucial difference between Lippmann and Dewey. Each tries to explain why Britain's propaganda worked so well. Lippmann attributes its success to people's lack of information and sophistication; in the language of science, which we will get to know, this guess is a *hypothesis*. Dewey rejects Lippmann's innate incompetence hypothesis and presents his own guess. He further observes that "until secrecy, prejudice, bias, misrepresentation, and propaganda as well as sheer ignorance are replaced by inquiry and publicity," there is no way to determine "how apt for judgment of social policies the existing intelligence of the masses may be." Here, Dewey recognizes that Lippmann's hypothesis has never been tested. These two hypotheses determine the rest of their arguments. Each forecasts the impact of improving public education. Lippmann predicts it would not change anything. This deduction leads him to recommend technocracy, putting experts in charge. Dewey, in contrast, thinks improving public education would work wonders.

Both of their arguments should make you a bit a suspicious, because they skip through a crucial question—what does adequate public education look like? Neither, in my opinion, provides a good answer. Here, we should criticize Dewey more than Lippmann, if only because Lippmann thinks public education will not do any good, no matter what it looks like. Dewey seems so fixated on rebutting Lippmann that he glosses over his own ideas. Some irony comes from Dewey's philosophy. In other works, he preaches pragmatism; with Charles Peirce and William James, he founded a school of philosophy devoted to "the active adaptation of the human organism to its environment" (the *Internet Encyclopedia of Philosophy*). Dewey preferred working to make life better to wrestling with metaphysical questions. When it came to writing *The Public and Its Problems*, he appears to have skipped specifics. (In his defense, Dewey spent much of his life trying to enact his vision of education reform.)

Nevertheless, if we take Lippmann's critique seriously while trying to keep faith with Dewey, we need to set standards for public education along with discussing public opinion. I want to phrase this goal as a question to drive our investigations. The question, which we will struggle to answer, is what kind of public education we will demand before we take public opinion seriously. The rest of the chapter lays a foundation for my answer. Observe that human conversation—specifically, asking and answering questions—forms the heart of polling results. Our public education concern asks what stands behind the answers people give. The core lesson that contrasting Lippmann and Dewey teaches is that the more thought, feeling, information, and education (or whatever else) there is standing behind answers, the better it is for democracy. Alternatively, citizens may be like parrots, driven by experts or the media to squawk out judgments they really don't understand. Let me recount a study that illustrates this point—like too many studies, this one reinforces Lippmann's argument.

In 1978 George Bishop and his colleagues polled Cincinnati residents, asking "Some people say that the 1975 Public Affairs Act should be repealed. Do you agree or disagree with this idea?" 15.6 percent of the respondents agreed, 17.6 percent disagreed, and 66.8 percent spontaneously said some version of "I don't know" (see *Public Opinion Quarterly 44*, starting on 198). So far, the public's view seems pretty clear—most people have no idea and the rest barely favor repeal. Once I reveal the backdrop, everything changes. These intrepid investigators made up the 1975 Public Affairs Act—it was a total fiction! Now what do we think? While most respondents—the people answering the question—said they didn't know, a significant number gave an opinion on something that does not exist. (We presume this result does not depend on factors, like their location, the timing, or the introductory phrase "some people say.") Seen in the new light, the two thirds responding "don't know" gave the "right" answer, while the third expressing an opinion comes across badly. The lesson: questions and answers look smart or dumb only with respect to the context surrounding both. In this study, nothing lay behind a third of the expressions, because we know the act did not exist.

We could look at this study as a trap: anyone saying something with substance ends up looking dumb. What's more, pollsters have ways to discourage people from babbling about things they do not know. They ask filter questions, like "have you thought much about this issue," before the pertinent question. When Bishop used filters, for instance, don't know responses went up to roughly 92 percent. Pollsters can also put forward the "don't know" option more vigorously. Yet, the general problem this study illustrates haunts public opinion research. Are answers based on substance, or on something else? Maybe respondents are trying to appear knowledgeable or agreeable—or just to get done sooner. To the extent that anything other than an informed opinion underlies answers, we do not want to value it very much.

POLITICAL SCIENCE 101:
WHAT EVERY CITIZEN OUGHT TO KNOW!

To gain an understanding of public opinion, we need theory. Public opinion theories try to identify all the important contextual elements causing particular answers to survey questions. This theory, my organized intuitions as how the parts of our political system interact to produce public judgment, guides our investigation. Before detailing the theory, we need to establish a few definitions. These words may be familiar, but successful political science requires more precision if they are to do their job. We will also take this opportunity to delve into the nature of power and into what makes democracy special. Successfully completing this review certifies you as a beginning political scientist, ready for investigation.

Politics is the authoritative redistribution of resources. Within this definition, pretty much anything counts as a resource: money, goods, power, or love (maybe not love). Redistribution covers the taking from some and the giving to others; the "re" highlights that resources do not come from outside the system—thus, saying that we tax ourselves to raise money to give ourselves makes a weird kind of sense. The key word is authoritative. In a nutshell, authority translates as compulsion—you *have* to take part. This adjective meshes politics with power. To have power entails having the ability to influence people to do (thinking and feeling included) anything that they wouldn't otherwise. If you have authority, you have power.

A quick anecdote unveils political authority's hallmark. Imagine yourself on vacation, during spring break perhaps, driving a borrowed Toyota Camry. You cruise down the highway at 90 miles an hour as your friends scream "faster, faster!" Suddenly a car pulls alongside; its driver commands you to "slow it down." What next? In this situation, many (if not most) would respond negatively, some perhaps with an obscene gesture. Now imagine that the interloping car has decals on the doors and some lettering on the back. Give the driver a silly hat and maybe a gun. These symbols of authority alter the reaction, and we cheerfully slow. Why are we cheerful? First, we avoided punishment, a speeding ticket or worse; resistance would lead to more cars, helicopters, and jail. Less obviously, we feel some compulsion to drive safely. All people except for some sociopaths want to be good citizens and to do the right thing. This internal respect for law is the heart of democratic authority.

A TYPOLOGY OF POWER

Governments monopolize one type of power called coercion (another definition). Coercive power equals force, and states use it regularly. People go to jail for breaking the law. In addition, states prevent others from coercing their citizens. When the unauthorized use force, we call them invaders, vigilantes or criminals, and governments try to stop them. Real statecraft benefits from two more subtle forms of power. The first, incentive or economic power, equals bribery: I get a tax credit when I buy an efficient car. Governments, especially democracies, prefer bribery if only because coercion makes people unhappy. Still, bribery has problems. Incentive power, like coercive power, costs a lot, and these costs also tend to escalate. At first a small bribe or show of force gets citizens to behave; next time, more is a required. Eventually, incentive-based states spend everything on bribes; see ancient Rome, under bread and circuses. States run on coercion spend too much on order, see totalitarian regime. Once the resources vanish, the state does, too—so coercion and bribery have built-in limits. The third kind of power, persuasion, supplies a deceptively simple solution, bringing us to another tale.

Every night or so, my wife and I try to bathe the kids. As much as they like the water, they resist the scrubbing they need. Some nights they want nothing to do with the tub. As good parents (read: authorities), we use power. We could (and sometimes do) use coercion; we pick them up and plop them in the tub—force, pure and simple. As they grow, coercion gets tougher, and it always creates misery. Sometimes we use bribery, offering an incentive. We reward bathing with ice cream, which they love. Sure enough, everyone runs to the tub, shouting "ice cream!" Of course, the cost goes up: today ice cream, tomorrow a toy. Persuasion takes a superior route to influence.

Persuasion towers, almost magically, above other kinds of power, so much so that Habermas (who we will meet) gives it the striking name the "unforced force." As adults, all of us bathe fairly regularly. Part of this behavior stems from fear of sanction; people tend to avoid the filthy. Most of it stems from childhood, when someone persuaded us to bathe. The magic lay in the fact that persuasion costs a good deal less then coercion or bribery. It may take effort to find the right message, the persuasive key to unlock the desired behavior, but we use it freely once found. The real magic is that when we persuade someone to do what we want, they keep on doing it, even if we disappear. In this way, persuasion is self-enforcing. To top things off, successful persuasion is voluntary, keeping everyone happy. Cheap, effective, and satisfying, persuasion easily beats its power colleagues. Few political philosophers fail to admit that the use of persuasion leads to superior governance. Even though no one really knows the secret of persuasion, as chapter 6 details, it defines democracy—governance by collective self persuasion.

DEMOCRACY'S REQUIREMENTS

A glance at humanity's story reveals an agonizingly slow progression: the gradual transfer of power away from the few toward the many. Though this development has stopped or reversed on occasion, no one can miss the trend. Unlike our ancestors who took divine right kings for granted, we see dictators—Kim Jong-Il, Saddam Hussein, and their ilk—as relics. Americans tend to dread or laugh at the countries these dictators run, and to pity the people they rule. Yet, while humans yearn for the freedom and stability successful democracy brings, debates over what democracy means and how it works continue. Many critics, like our friend Walter Lippmann, still question the ability of the people to rule, and offer reforms that would make governance less democratic.

The number of people holding power separates one kind of government from another. The basest is autocracy, rule by one—the aforementioned dictator.

Persuasion still works here, though only one person sits in the audience. With monarchies, a type of autocracy, commoners and nobles alike try to persuade the king or queen to endorse their way of thinking. As the number in power expands we move to oligarchy, rule by few. Theocracies, government by religion, usually survive as oligarchies in which the official religion's leaders pull the strings. Lippmann recommends technocracy, a government of experts that Dewey correctly categorizes as an oligarchy. In each of these, the only way to change things—short of rebellion—is to persuade the small group in power. Not surprisingly, oligarchs frown when common folk rock their boat. These states, more often than not, treat dissenters to generous doses of coercion.

Now we come to precious democracy, a government—in Lincoln's words—of the people, by the people, for the people. Beyond praising democracy, I want to develop some useful points. Specifically, let us examine three conditions political philosophers propose to summarize democratic governance. (For those who wish to know more, I recommend David Held's excellent *Models of Democracy*.) When the practices within a state satisfy these conditions, then the people hold power—they are able to persuade themselves—and we have democracy; if they do not, something is awry and the claim to democracy is suspect. Ultimately, these conditions will help us isolate the role polling and public education must play.

MAJORITY RULE, MINORITY PROTECTION

The first condition is easy. Generally, when a majority wants something, the government does it. Majority is mathematically defined as half the citizens—50 percent—plus just one. Any smaller group embodies a minority. By definition, if we do what a minority wants, we have an oligarchy, so that route doesn't work.

Democracies also require minority protection, the second condition, which is the grand exception to majority rule. The theoretical reason for this exception should be readily apparent. Majorities tend to chip away at minority power. The famous founding fathers worried about a "tyranny of the majority"—that the poor would vote to redistribute the rich's money to themselves, creating a legal Robin Hood. Partially to avoid this outcome, they invented our complicated government, including checks and balances and so on. They created the Bill of Rights to make the minority's protections clear to everyone. Finally, they set up the courts, which most scholars recognize as a counter-majoritarian institution. The Supreme Court, for example, can overturn a law that the president, the Congress, and everyone else other than five of its nine members want.

The more pragmatic reason for setting up minority protection arises from the hope of avoiding a permanent majority, a beast that spells trouble because it comes with permanent minorities. Think about Iraq, where ethnicity determines politics; the Shiites form a majority that will last into the foreseeable future, leaving the Kurds and Sunnis as permanent minorities. Naturally, minorities live in anxiety, even with democratic elections, because they always lose. Constitutions try to protect minorities; more pragmatic protection arises when the majority anticipates losing power and turning into a minority. Remaking citizens' political identities would supply a great but unlikely solution in Iraq. In the United States, our relatively fluid electoral coalitions have produced a history that helps ensure that majorities, after they lose members, safely become minorities and work peacefully toward putting together a new majority.

We need some more background for the last condition, freedom of expression, due to its special relevance to public opinion.

A THEORY OF PUBLIC JUDGMENT

How does government meet democracy's conditions in everyday politics? What are the nuts and bolts? Many political scientists who study our political system start with the familiar three branches and move on to their intricacies; we will take a different course. We shall focus on the actions of politicians, the media, and citizens, and on how they create public judgments.

More than a definition, a theory (again) describes how actors come together to cause outcomes. Theories also tell us where to look for evidence to test hypotheses, like our question about public education. To be silly, what if we thought sunspots lead democracies to war? We might look for sunspots in 1917 and 2003. Of course, this by itself would not prove a causal relationship (discussed in chapter 4), but this theory would have us start there. When searching for answers, it doesn't hurt to start with something sensible. Our working theory tries to specify what affects people's responses to poll questions, going beyond the question and answers to the surrounding environs.

In this theory's view, politicians do almost all of the political work as they compete for power. The media gathers information, generally from politicians, and passes it to the people. Citizens ultimately judge this competition. Along with these roles, this view also highlights each actor's goals. Politicians seek public support (or acquiescence), knowing that its lack can rob them of their livelihood. Journalists, in contrast, are less concerned with support and generally accept public attention in its place. The public awards power according to their whim or will. Finally, notice the interdependence.

Politicians use the media to reach citizens. Citizens need the media to judge between politicians. The media requires politicians as sources, and citizens as audience.

This theory does not specify everything. A public opinion theory could go back to the beginning of time and list everything that happened since then. Not only would this be a lot of work, we prudently suspect that most happenings have little impact. We want to bore in on the most important. This reductionism often gets criticized, but it saves time and helps our thinking. Conversely, we only have to look to Lippmann to see simplification's danger. We need to weigh whether each factor has sufficient import to warrant inclusion. As I said, our investigation skirts some distinctions, like the three branches, that many find indispensable. It is also pretty vague; we will fill it in as we progress.

This simple theory does capture several essentials: each actor's role, motivations, and interdependence. By design, it draws attention to the division of labor between politicians, and citizens, and then puts the media between these two. Thus, this particular theory of public judgment delineates what some call the political culture, the informal side of politics. In my view, these features work alongside the formal features of our government, like the presidency or the Congress. Many conceive of governance as two parallel systems. On one side we have specified procedures and institutions; on the other we have the media, parties, and citizens. Significantly, the two systems connect at many points, like elections. When people vote, the informal system selects the formal system's officeholders.

You may be wondering where pollsters fit. Our interest lay with pollsters who work with or through the media (we will not worry about others). Let me to switch to a common metaphor—the court of public opinion. Within this court, politicians play the lawyers (or defendants), and citizens take on the role of jury. The media serves as presiding judge. In jury trials, presiding judges do not render verdicts; instead they control the courtroom, maintaining order, refereeing between the lawyers and—crucially—deciding what the jury hears. If you watch enough *Law and Order*, for instance, you are acquainted with attorneys' objections; in successful objections, the judge rules that the jury should not hear certain testimony. In politics, the media plays a comparable role.

This analogy underlines the media's importance. People generally spend their meager allocation of political attention with the media, as Lippmann thinks. In our polity (jargon for society's political aspects), the media filters public information. In brief, the media has only a small window to report on a day's worth of political activities—the space within a daily paper or news show. Politicians struggle to grab the media's attention. In doing their job, the media pick the best, and hopefully most important, stories. For instance, Iraq, unsurprisingly, controlled the news of the time while other events silently slipped by. Researchers call this process agenda-setting. Effectively, then, the media determines where public education starts and stops, deciding what things citizens notice and what things they ignore.

Within the media, pollsters perform the task of constructing and announcing public judgments, serving as the court's bailiff. Conflict drives politics. Every potential government action has politicians pushing and pulling it every which way, trying to mold the outcome to fit their goals. On big issues (though predicting which issues will command attention is difficult) the mechanics of our system generally promise that political parties take different sides. So once the media graces an issue with coverage, we typically see a loose confederation of Republicans arguing that we should go one direction while a corresponding group of Democrats tries to sell the reverse. Pollsters allow the public to judge these competitions via sample surveys. Seen this way, pollsters regulate the precise expression of public judgment. With this theory of how things work, the puzzle that is our investigation requires one more piece to start.

MASS INFORMED CONSENT

To this point, our theory of public judgment covers every instance, including the mistakes we discussed, in other words, it covers bad public judgments as well as good (if they exist). We need more, a way to distinguish when the political system is operating well from when it operates not so well—a standard for good public judgment. This task of separating good politics from bad is so important that political philosophers discuss it under the special heading of legitimation. While all political decisions possess authority; in proper terminology, good decisions have legitimacy that bad decisions lack. Further, legitimate authority, like our state trooper, merits respect. Knowing what makes certain decisions legitimate will answer our question about what kind of public education we will demand before we take public opinion seriously.

As you might suspect, the book's title—mass informed consent—names the standard. Not coincidentally, this standard, in combination with the theory, gives us the tools to sift through the political system and figure out where to place the blame for mistakes.

FREEDOM OF SPEECH

Democracy's third condition, freedom of expression, steers us toward understanding legitimacy and mass informed consent. We know that elections reward majorities with formal power. To reiterate: after losing an election, the minority struggles to add enough members to retake power, just as the majority tries to keep the power. This struggle features persuasion: the minority has to persuade majority members to defect and join them, or must find new blood to win. Minority protection permits this process to run smoothly. Freedom of expression is such a weighty aspect of minority protection that political philosophers often see it as a democratic condition by itself. Our Bill of Rights trumpets its significance by putting free speech in its first amendment. Without freedom of expression, the minority would not have the chance to take back power, and democracy would vanish.

There is a crucial caveat. As a practical matter, 10 people, even a thousand, can practice free speech with ease. But among 300 million citizens, we need to divide effective speech from free speech. The problem, of course, is that now matter how loud you scream, you cannot effectively communicate with that many; you need assistance. Although the Internet may offer another route (see chapter 7), current politics mandates the use of broadcast technology, such as newspapers and television, for effective speech. In reality, if you barge into a radio station and grab the microphone to decry some outrage or read poetry, you will be arrested; someone will stop you from reaching the public. This state of affairs puts the media into a special position. Some suggest that representation bypasses the media's monopoly; we vote for people who speak for us and fulfill our right of expression. At most, this kind of representation only affects the formal part of our system; it does not meet the needs of the informal court of public opinion.

In politics today, communication costs money. The Supreme Court affirmed this notion in the 1976 *Buckley* decision. They ruled that limits on political spending deny the rich their free speech rights. Together with our theory of public judgment, the notion of effective speech reveals how this ruling exposes us to the danger of plutocracy, an oligarchy of the rich. Ads are expensive. The expense also goes up with their effectiveness (technically their reach), so a Super Bowl ad watched by millions carries a mind bending price tag. Late-night infomercials, seen mainly by insomniacs, still cost something. Thus, while persuasion is free and everyone can buy all the ads they can afford, only the rich have the money to afford them. When the rich control public education, according to our theory, they determine public judgment. This line of thought signals the broader point that imbalances in communication resources—effectively propaganda—threaten democratic legitimacy.

Off hand, we can list the factors that mitigate this plutocratic danger. First, the political bottom line only tallies votes and some evidence—one of our studies, for one—shows that the volume of communication does not necessarily translate into votes. In chapter 6 we will see that citizens have the potential to reject, as well as accept, any communication. Second, in the mass media, numbers count. Although large conglomerates own the media (see Ben Bagdikian's *Media Monopoly*), they care intensely about ratings, so people, collectively, control what is aired. Third, the not so rich have some money, and can pool it for political use. (The Internet may be particularly important here.) Fourth, as already raised, the Internet may also offer a way to equalize the resources available for political communication.

Getting back to the main point, the notion of effective speech applies to the listener as well as the speaker. In so doing, it sets the stage for elaborating upon the requirements for public education. No one really knows how persuasion works, in the following sense: the English language has an infinite number of sentences (see Steven Pinker's book *How the Mind Works*), so any persuasive attempt selects from an infinite number of messages. No living being can know for certain which will succeed. In the real world, political communication runs largely on guesswork and intuition. We can, however, observe certain clues that get to good persuasion's core. Jurgen Habermas argues that legitimate persuasive attempts equalize the speaker's power relative to the listener. Good persuasion, then, requires that audiences can freely reject claims and, in this way, enhances the audience's autonomy. Propaganda, in contrast, creates an environment where audiences lack choice.

Autonomy (read freedom of choice), stands as a paramount human value in ethical philosophy—ethicists study what makes right, not wrong. Within these discussions about protecting autonomy lies the best practical discussion of propaganda and free will. As you see, I christened our standard "mass informed consent" because my reasoning is based on ethical work concerning informed consent, a process that ensures free choice.

When we go in for surgery, the doctors sit down with us to discuss the procedure. After this discussion they hand us a form by which we attest to our willingness. This procedure gives the patient legal responsibility and shields the surgeons from lawsuits. The protection does not come from the signature alone; it also comes from the discussion. What's more, it cannot be just any discussion; talking about the weather, for instance, would not grant any legal protection. The discussion has to educate the patient about the surgery's risks and benefits. If this education fails, in other words, if the patient does not comprehend the choice, the signature is worthless. The education also must be complete. For example, if we explode on the operating table, and the surgeons failed to warn us about that possibility, the surgeon faces serious trouble. On the other hand, if they did warn us—then tough luck.

Informed consent establishes the responsibility of the individual. In so doing, informed consent delicately balances the patient's autonomy with the doctor's expertise. If doctors operate without any patient input, they would trample over the patient's liberty, probably needing to use bribery or force. Put bluntly, safeguarding autonomy mandates the use of persuasion. On the flip side, patients cannot demand any kind of treatment; medical ethics oblige doctors to refuse treatments that run counter to the patient's best interest. This obligation reflects the doctor's expertise.

Social science calls this circumstance a principal agent problem, wherein the patient, as principal, must make a decision based on information received from an agent, the doctor. Principal agent relationships raise the issue of trust; when we trust agents to act in our interest, no one worries. Imagine we are selling our house. We want to get the highest price possible, but we have little idea what the house is really worth. Our real estate agent suggests a price, and we accept that price, trusting the agent's experience. Should the agent's cousin turn up the next day and buy our house, we would be outraged. (The law actually criminalizes this particular kind of abuse.) Going back to Lippmann and Dewey, you can see that we face the same situation with regard to politicians and the media. In any situation, they may convince citizens to do something against their self-interest.

This loose description allows us to apply medical informed consent to politics. In light of our theory, informed consent demands that politicians and the media deliver sufficient education before the judgments that citizens render can be legitimate. Thus, the informed consent logic applies to our primary question by detailing a standard for public education that compels us to take public opinion seriously. We will talk about this standard more, but for now we need to adapt individual informed consent to mass politics.

After the horrifying Tuskegee Syphilis Study became public in 1972, Congress set up the National Commission for the Protection of Human Subjects of Biomedical and Behavioral Research. This commission produced 1979's Belmont Report, also known as Ethical Principles and Guidelines for the Protection of Human Subjects, which gives the foremost singular statement regarding informed consent (it is downloadable on the Web). The report specifies that patient competence is the first prerequisite of informed consent. The young, mentally infirm, and temporarily impaired cannot understand the choice, so their consent never counts. In these cases, someone must stand in for the patient; a guardian (this label echoes Plato's use). Next, consent has to be voluntary (read: free from coercion); doctors cannot hold a gun to the patient's head. The report rules out subtle coercion as well. Unlike television, doctors cannot shake patients, yelling "without this treatment you will die." (I won't bring up political ads that threaten collapse if the other candidate wins.) The report instead mandates that doctors couch risks in probabilities to reduce tension. Finally, the doctor must present all risks and benefits that may affect the patient's well-being. Naturally, omissions or misrepresentations impede informed consent. Finally, the patient has to understand—an amazingly difficult goal, if only because we lack instruments with which to reliably measure deep understanding.

Certainly these guidelines address difficult situations, but I believe that medicine is easier than politics. With any particular procedure, experts know the relatively finite set of pros and cons. In politics, the list of risks and benefits is itself subject to competition, as is the right precedent. Was Iraq really more like World War II, or Viet Nam, for example? Next, in medical situations the doctors generally are on the same team. In politics, the players work for different teams, and the public's decision determines whether they win or lose. In practice, this means that their messages often conflict. Third, doctors do not need intermediaries to reach patients; in politics, the media may come between the public and necessary information. The fourth, and perhaps most important, difference recalls problem structure. In medicine it is pretty clear what the consent gives the doctor permission to do. In contrast, pollsters often define situations for respondents. This burden, as discussed in the next chapter, can create all kinds of problems. Within a given question, for instance, pollsters can provide specific information, reframe the decision or offer different options. Moreover, other pollsters often ask different questions on the same topic! At minimum, these possibilities mean that we need some way to disambiguate the verdict polling renders.

This analogy to medicine reinforces the crucial point; if nothing stands behind polling results then we should discard them. Consider *Manufacturing Consent*, another idea of Lippmann's that became the title of a book by Noam Chomsky and Edward S. Herman. We admit that jury decisions can go wrong; if a member has been bribed or slept through the trial, we want the verdict thrown out. Chomsky and Herman (and others) suggest we should throw out public opinion in the same way. The same holds if jurors are unduly influenced by one side, or if a patient merely repeats what the doctors says. In these cases, a top-down process whereby politicians use the media to propagandize the public into supporting actions against their own self-interest replaces the bottom-up process of citizens' freely charting the course of government. Further, Chomsky and Herman correctly conclude that when this happens, an appearance of democracy masks an oligarchy.

The great political scientist V. O. Key, one of the select few to win the field's unanimous respect, restates the *Manufacturing Consent* problem this way in *The Responsible Electorate*:

> It is too early to conclude that governments can ignore public opinion or that democratic government amounts only to a hoax, a ritual whose performance serves only to delude the people and thereby to convert them into willing

subjects of the powers that be. . . . Yet the sharp definition of the role of public opinion as it affects different kinds of policies under different types of situations presents an analytical problem of extraordinary difficulty. That problem, however, should not lead us to ignore, or to deny, the phenomenon of the conduct of enormous governmental operations in a manner that by and large wins the support of a citizenry of millions and is in the main in accord with their preferences. Given control of the apparatus of authority, to govern is easy; but to govern without heavy reliance on the machinery of coercion is a high art. (7)

To me, these views boil down to the claim that public persuasion may not meet the informed consent standards: competence, free choice, and full information.

In moving to politics, mass informed consent requires more than competence, free choice, and full information. It also demands that pollsters faithfully convey the issue at hand and that analysts minimize any equivocation in their interpretation of poll results. Finally, people, the media and politicians have to understand the results—and what lay behind the public's judgment—well enough to respect them. As critics of our system may acknowledge, this is a tall order. This goal also provides this book with a narrative structure that most public opinion texts lack. All the information I will present is organized around making the broader point about polling's place in democracy. In addition, all chapters (except the second) combine a concrete claim about polling with a supporting scientific lesson; each chapter then offers an empirical investigation that provides evidence consistent with the claim. Thus, in addition to learning about polling, we will also become acquainted with scientific research. Let me preview the point, lesson and study each chapter contains.

CHAPTER OUTLINE

Chapter 2: The Yes, No, and Don't Knows of Political Polling

After you turn the page, we will wrestle with the fundamentals of polling, going over the three ingredients all sample surveys possess: random sampling, interviewing, and aggregation. We will ponder the magic of random sampling, which allows roughly a thousand people to speak for almost 300 million Americans. Among other implications, this knowledge will emphasize the tremendous power of polling as a medium for public speech. Subsequently, we will review polling's history and entertain some of its most significant critics. Even as we grant parts of the critics' arguments, I shall present a case for polling's necessity in contemporary governance. I hope my responses will convince you that sample surveys merit our respect. Finally, we will interview some leading pollsters in order to become more familiar with the work they do. These interviews form a protostudy that will reveal something about pollsters' motivations and perspectives as well.

Chapter 3: Gently Introducing Science, Starring the Median Voter Model, and a Test of Citizens' Independence

This chapter is devoted to social science. After a prelude clarifying background matters, such as why social science lags behind physical science, we will undertake a crash course on empirical investigation and how it produces knowledge. Then, we shall dive into the political science's store of knowledge, opening with the amazing Median Voter Model—the best available framework for summarizing Americans' political behavior. This chapter ends with a real study that addresses the question: can the public think independently? This relatively uncomplicated investigation uses an experimental design—perhaps the fundamental research method—to examine the relationship between media frames and citizens' attitudes toward partial birth abortion. In the course of analyzing this experiment's results, we will learn about the crosstab and significance testing, the conceptual underpinnings of statistical thinking. These tools help separate meaningful observations from chance activity. Not to spoil the ending, this study confirms that citizens are capable of independent thought.

Chapter 4: Why Do Americans Favor Some Things yet Oppose Others? and, Explaining Republican Success against Partial Birth Abortion

Here, we concentrate on the interview, outlining the forces (called variables in scientific lingo) driving Americans' responses to poll questions. To aid our examination, we will try out a new tool, the correlation coefficient, a number that captures the strength of a crosstab's relationship. We will use this statistic to score a replay of the game that began public opinion research. Next, we will jump to the present and explicate the Zaller model—the most advanced thinking political science has to offer on survey response. We shall also consider this model's normative overtones, as well, seeing where it agrees with Lippmann and going over my objections. This chapter's study then applies this model to complete our look at attitudes toward banning partial birth abortion. After tracing the term's origin, we use the idea of correlation to chart how this label, accompanied by the use of the word "baby," passed through the Supreme Court, the United States Congress, and the *New York Times* to determine the public's attitude toward this medical procedure.

Chapter 5: Questions Are Just as Important as Answers, Particularly in a Study of Public Opinion on the Iraq Invasion

This portion revisits the 2003 Iraq invasion to fill out our theory of public judgment—specifically, in terms of how to use sample surveys to guide governance. We will take on the question wording problem, which arises whenever poll results addressing the same topic seem to contradict each other. Resolving this issue will entail going over a substantial chunk of the public opinion literature, including split-half studies and trend analysis. I shall propose that multiple regression—the most potent tool in a statisticians' kit—offers a great way to resolve the interpretation of poll results. We shall learn about regression in order to use it in our study of public opinion prior to the start of the Iraq war. This research into the effects of question wording will show, contrary to widespread belief, that public support for the war was nuanced and highly contingent on the truth of the administration's message. Pollsters, in my opinion, were the only professional group to do their job properly during this time. They asked enough of the right questions to uncover the public's reason for endorsing the war, and what factors would have led the public to withhold support.

Chapter 6: Debunking Manipulation Myths, Featuring the Infamous Harry and Louise

Knowledge about polling and how to interpret poll results allows us to move on to study the provision of political information. This assessment requires that we go over persuasion, legitimate governance's key, and define propaganda—bad persuasion. As no one knows precisely what makes a message persuasive, some uncertainty extends to sample survey responses. I will argue that this unpredictability has value. This idea prompts our final study, a look at the myth of Harry and Louise, one of the most damaging stories in political folklore. Though many scholars attribute the demise of the Clinton Health Care Plan in 1994—not to mention Barack Obama's unwillingness to take on insurance companies in 2010—to these television ads, our evidence will show that the public was not so easily swayed. Here, another use of regression will demonstrate that perceptions of change in public support related to a change in question wording. Further analysis suggests that the media and, to a lesser extent, pollsters should be blamed for erroneously spreading the propaganda story and helping bring down the Clinton plan and contributing to misperceptions of political power.

Chapter 7: Political Reforms and Thoughts on Media Old and New

Our work ends with a discussion of what will improve public judgment: more precisely, how we can ensure that poll results meet the standard of mass informed consent, and how these results can play a larger role in our politics. This chapter starts with the status quo, detailing the difference between "normal" citizens and political elites. This difference gives rise to interest group politics, which is predicated on distaste for polling. Next, we delve into education's twin meanings: general schooling and more specific political information. After talking about skills necessary to citizenship, we turn to the media—old and new. Here, I spotlight the distinctions between traditional media and what new technologies offer. In particular, we focus on government regulation and content financing. The book concludes with a list of recommendations covering what can be done to improve democracy from the standpoint of citizens, politicians, and the media.

Chapter 2

The Yes, No, and Don't Knows of Political Polling

Addressing—much less resolving—the issues we have raised calls for us to learn about polling itself. We have all heard of polling, especially if we follow the news, but that does not guarantee that we know enough about what lay behind a poll's results to evaluate things properly. To take the most important aspect, most of us know that sample surveys and other offerings like call-in, e-mail, or cell "polls" differ, possibly because good media constantly states: "this is not a scientific sample" (though they keep doing them). We know that the former are "real" and that the latter do not "count." So when a news station asks viewers to e-mail in stating whether they support certain policies, serious observers do not care when, for example, 90 percent say yes. And even though sometimes the 90 percent may be surprising, it still lacks the majesty of a sample survey result. This chapter pinpoints that difference—which we call self-selection—and others by scrutinizing public opinion polling's mechanics. By the end, you should understand polling's foundation and should be able to imagine what it would take to create your own poll results.

We may also recognize the tremendous power of polling as a medium for public speech. This power goes far beyond talking to your neighbor, posting on the Internet, or even appearing on television. Polling does no less than allow around a thousand people to speak for everyone in the nation. This fact bears repeating. Polling empowers a thousand or so carefully selected people to represent all 300 million U.S. citizens. Careful selection is polling's crucial ingredient, and absolutely must use the proven technique of random sampling. Like good media point out, random sampling makes a poll "scientific." Beware of any substitute! We will discuss why claims about public opinion that do not use random sampling are suspicious. In addition, we shall touch upon the other two ingredients that sample surveys require: interviewing and aggregation.

In talking about sampling, the almost supernatural source of polling's mojo, we quickly review polling's history, encountering George Gallup, polling's patron saint, and some of polling's foes. Next, we will examine the moral status of results and talk to leading pollsters. These professionals perform a remarkable service—one that modern democracy makes essential. In interviewing these interviewers we will discover that it takes more than sampling to get results. Before we start, I have to clarify one thing—my use of poll always refers only to public polls. Polling has non-political uses; businesses utilize polls in marketing, for instance. Likewise, not all political polls count as public polls. Candidates depend on private polls to win elections, and researchers apply them to the study of political behavior. So long as they employ random sampling, they are proper polls. Their aims, however, preclude more than a passing mention. Public polls, from start to finish, have a democratic purpose—to accurately report public opinion to everyone—and public pollsters generally work for or with media organizations.

Let me bring up a misuse of the polling concept that you may have already heard about—something called "push" polls. Despite their name, push polls actually are despicable attempts to use polling's credibility to spread rumors. To cite a notorious example, it is alleged that in the 2000 Republican primary some of George W. Bush's supporters, not affiliated with his campaign, called voters to ask, "Would you be less likely to vote for John McCain for president if you knew he fathered an illegitimate black child?" By doing so, these so-called pollsters disguised as a poll what was actually an attempt to plant an unsubstantiated charge in people's minds. Compounding their lies, push polls never intend to measure public opinion. If you witness this activity, you ought to report the culprits on the Internet, to the media, and to election authorities. In stark contrast, I believe citizens have a duty to respond to legitimate polls, which will authenticate themselves as necessary.

POLLING AND PUBLIC OPINION

The idea of public opinion goes back to Jacques Necker, the otherwise forgotten finance minister of France's King Louis XVI. Having read *A Tale of Two Cites*, you may know Louis (pronounced LOO-wee) as Queen Marie Antoinette's husband; history accuses her of replying "let them eat cake" when she was told people were starving. Necker's job was to collect the taxes needed to keep the monarchy in luxury during the period when the French started to question Louis' "divine right." This challenge drove Necker to contemplation, wherein he defined public opinion as the invisible power of just authority. No fool, Necker realized his job would be easier if the people genuinely supported Louis. When that support evaporated, Louis and Marie's careers came to an abrupt end. Public opinion, to use Necker's term, turned decisively against the king. This definition predates the invention of polling by a wide margin. Nevertheless, Necker's view remains roughly correct.

Given this definition and the existence of polls, you might think that polls and public opinion are obviously related. Indeed, some researchers automatically assume that they study public opinion whenever they use polls. Should you question them about the tie between the two, they will look at you strangely—the thought never occurs to them. Polls do relate to public opinion, but we need to pin down this link to appreciate democracy's need for polling.

To start, few openly question the value of democracy today, and about the same number question the public's status as democracy's ultimate judge. Yet, as Walter Lippmann showed, this unanimity does not extend to public opinion. Even less support reaches polling. This discontinuity strikes me as odd. Early political philosophers, such as our Founding Fathers, usually talked about public opinion and democracy in the same breath. More to the point, initial assaults on public opinion invariably attacked democracy as well. Yet in the face of near universal support for democracy, the con side in the debate over polling's value lingers. Let us clarify polling's rationale by talking about four alternative ways to measure public opinion.

Imagine that the president wakes up confronting a dire decision—not an invasion, but still something important. The president wants to respect democratic values (or may merely care about reelection) and needs to know what the public thinks. What now? First, there are formal methods prescribed in the Constitution. Each geographic area in the United States has designated representatives. The president might call a senator to get some input. While helpful, this method effectively pushes the problem down a level. California's senators represent over 30 million people! Even members of Congress speak for more than half a million. How do they know what their constituents want?

Second, the president might call politics' less formal workers. If the problem concerns cars, the president messages the United Auto Workers' chief, the employees' representative. Or the president might call the CEO of General Motors, who embodies automobile manufacturing interests. This contrast leads me to doubt informal informants' ultimate value. Their position limits their authority: they speak for a slice of the people—not the whole pie. The conventional name for these slices, "special interests," signals that they do not represent everyone. While many automatically scorn special interests and their lobbyist minions, they do have a democratic role. They provide information about what their employers (be they union members, auto companies, or foreign governments) desire. However, their task precludes representing the whole. The wise shiver whenever lobbyists claim to advance the *common* good.

Third, the president can look to the news media. After all, the news presumably covers what the public thinks. The media also pay for nearly all the polls we care about. Even so, we need to ask whether the media represents citizens in the absence of polling. Before polling's invention the media certainly made this claim; editors and reporters regularly spoke about public opinion, basing their views on their contact with citizens and their intuitions about the people's wants. To boost their credibility, they still publish some letters to the editor they receive. Would this summary of media contacts offer sufficient information on public opinion without polling? I think not.

Fourth, the president can ask his party. Today, we probably don't think of Republicans and Democrats as sources of public opinion information, because parties have shrunk. They used to be huge organizations that ran local politics; today, they are ghosts of their older selves. National conventions, for instance, were assemblies of the faithful that choose the presidential candidate from the time of Andrew Jackson to the 1950s. More recent conventions pretend to ratify primary voters' decisions. The parties' former power came from their workers, organized down to the precinct and up to the "boss." Vestiges of this system remain—you can volunteer to be a precinct captain, which should tell you how weak this position has become.

At the height of party power, precinct captains were the local government. A precinct covered a neighborhood, small enough for the captain to know the residents. Their job was to get the party votes; in return, they helped voters—potholes were filled, disability checks came, and the like. Today, members of Congress perform this ombudsman service, and it plays no small part in incumbents' reelections. The captains' power came from the party; they toiled at the lowest level of a pyramid with a chain of authority all the way to the top. Equally significantly, precinct captains were not outsiders; they had to come from and live in their precincts to do their job. With a few horrible exceptions, such as African American disenfranchisement, every ethnic group had precinct captains, and they blanketed cities, towns, and farms. The bosses depended on this legion for good public opinion data. Polling contributed to the demise of parties by reducing the cost of this vital knowledge.

POLLING AS A TECHNOLOGY

Without polling (or asking everyone), presidents, legislators, lobbyists, and media speculate about public opinion—each extrapolates from their contacts or experience to the entire public. Politicians imagine how people will react to proposals. Lobbyists perceive everyone's hopes or fears. The media has a special sensitivity to what audiences find interesting. Each needs polling as much we do to measure public opinion accurately. Further, little guarantees that their views are free of bias, particularly when it comes to lobbyists and others with political agendas. If they talk to average people, they may well focus on those who share their goals. Political parties used to do better. Hundreds of thousands of people living in neighborhoods across the nation can recount the goings on of their neighbors. Before polling, they provided the best account of public opinion. This system, however, was expensive, and what has been labeled corruption—hiring party workers into civil service, for example—paid for it. Somewhat regrettably, it has vanished, never to be seen again.

Our imaginary president, not to mention everyone else, needs technology to measure public opinion. The best democracy arises "if the will of the majority of citizens were to become ascertainable at all times." Those words belong to James Bryce—an English scholar who visited our country in the 1880s. Bryce was another Alexis de Tocqueville, an outsider who came to America to learn how our country worked and take these lessons back to the old world. If you saw the film *Borat*, you are loosely familiar with how this works. Bryce, however, came to the United States later than Tocqueville (and ahead of Borat), at the moment when immediate communication began to shape the political system we still use.

His 1889 book *The American Commonwealth* emphasizes public opinion's place in political evolution, outlining four stages in the development of governance. First, Bryce tells of times when "public opinion was static and passive, acquiescing in the exercise of unquestioned political authority by the dominant group," (imagine ancient Egypt run by the dictatorial pharaoh, or the North Korea of today). This stage's public opinion, such as it existed, supports the leader—or else. Bryce's second stage dawns as people come to understand their power. This awakening causes "conflict" between citizens and rulers, such as took place during the French Revolution. Bryce observed the third stage in 1890s America, when public opinion became an active force, taking the form of periodic elections. Finally, he made an incredible prediction: political evolution would bring a fourth stage into being, when governance has continuous access to public opinion. We live in Bryce's future, when polling satisfies this need to know the people's will.

How well does polling do this job of letting the people speak? We need standards to answer this question. Think about the lightbulb, a wonder of technology. To shorten a long story, humans needed the sun to see. With fire, things improved. Later, inventors built expensive lamps to refine fire and allow the rich to enjoy constant light. Finally, the incandescent bulb extended this luxury to everyone. What makes electric light so good? A number of reasons pop out, and we can use three as technology benchmarks. It is quick—flip a switch, and you get light. It is relatively cheap—wiring a house and buying electricity replaces gathering or storing fuel. It is reliable—unless the light breaks, it always shines. Savings of time and money, along with dependability, are reasonable things to want that other paths to public opinion do not offer.

Measurement technologies confront two more benchmarks—precision and accuracy. Measurement theory—and there are books on such things—uses the connection between a measure and the truth to define these additional standards. Hence, precision and accuracy describe aspects of the correspondence between the measured and the measurement. Precision covers vagueness. It suffices when a friend's directions refer to a place you both know, but laying a sewer to the same spot demands more precision. In the same way, "30 percent approve of the job George W. Bush is doing as president" is more precise than "most people do not like George W. Bush." Accuracy has the same standing. Measurement theory ties accuracy to bias; thus, a biased measure systematically deviates from the true value. A broken tape measure, for example, could have bias if it always underreports the true length. Similarly, lobbyists often present inaccurate views of public opinion because their reports are skewed toward their agenda.

Stepping back, this view invites us to regard polling as a technology. The point is not to become a pollster (though I would not protest if you were inspired!), but to understand how polling beats other methods of ascertaining the public will. In addition, knowing a tad about how something works helps us use it better. We do not need to be an electrician to trace the cord when a bulb goes out. Knowing what results mean requires learning about polling. Thinking about polling as a technology also lets us categorize objections to polling. For instance, when people claim that questions are biased, our thoughts move toward investigating the correspondence between a result and some "true" value. Finally, this technological perspective highlights the fact that polling is a tool, so we can ask whether polling is the right tool. We can imagine ways to improve polling or better technologies, like the great writer Isaac Asimov.

Asimov, a science fiction master, foresaw "computer-assisted elections" when he observed sample surveys' early popularity. He wrote the short story *Franchise* in 1955, which takes the logic of polling to an extreme. Asimov's character, Norman Muller, was picked as the typical American. He was the sole "elector" in a future election—in 2008, no less. On election day, to great fanfare, Muller goes to the poll and votes. After he leaves, reporters pester him, asking who won. The twist is that Muller has no idea; he wasn't given a ballot with names; instead, he answered unusual questions. A computer did the remaining work. The machine decided, first, that Muller's dispositional mix assured he would pick a winner; then it extrapolated from his responses to decide who won, essentially using a sample of one. This story remains science fiction; nevertheless, what polls do is only slightly less fantastic. We can't extrapolate from a sample size of one, but polling does let roughly a thousand people stand for over 300 million.

WHAT MAKES A POLL SCIENTIFIC?

Sample surveys have three ingredients: random sampling, interviewing, and aggregation. Random sampling identifies a population and selects the respondents. Interviewing consists of asking each respondent the poll's questions and recording their responses—a respect for interviewing is the most important thing to take away from this book. Aggregation sums the responses into results. The three together do the job of measuring public opinion. Every poll that successfully combines them produces results that truly represent the population within a known, relatively small, margin of sampling error. Let's lift the curtain to see how this works.

THE MAGIC OF RANDOM SAMPLING

As the name suggests, the people, technically *respondents*, to whom pollsters talk must be selected randomly. Using a lottery, for instance, is fine, but sampling methods that do not use chance will not work. Going over some great disasters in the history of predicting electoral outcomes should make this point crystal clear. Many public opinion textbooks cover these fiascos as cautionary tales for young pollsters because they tie the mistake to a lack of random sampling.

BELLWETHERS

Those versed in political Americana will remember the saying "as Maine goes, so goes the nation." This aphorism encapsulates the notion of a bellwether, a smaller area whose choice predicts that of the whole.

Maine's fame stems from the way that the party of its governor (who is elected in September) matched the party whose candidate was elected president in November every year from 1832 to 1932 except for 1848, 1856, 1880, 1884, 1892, 1912, and 1916. In other words, Maine got 19 of 26 Presidential elections right—a darn good batting average of .731. If Maine's choice had no relationship to the Presidential election—if it were what the jargon calls *independent*, we would expect them to match half the time (50 percent), exactly the same as the two sides of a flipped coin. While imperfect, Maine's track record was enough to scare Presidential candidates whose party lost Maine's gubernatorial race. But we need to know the why of it all.

Maine's success could be pure coincidence. If Maine's choice had nothing to do with electing the President, Maine's voters may have done better than average over a short stretch, like 26 elections, due to chance. Superstitions often grow out of coincidence: perhaps I play ball exceptionally well one time I wear red socks; I might continue to wear them as if they really did help. If chance is the reason, then [residential candidates' unease would be like that after having a black cat cross one's path. Alternatively, Maine could be a decisive tipping point, like the median voter in the next chapter. If elections in other states alternate their choice of candidates in such a way for the outcome to balance evenly, Maine's voters could pick the winner. Empirical investigation quickly dispels this idea.

Lastly, the behavior of Maine's voters may resemble the behavior of all voters. Marketing often employs this logic. When fast food restaurants try out sandwiches, they frequently use Columbus, Ohio—America's supposed market research capitol. They believe that Columbus's food sense is closer to average than that of Boston or New Orleans; in this sense Columbus is more representative. Thus, if a sandwich works in Columbus, chances are it will be generally successful. Consumer companies are right to use a typical city; on the other hand, fast food involves more than voting. Marketers cannot mail out sandwiches to get reactions. Likewise, restaurants are not overly concerned with accuracy; they are happy if a product sells well. In politics, sample surveys are more precise and more accurate than any bellwether.

STRAW POLLS

Many of us have been in "straw" polls, which seeks only to divine a nonbinding choice that indicates where a collective choice may head. Juries, for example, take straw polls to shirk deliberation; if everyone agrees on the verdict, they are done. If they disagree, people are free to change their minds. The results influence but do not determine the outcome. Like *push poll*, *straw poll* is a misnomer. The expression comes from farmers who throw straw into the air to see the wind's direction. Around Andrew Jackson's time, the start of popular politics induced newspapers to straw poll electoral outcomes. They would quiz the "man on the street" and tally the answers to produce a prediction. With juries, straw polls work, because the sample is exhaustive: every juror expresses an opinion. With elections, straw polling's mechanism (often called a *sample of convenience*) is dreadfully unreliable.

The story of the most famous straw polling mistake starts in 1916. *Literary Digest* magazine, wanting to increase circulation, glommed onto the idea of predicting the next president. They mailed millions of postcards to ask people who they would vote for and counted the returns. Long before election day, they published their results, correctly predicting that Woodrow Wilson would win. Nearly everyone saw this as a tremendous accomplishment; the *Literary Digest* "poll" went on to fame and fortune. In 1920, 1924, 1928, and 1932 the magazine repeated its success, correctly predicting the wins of Warren Harding, Calvin Coolidge, Herbert Hoover, and Franklin Delano Roosevelt. In 1936 they called the election for Alf Landon—but wait; who is Alf Landon? The *Digest* was in big trouble. With their first five predictions' perfect record, their poll was a national institution and few doubted they would succeed again. But their confident 1936 prediction caused a furor when Franklin Delano Roosevelt won reelection.

Looking back, their mistake is obvious. Although *Literary Digest* sent out 10 million postcards and 2 million people (20 percent) mailed back intended votes, the results were worthless. The list of addresses came from three sources: subscribers, automobile owners, and telephone users. At the time, only the wealthy could afford such luxuries and, consequently, be on the lists. Thus, the *Digest* really asked how the well-off would vote—and sure enough, they supported Republican Alf Landon. Prior to 1936 the political gap between rich and poor was small enough that their straw poll produced the right answer, but during the Great Depression, this gap grew to expose the fatal flaw.

This upset catapulted the new industry of scientific polling to prominence when a young George Gallup used sample surveys to predict that Roosevelt would win. He randomly sampled a mere 50,000 people. Before the election, everyone made fun of Gallup. How could 50,000 do as well as 2 million? Well, of course, we know they can; Gallup was right and the *Literary Digest* was wrong. His company remains successful while that magazine folded, barely remembered past this tale of their fatal mistake.

TRUE RANDOM SAMPLING

So how did 50,000 beat 2 million? Past that, what logic tells us that roughly a thousand Americans can faithfully represent all 300 million? At the outset, it's hard to believe that 1 in 300,000 citizens, 0.000003, can do the job; surely, we sympathize with those who ridiculed Gallup. The magic lay not in the numbers but in picking the right people—Asimov was right to focus on selection! This process relies on randomness. A good analogy concerns macaroni and cheese: should we taste it right after we dump cheese into cooked noodles, we get either a plain noodle (no cheese) or a lump of cheese, so we mix it up. As we stir, the difference between one taste and another gets smaller. With sufficient mixing, any taste is roughly the same because the pot's contents are homogenous or, equivalently, the cheese and pasta are randomly spread. Now, any taste is representative of the whole. Random sampling does this to the population, mixing it so well that it is like putting the mac and cheese into a blender.

To pollsters, *population* has a technical meaning—the group we want to understand or those represented. It is important to keep the population criteria in mind when examining poll results, because these results, intentionally and literally, only represent that population. Political polls often focus on registered or "likely" voters, in which case the unregistered or "unlikely" are not represented. Thus, if a pollster wants to predict an election and guesses badly about who will vote, the poll will be wrong.

The *sample* is a randomly selected subset. The process of choosing the sample has two parts: first, pollsters list everyone in the population, and second, they use chance to choose who to contact. Listing everyone in the United States is no easy task. Pollsters today typically use a sampling procedure called random digit dialing, or RDD. This term may give the wrong impression; pollsters do not pick up the phone and start making calls. Rather, knowing something about how phone companies assign numbers, they list the country's residences and select a random set to call.

RDD's way of choosing respondents is light years ahead of the *Literary Digest's* postcards, yet it has problems, too. One major issue concerns response rate—the percentage of those called who answer the phone and participate. If refusal itself is random, refusals can be replaced with another random choice. Systematic refusals affect the results by decreasing the representation of groups that tend to not participate. College students, for instance, frequently ignore pollsters, so the quality of their representation goes down. Pollsters, well aware of this problem, try to get everyone to answer, and as said, we ought to agree. They can also deal with refusal by adjusting results, to weight them so the numbers reflect reality more closely. If only half the sample's college students respond, one might double count their answers to make up for the refusals. Still, weighting procedures are imperfect. Nothing ensures that the answering college students are like the refusals, so pollsters tend to weight on a case-by-case basis.

In addition, polling has to adapt to changes in communication technology. In Gallup's day, field workers traveled the country, locating the selected respondents and conducting interviews in person. When telephones penetrated every household, this expensive method gave way to call centers. Presently, telephones remain the standard way to contact respondents. Technology continues to advance, and cell phones create new obstacles. They make listing the population and contacting respondents harder, forcing pollsters to compensate. Some polls have turned to using the Internet. While generally cheaper, this method lacks the intimacy of telephone conversations. Then again, changes in communication technology have no effect on the logic of random sampling. The representative value of a random sample from an identified population is certain.

Critically, mathematics tells us exactly how well the sample represents the population. Known as *sampling error*, this concept and its formula are well known to all who work with polls. We know it, too; sampling error is the plus or minus 3 percent that good media tack on to poll results. Sampling error tells us that the true result (from the entire population) will be within a specified range—namely, from the result minus the sampling error to the result plus the sampling error 95 percent of the time. In this way, sampling error indicates the range in which the true value is likely to fall given the result. Sampling error can be seen as the price of representation, if we interviewed everyone in the population, sampling error would be 0. Notice also that the sampling error concerns the precision of poll results; smaller sampling error makes for tighter predictions about the population.

Without going into sampling error formulae in detail (consult the Internet if you're interested), allow me go over how sampling error relates to the sizes of the sample and population. This table lists population sizes across the top and sample sizes down the left side. The numbers that these categories index are estimates of the sampling error for that sample and population size.

Sample	*Population*			
	3,000	*300,000*	*3 million*	*300 million*
500	4	4.38	4.38	4.38
1500	1.79	2.52	2.53	2.53
2500	0.8	1.95	1.96	1.96
3500	–	1.65	1.66	1.66

If our population is 300 million, roughly the size of the United States, and we randomly select 500 people to interview, then the sampling error is 4.38. Hence, if we ask people, "Do you approve or disapprove of the job the president is doing?" and the answer for the entire population—which we do not know—is 50 percent, then the poll would report a result of between 45.62 and 54.38 95 percent of the time. Consequently, adding and subtracting 4.5 percent to a poll result gives the likely range of the true value. Notice how sampling error makes arguments over small polling differences inane. If one result is 50 percent and another is 51, sampling error makes them virtually identical. Put another way, the difference between two poll results has to be greater than the sample error if it is to be meaningful.

As the sample size increases, sampling error slowly falls. With a sample of 1,500 in a national population, the sampling error is roughly 2.5, narrowing the range around 50 percent to 47.5 to 52.5. Looking at the whole table, you can see that sampling error does not decrease at the same rate as the sample size rises, nor do the two go up linearly as the population increases. With a sample of 500, for instance, the sampling error is the same whether we interview 300,000, 3 million, or 300 million. At the same time, if the population is small—3,000—and 2,500 people respond, the sample error is still 0.8, though we have polled almost all the population. National polls typically sample around a thousand respondents to represent Americans with a sampling error of roughly 3 percent. And that is it—all there is to polling's scientific basis.

A point that some discussions neglect is that random sampling ensures that poll results are unbiased. Consider a concrete case; imagine we sample 1,000 males to find out American men's average height. We know the true answer is around five feet, eight inches, so the most likely result from the sample is also five feet, eight inches—there is no bias that would cause us to expect a higher or lower result. This lack of bias extends to any measured characteristic—physical, psychological (IQ), economic (income), social (education), or political. The same logic entails that bigger errors are more unlikely than smaller errors. For example, we could draw a sample from the general population in which all the respondents are women, but we can also win the lottery: both are possible, but vanishingly rare. Further, pollsters can use known characteristics, like age, to check a sample's randomization. If a national sample has only old people, then that sample is extraordinary.

Other elements of polling can create problems, too, which usually revolve around determining exactly who or what the sample represents. We alluded to one issue, population definition; a sample of registered voters does not represent the unregistered, but there is more—time for another story.

With his 1936 success, George Gallup and sample surveys entered American life. However, Gallup's celebrated record has its errors. Everybody has heard of his most famous mistake, due to the famous photograph that indelibly etched itself into political memory. The photo has Harry Truman holding up a newspaper, the *Chicago Daily Tribune* of November 1948; the headline screams "Dewey Defeats Truman," yet Truman smiles triumphantly. Why? He won. The faulty headline traces to a polling error. Although Gallup used random sampling, he based his prediction on results from the wrong time. Specifically, he quit polling two weeks before the election, presumably when Dewey was still winning. Gallup was mortified on election day; the lesson is that the timing of polls (and other factors we will discuss) may influence results.

A similar error occurred in the 2008 New Hampshire Democratic presidential primary. The Sunday before the election nine polls indicated that Barack Obama would not only win, but win by 10 percentage points. That number is important, because it is well beyond the sample error range. Hillary Clinton actually won the primary, leading everyone to ask what went wrong. Most observers concluded that a press conference held on Monday—after polling ended but in time to change the outcome—pushed voters to Clinton. In polling's defense, I propose that the other methods to measure public opinion we listed probably would have done worse in both cases. More to the point, once pollsters analyze these mistakes, they try to avoid them in the future.

A final crucial aspect of random sampling can also be overlooked. Random sampling's representation runs both ways, so that your thoughts and feelings about a thousand randomly sampled Americans necessarily capture your attitude toward all of us. Take a scenario based on Lippmann's conception of stereotypes. Someone who has an idiot for a neighbor or who watched *Jackass the Movie* may discount poll results when they hear them, reckoning that people are idiots. Leaving aside issues that we will discuss in chapter 6, this person is extrapolating from a sample of one to every American. In reality, a poll with a thousand respondents is far more diverse than any one person—diverse enough, in fact, to represent the whole country. So although there may be idiots in the sample, the likelihood of it being a sample of idiots is nearly nonexistent—unless you believe that everyone in the United States is an idiot.

POLLING AND DEMOCRACY

Understanding the representation that random sampling offers launches our discussion of what polls can and cannot do. This discussion has strong normative overtones, because talking about polling's purpose must include questioning polling's moral status. My answer tracks the three ingredients. Sampling replaces exhaustive or haphazard attempts to contact citizens with a subset that stands in a mathematically defined margin. To me, this hints at a moral equivalence between the sample and the population. The interview, then, quizzes respondents and records answers; this process requires deeper examination. To take one example, pollsters' control over choosing topics and formulating questions demands that we examine their motives. Here, we will look into pollsters' backgrounds and the pressures they face. We can ask a similar question about respondents, focusing first on the prima facie case for taking their answers seriously, which prepares us for the rest of the book.

Aggregation, the third and least complex ingredient, offers a place to greet some of polling's more thoughtful critiques. This process of adding up answers to poll questions to produce results is so undemanding that most researchers ignore it completely. Of course, this ingredient is essential; without it, polling results (and the enterprise) disappear. Furthermore, when critics dismiss aggregation they pointedly suggest that polling does not measure public opinion. In contrast, pollsters and researchers rarely bother to defend their belief that polling and public opinion are synonyms. When criticism meets inattention, this discussion breaks down. Critics refuse to acknowledge the value of polling while others go on producing, studying and trying to publicize sample survey results.

This book could restart this conversation by defining polling's purpose more narrowly, explaining that polling is only the best technology for measuring public opinion. My view implies that the here and now requires polling to know public opinion, effectively linking the terms. I do not expect to convince polling's critics; a Lippmann zombie would not change sides and cheerfully accept pollsters' offerings as good guides for governance. This exercise has another purpose. These claims push us to a unified democratic theory that specifies the role public polling should play in democratic governance. In this endeavor, the principle of sympathetic utility may speed our pursuit.

Sympathetic utility calls for recognizing that most serious commentary has value, so synthesis is better than rejection. All too often, scholarly discourse, like that of pollsters and critics, ends with *I am right, you are wrong, goodbye*. To achieve synthesis, we integrate worthwhile ideas into our own. Accordingly, I shall try to turn the criticism of polling into a more precise statement about polling's function. Keep in mind that if I succeed, we have only made an opening step. Should we agree that polling measures public opinion satisfactorily, we still must determine whether public opinion itself has value. And if we decide that it does, we then need to figure out how that value can be extracted and enhanced.

SOME GENERAL ATTACKS ON POLLING

Throughout its brief history, polling's foes (eminent social scientists included) have bashed sample surveys and the people they represent. Early dismissals generally reworked ancient criticisms of democracy into more palatable forms. Lindsey Rogers tossed off a surprisingly fierce slam in his 1949 book *The Pollsters*. Mocking the title of Gallup's book, Rogers concludes, "[I]nstead of feeling the *Pulse of Democracy*, Dr. Gallup listens to baby talk." Foreshadowing many later works on polling, Rogers goes on to lists flaws that foil polls' attempts to portray public opinion in his view: the lack of information behind opinions, the inability to reflect variations in intensity or conviction as well as possible discrepancies between announced opinion and private thought or between response and behavior. His recommendation, nevertheless, is fairly boring; basically, he restates the "trustee" argument of Edmund Burke

Burke is a favorite of polling's detractors. After witnessing France's turmoil, he published *Reflections on the Revolution in France* in 1790. Amazingly, Burke foresaw the "reign of terror" before it happened. In that phase of the revolution the mob, under Robespierre, adopted a new way of dealing with its enemies—public execution. A whiff of suspicion was sufficient to send French aristocrats to the guillotine. Soon things got out of hand, and any suspected enemy of the revolution was murdered. Thousands died, many of whom were undoubtedly innocent. This tragedy gave mobs the bad name that somewhat absurdly weaves through many treatments of public opinion.

Burke contrasts the fairly orderly American Revolution with the French chaos, laying the groundwork for the trustee argument. He claims that the Founding Fathers' wisdom prevented the mob's takeover and accompanying bloodbath in the United States. He proposes that elected representatives should exercise their own judgment and ignore "momentary passions." This argument maintains that representatives should not act like delegates, merely repeating the public's whims. Instead, they ought to be trustees, ignoring public opinion whenever they deem it necessary to protect the public's interests.

A similar attack on polls came from Gabriel Almond, a social scientist revered for his investigation of civic culture. In his 1950 book *The American People and Foreign Policy*, Almond argues that public opinion should not guide international relations, because "citizens have formless and plastic moods which undergo frequent alteration in response to changes in events." Almond argues that the government has to ignore public opinion to maintain consistent policies. For all intents, Almond rehashes one of the central arguments in the *Federalist Papers*. Burke's wise Founding Fathers designed a system of checks and balances and separation of powers not only to keep officeholders from abusing their authority but also to prevent a "tyranny of the majority." Our founders feared that democracy would bring frequent rebellions that would prevent stable government.

This fear was not unreasonable. Right before the constitutional convention in 1787, Daniel Shays, a former continental army officer, led a rebellion in western Massachusetts against state taxes. If Shays could do it, remarks went, anyone could. The Founding Fathers themselves had revolted, making it difficult for them to question Shays' legitimacy. Instead, they tried to craft a representative government that would respond to the people, yet not react mechanically. Imagine that some desire hits everyone save officeholders, who vehemently oppose it. The representatives invoke Burke to justify their intransigence. Within two years, citizens could award challengers every seat in the House, but up to four years would pass before they could change two-thirds of the Senate and the President. Then, a Senate minority can filibuster and the Supreme Court can rule it unconstitutional. This scheme purposefully slows down government's reactions; Almond just favors a bit more movement on the continuum from participatory to representative governance.

One significant detail, however, separates Burke and the Founders from Rogers and Almond. The former worked in Bryce's third stage, before the invention of quick, cheap, and reliable technology for measuring public opinion. We can suspect that some founders may not have reacted so negatively to polls. Thomas Jefferson, for one, embodied a line of thought that encourages participation. Moreover, his stance prevails, leading, for instance, to expand voting rights, which have moved decidedly away from franchising only white male property owners. Other forces, chiefly related to communication technology, also influenced the founder's structure. When it takes days for a letter from Boston to reach Washington, the capitol's residents, like the Parisian mob, can wield inordinate influence, and officeholders have a stronger rationale for using their own judgment. Last but not least, we come to a more normative point that we shall develop below—if you trust people to elect leaders, why don't you trust them more?

AN INITIAL RESPONSE

Having acknowledged the value of random sampling, we can expand the idea of trust into a preliminary rebuttal to Rogers, Almond, and their anti-polling comrades. If we assume that pollsters act in good faith (we look into their motives below), using the technology appropriately to try and measure public opinion, then it seems reasonable to see polling's problems as treatable diseases rather than as fatal flaws. To analogize, the *Diagnostic and*

Statistical Manual of Mental Disorders provides an extensive list of the problems afflicting human minds. Its fourth edition, updated in 2000, lists 297 disorders. Although these disorders are present in all humans, no one person has every disorder. Furthermore, we do not find humans defective, despite their having the potential for all these ailments. We could make similar analogies to cars, electronics, and houses; they are useful enough that we treasure them in the face of their vulnerabilities and try to fix them when they break.

There is a deeper moral justification for taking poll results seriously that uses the principle of "performative utterance." Jurgen Habermas, who we will discuss further, observes that certain things are true by virtue of saying them. In saying "I promise to do X," one has indeed promised to do X (unless the statement was sarcasm). Linguistic philosophers categorize this kind of speech as performative, or self-executing. Habermas notes that political expressions, like respondents' answers and other candidate's speeches, share this performative property. When a respondent states "I support X" or answers "Yes" to "Do you support X?" the only plausible impression is that they support X at the moment they make the statement. Thus, in practically all cases, we have no reason to doubt the sincerity of anyone's answers at the time of the interview. (The qualifier "'t the moment" will lead us to empirical research into the dynamics surrounding these expressions.)

Combining the mathematics of sampling with survey response's performative property logically entails that sample survey results express the public's preferences with respect to that moment and question. This two-part foundation should stave off more expansive critiques of polling well enough for us to move on to more specific assaults.

CRITICISMS OF AGGREGATION

One thoughtful and specific condemnation of polling flows from Jean-Jacques Rousseau's definition of the general will. Rousseau (pronounced roo-SO) published *The Social Contract* in 1762 (again with the French Revolution). He defines the general will as "citizens' desires when they think about the community as a whole" and, naturally, argues that it legitimates governance. This definition seems uncontroversial at first glance, but the codicil "as a whole" directs Rousseau's meaning in a way that may conflict with sample surveys. His whole is the object of citizens' desires that comprise general will, implying that desires with other objects do not. Thus, the general will is not the mere aggregation of the public's opinions. Scholars say that the general will captures "refined" preferences, where the refinement process separates worthy desires—those that concern the whole—from the rest.

Gustav Le Bon (hard for non-French to pronounce correctly) built upon Rousseau's classification. In *The Crowd*, which appeared in 1896, Le Bon compares the public with the mob—elitists' favorite target. He tries to distinguish legitimate publics from illegitimate mobs by describing the refinement citizens' desires require to become the general will. The public, to Le Bon, transforms into a self-aware entity through a reasoning process, whereas the mob is a highly emotional collection of individuals. Le Bon deduces that the singular public's wishes count as the general will, whereas the mob's aggregate desires do not. It is too easy to point out the flaws in Le Bon's psychological research; reason, for instance, does not exist without emotion (see Antonio Damasio's *Descartes' Error*). It seems unlikely at this time that the public is an emergent superentity, as well; conversely, one version of Le Bon's thinking is not so different from John Dewey's.

We should take time to recognize that Le Bon's ideas stem from adverse political conditions. Bryce's England, for instance, had its last major political tremor in 1688, a tame coup named the Glorious Revolution. By Le Bon's time, France had withstood four colossal disruptions—1789, a civil uprising in 1830, a rebellion in 1848, and a near civil war in 1871. The last event was unusually bad; in the aftermath of their defeat by the Prussians, Parisians created a revolutionary government, the Commune, which attempted to duplicate the reign of terror's excesses. This backdrop makes Le Bon's wish to smother emotional politics more alluring. Other observers and the great Habermas have picked up on his idea, cherishing political deliberation and identifying it as a prerequisite of democratic legitimacy—but we will continue this discussion later.

At the moment, it seems these ideas about public rationality often confuse standards for good public opinion with public opinion itself. Thus, Le Bon's proposal that reasoned opinion provides a better foundation for governance than whatever crazy mobs offer does not contradict the belief that polls are the best measure of public opinion. In this vein, we can isolate processes, such as education or deliberation, that may enhance public opinion, from polling—its measure. A thought experiment may substantiate this claim. Imagine a poll taken of the French people as the guillotine was chopping; we suspect that in a propaganda-free environment, they may not have been so supportive. The word propaganda recalls Dewey's argument with Lippmann (as well as the claim that forms chapter 6) that the citizens can learn and make good decisions, and communicate them through poll results. There is, however, an alternative interpretation of Rousseau and Le Bon that attacks polling at a fundamental level.

THE PRICE OF MEASUREMENT

In 1948, Herbert Blumler, a contemporary of Rogers and Almond, penned the *American Sociological Review* article "Public opinion and public opinion polling," which presents an original, and potentially devastating, assessment of polls. Following Le Bon, his central assertion is that public opinion is an organic whole, not "one person, one vote"—read: an aggregation. He proposes that public opinion is a conglomerate of group interests that encompasses the attitudes of group leaders, carefully tuned by their intensity and relative political power. Further, since he regards things like intensity as unquantifiable, attempts to weight poll results to account for these factors are doomed. Blumler concludes that poll results will always misrepresent what he calls public opinion. Susan Herbst (in *Numbered Voices*, 1995) self-consciously extends Blumler's argument; she recommends discovering public opinion through a "clan" model that captures citizens' interaction with governance by talking to group leaders, lobbyists, and the media. Herbst and Blumler also highlight what they see as inherent flaws in polling—chiefly survey respondents' lack of agenda control and initiative.

Other prominent scholars echo this unease. Perhaps the most important public opinion researcher (chapter 4), Philip Converse, acknowledges that polling uncovers less intense opinions than voluntary expression in 1965's *American Political Science Review*. John Geer's 1996 *From Tea Leaves to Opinion Polls* argues that politics required leadership prior to polling, implying that polling obviates this need in his history of polling. In a standard text, *American Public Opinion*, Robert Erickson observes "where it had once been a behavior, public opinion is now mostly a summation of attitudes. In fact, the citizen is relieved of all initiative whatsoever."

Some scholars dismiss these critiques, in the words of V. O. Key from 1961's *Public Opinion and American Democracy*:

> For purposes of political analysis one need not strain painfully toward the formation of a theoretical representation of an eerie entity called "public opinion." One need not seek to find "the" public embodied in some kind of amorphous social structure that goes through recurring patterns of action as it reaches a decision. "Public opinion" in this discussion may simply be taken to mean those opinions held by private persons which governments find it prudent to heed.

Gallup uses less academic language:

> Polling is merely an instrument for gauging public opinion. When a president, or any other leader, pays attention to poll results, he is, in effect, paying attention to the views of the people. Any other interpretation is nonsense.

My amendment synthesizes Blumler's critique; essentially he assigns a price to polling, offering a choice: pay the price (and maybe find a substitute) or abandon the use of polls. Clearly, I advocate polling, so I suggest that we clarify its price by defining agency, and that we then address agenda control, intensity, and leadership. Agency, in their sense, refers to the capacity to act; this idea connects to freedom, as in free agent. Lacking agency, one loses initiative and the ability to act autonomously. This characterization uncovers the horror nested within the critics' claim. Further, this threat is not implausible. Polling typically discourages respondents from talking freely; for instance, it asks standardized questions and limits the range answers can take. These constraints lead polling texts to prominently feature discussions about outwardly trivial details, like whether interviews should prompt respondents to say "do not know."

Moreover, we do not call polling organizations, as we might call politicians; rather, they call us. Pollsters (or whoever pays the bill) determines the poll's timing and topic; thus they control the agenda—to use the correct term. When a pollster calls, they may ask open-ended questions, like "What do you think is the most important problem facing the United States?" but respondents cannot drive the interview. In a survey on abortion, one would not expect respondents to start venting about the economy, though that may be their primary concern. Polls also have trouble letting respondents fully express the intensity of opinion within topics. While pollsters may ask if we care about the environment strongly, not so strongly or not at all; it does not give the person who lives in a tree more weight than the person who bumper-stickers their car. In sum, polling measures reactions not actions. Does polling's advantage in measurement make it worth giving up agency, agenda control, and the ability to capture the full range of political preferences' intensity? Of course I, like Key and Gallup, enthusiastically say yes.

AGGREGATION'S TRUE WORTH

Consider two points in defense of aggregation. First, polling allows us to separate things like agency and initiative from public judgment. At one level, these alternative public opinion indicators still exist. We have the freedom to talk with whom we wish, and they can decide whether to listen. In this way, polling supplements earlier modalities, even if polls push these mechanisms to change. More generally, polling's existence has changed our political system by letting us separate public judgment from other processes, like agenda setting. Not inconsequently, this shift also allows other political actors to pay part of aggregation's price. In large part, the functions that Blumler and others attribute to public opinion involve advocacy, so we can reasonably admit that polling divides citizens into advocates and judges. This division of labor has the potential to enhance democracy for all.

When agents, whether individuals or groups, exercise initiative and seek government action, their efforts open with attempts to put their ideas into play. In political science jargon, they try to set the agenda. The fact that government can only do so much creates a struggle for the government's time—read: agenda control. This competition is a democratic hallmark. Dictators set agendas in totalitarian regimes, whereas democracies hold sacred the freedoms of speech, petition, and assembly. In general, agenda-setting fights operate at two levels—private affairs such as lobbying officeholders, and more public stabs at grabbing media coverage and winning mass support. There is no sharp division between the two; competitors decide which route to take (or use both), freely changing tactics at any time. All the agents we listed, such as presidents, legislators, and lobbyists, play this game every day. The media also plays—whether actively, by allocating coverage to other players, or passively, by ignoring them.

Our theory of public judgment, spelled out in the last chapter, covers the commonly visible aspects of this competition—the fight for public attention and support. In fighting over agendas, politicians and others "make the case" for their plans, trying to persuade the public to support their goals. As they do, their disjointed, overlapping, and competing messages produce the flow of information directed at the public. Before the book's end we will say more about the quality of this information, and about some ways of improving it. For now, we can place polls in this process.

Polls let citizens judge this competition—the second point. Thinking public opinion is some immeasurable organic whole leaves every political debate unresolved, a bubbling mix with no end. True, in democracy every policy can be challenged, so there is no final outcome. However, polling allows citizens to give concrete input at distinct points in time, fostering closure. These results are no more than judgments about the questions put before them, if only because polling is reactive. Yet, given the foundation we discussed, all citizens get the chance to speak within the limits raised by polling's critics.

How can the citizenry be heard without polls? The other methods discussed speak for population segments; either intentionally or not, they do not represent everyone equally. In giving everyone this chance, however limited, polls counterbalance special interests. Effectively then, polls can change democratic politics from a competition between interests to a competition among interests for the public's favor. This feature is polling's trump card;

even elections—which no one disputes as essential to democracy—lack the ability to speak for all. We should pause to elaborate.

POLLS VERSUS ELECTIONS

What exactly is the moral difference between sample surveys and elections— why do we need both? I trust this comparison is not far-fetched. At bottom, both offer measures of public opinion, yet elections give rise to few norma- tive disputes. In *Federalist 53*, no less than James Madison repeats the apho- rism "where annual elections end, tyranny begins." Hmm why, then, did we get longer terms for legislators and the presidency? Anyway, Madison lived in Bryce's third stage, too—a time when no one would think of democracy without elections but before the invention of sample surveys. My goal, in bringing up elections, is to reassign some of their moral standing to polling.

George Gallup uses a similar argument in his works. Besides being a poll- ster, Gallup was a businessman, and his book, *The Pulse of Democracy*, is equal parts sales pitch and political philosophy. Nevertheless, his arguments have worth. Driven by Bryce's vision and with the attention from his role in the *Literary Digest* fiasco, Gallup spotlights polling's critics' not looking for customers. He talks about the way polling counterbalances special interests by providing a less biased way to assess public opinion. Here, he picks on absolute dictators. One might shrink from this equation, but as the most spe- cial of special interests, dictators put the needs of one—themselves—above the needs of all. Gallup argues that dictators and special interests preempt the people, whereas polls and elections tap their will.

So similar are polls and elections that Gallup calls his product the "miniature electorate" or "instant referendum." Indeed, they have a lot in common; polls and elections rely on aggregation—the *one person, one voice* rule. Likewise, both are unbiased in the sense we defined. More profoundly, the preferences expressed in polls and elections share the same psychological mechanism. This mechanism, which we shall discuss throughout the book, meshes citizens' dispositions with whatever they see and hear to produce choices. Researchers tacitly acknowledge this point when they use sample surveys to study electoral behavior. In fact, the bulk of public opinion research's find- ings apply to elections and vice versa. Moreover, some reflection reveals that the arguments of Lippmann and Dewey apply as much to elections as they do to polls. The same is true for nearly all polling critiques; Rogers, for one, can just as easily classify electoral outcomes as "baby talk."

The agency critique in particular applies as much to elections as polls, with one exception. Both votes and poll responses are private and anonymous expressions, in which external forces heavily circumscribe the format. Nominating processes, for instance, determine electoral choices, leaving write-in candidates with infinitesimally small prospects. Thus, the ballots voters cast are as reactive as the judgments respondents render. The argument about initiative applies to elections, as well. Voters exercise no initiative beyond deciding to go the polls—that is the sole exception (though polling is also voluntary in a loose sense). At the same time, everyone is free to seek nomination and electoral victory, regardless of their likelihood of success.

As we turn to their status, elections and polls part ways. Ancient and entangled in democratic tradition, contemporary elections are tightly regulated. Not only do we specify their timing, the manner of voting and the tallying procedure, the law awards the victor real power. Hence, elections are binding—who or whatever wins takes office or becomes law. A more subtle "focal" property accompanies this legal stature. As regular and expected events, elections attract attention and effort. Elections are able to energize the nation, shifting candidates, organizations, and the media into high gear. Citizens, for the most part, respond to this activity by tuning into political news. Last, the electoral season ends with a distinct outcome. Thus, tradition and law stand in back of elections, assuring their importance, while polling, the relative newcomer, battles for respect.

On the other hand, elections have some salient disadvantages; the same forces that thrust elections to democracy's front and center deprive them of flexibility. Polling, in contrast, is an extraordinarily elastic enterprise, if only because polls cost so much less. Polls do impose the extra charge of sampling error because their interviews do not exhaust (no pun intended) the population. Nevertheless, for the price of one national election, we can afford hundreds if not thousands of sample surveys. Within polls, the range of questions and answers, if limited, is still broader than ballots offer. One poll can also ask more questions than any election. To conclude, compare the role of registrars, who oversee elections, to pollsters. Superficially, they fulfill the same duty by supervising a conduit for public judgment. Conversely, the registrar's discretion is so limited that their actions are seldom controversial; the same cannot be said for pollsters. Pollsters have more to do—choosing the timing and topic, phrasing questions and reporting on their results—and thus substantially more potential influence.

Interpretation is one hefty difficulty that pollsters do not share with registrars. Elections rarely do more than ask a set of parallel questions that have unambiguous consequences. The implications of any poll are less precise. For now, I hope we see value in this lack of structure. Rather than dealing with answers in isolation, polls give us the opportunity to probe public opinion thoroughly. Naturally, this raises challenges: *how can we pursue this task systematically? will we get contradictory answers?* We will spend most of chapter 5 on these topics. In addition, polls offer a continuous read on public opinion rather than the periodic tastes of elections. In the spirit of Bryce, we can see this shortcoming in the September 11, 2001, tragedy. Everyone can admit how that event radically changed circumstances.

Of course, polls can never replace elections—nor should they. In truth, polls and elections supplement each other as methods for knowing public opinion. Exit polls epitomize this symbiosis. Exit polls are real polls, because they use random sampling; however, they sample precincts instead of sampling individuals or households. Pollsters cannot list all the individuals who will vote, so they list all the places where voting occurs. They then send interviewers to a sample of these locations. For example, in recent national elections interviewers were sent to 1,495 precincts. At each precinct, exit polls sample systemically, interviewing every tenth or twentieth voter, producing data that represents all the precincts in the election.

As we know, the media and other politicos depend on exit polls to figure out why citizens voted the way they did. Without them, it would be much harder to talk about things like mandates, because it would be harder to know what drove voters' judgments. Maybe we could try alternatives like examining campaign speeches, but we must suspect that directly talking to voters is better and that talking to a random sample is better than talking to just anyone. So, while imperfect—exit polls tend to ignore absentee voters, for example—they provide valuable insights that supplement the outcome. More broadly, sample surveys play a big part in elections; private polls influence campaign strategies while public polls help determine media coverage, including who will participate in debates, as well as the flow of campaign contributions. In so doing, they bear out Gallup's miniature electorate notion by serving as surrogates for the real thing.

On the flip side, polling and elections sometimes compete; in particular, the day-to-day reading of public opinion strains against Burke's trustee notion. Many politicians take a perverse pride in "not following the polls," suggesting they are leaders. Admirable to a point, this position can be taken to an extreme. Do we really want political leaders who ignore the public's demands? My answer is no. Yet, I also believe that not all poll results are created equal. The major task of this book; in concert with interpreting poll results, is to determine when we should take poll results seriously and expect political leaders to heed their call, and when they can be safely overlooked.

Now we ought to see polls and elections resemblance. Contemporary elections do not allow voters to exercise agency, do provide a poor measure of intensity, and do produce somewhat ambiguous outcomes in terms of a mandate. But these characteristics do not destroy polls' legitimacy. Elections do have the backing of law—rules that define voting, tallying, and winners' rewards. More importantly, although events periodically publicize their imperfections, elections persist as democracy's cornerstone. Even in the absence of laws to regulate polling, it seems that polls merit some of the same respect as building blocks in the structure of democracy.

To buttress this point and continue to this chapter's final topic, let us inspect what may be the worst question ever. In succinct language, Gallup recounts the German Reichstag election of November 12, 1933, which asked the following horror (try to read it aloud in a bad accent):

> Dost thou, German man or German woman, approve the policy of thy Reich government, and art thou ready to acknowledge this policy as the expression of thine own viewpoint and will, and solemnly pledge thyself to it?

As if that formulation was not bad enough, the instructions read:

> The voter in the plebiscite shall mark his cross on the green ballot under the printed "Yes." The circle "No" shall be left free.

Can anyone dream up a more evil question? Though this plebiscite had electoral trappings, the result is illegitimate. The fact that nearly everyone, over 40 million German citizens, "voted" yes means nothing because the measurement does not offer a valid read of public opinion. So, beyond sampling and the notion of performative utterance, what makes readings of public opinion valid? Let us start to answer this question by talking to pollsters, conceivably members of democracy's most important profession.

CRITICISMS OF POLLSTERS' POWER

Pollsters, as stated, have far more discretion then registrars in doing their job supervising a measure of public opinion. This discretion is not total; if they fail to use random sampling, for example, they are not polling. Similarly, professional codes lay out some best practices for the rest of polling's mechanical side. The American Association for Public Opinion Research (AAPOR) has guidelines (on their website) emphasizing disclosure, especially the details concerning sponsor, population definition, sample size, and question wording, along with specific results. Scholarly checks generally find that public polls adhere to these self-enforced rules. Then again, there has been less investigation of polling's "soft" side, choices of topics, timing, and question wordings—exactly where pollsters' discretion seems most menacing.

My favorite critic, Benjamin Ginsberg, argues that for all intents and purposes pollsters form part of a conspiracy that undermines popular control. His 1988 book *The Captive Public* concludes that pollsters "domesticate" public opinion, effectively rendering it impotent. Ginsberg values the old days, before polling was invented, when officeholders had to consult with group leaders and the like to craft policy; now he thinks polls assist officeholders in manufacturing support for their own ideas. Thus, by channeling public input, polls make it possible for the elite to get its way with a more controllable public. Others we have discussed also share this belief. I admit that Ginsberg is right in some circumstances; we have to learn which—that is, what poll results deserve condemnation, and which are free of taint. On the other hand, you are well aware that I do not endorse his view that polling itself is an evil enterprise.

One problem we have in judging polling overlaps its nature as a measurement technology. Usually the way we check rulers is to compare them to some agreeable standard, like the length light travels in 1/299,792,458 of a second—the definition of a meter. We should see that common standards beat more haphazard ones, like the foot, which used to be just that, the length of anyone's foot. Sadly, we should also see that agreeable standards are not always available to evaluate polling. Sometimes they are; many studies, notably Crespi's 1990 *Public Opinion, Polls, and Democracy*, show that preelection polls are accurate, in that they do an excellent job predicting the margin of victory. Much of the time, though, there is no standard to gauge poll results' accuracy.

To illustrate, Burns Roper, writing in 1990's *The Classics of Polling*, makes the widely accepted point that sampling error constitutes a minimum estimate of a given survey result's inaccuracy. He then claims that the "biggest potential source of error" comes from question wording—so "other" error combines with sampling error to create "total" error in his view. Another fact magnifies this potential pitfall. Although we know the sampling error of a given poll result to a mathematical certainty, this other error to which Roper refers is harder to assess (though we will try in our investigations). Consider one finding that did not make it into this book. Looking across 139 national poll questions addressing the 1990s Medicare funding crisis, questions containing the phrase "keep Medicare from going bankrupt" were associated with an average of 30 percent more support, with appropriate statistical controls, than those with an alternative phrase, such as "keep Medicare financially sound." If pollsters have discretion over putting words with such powerful effects in poll questions, then Ginsberg may be right in saying that pollsters have too much power.

Other pollster choices, like poll timing and topic, raise analogous concerns. In some sense, this worry reiterates an old koan concerning observation: "If a tree falls in a forest and no one is around to hear it, does it make a sound?"

Similarly, if no one polls on an issue, does public opinion exist? The expense of polling affects our answer. Though not as expensive as elections, polls still cost money, so someone has to pay for them. As a result, not every issue can be polled all the time. Public polls may be especially vulnerable in this area, if only because they are often funded by media organizations that have goals that may conflict with producing comprehensive public opinion data.

STUDY NUMERO UNO: GETTING TO KNOW SOME POLLSTERS

Instead of speculating further, my student Andy Levy and I decided to directly question some public pollsters. Our research indicates that this is the first attempt to talk to leading pollsters to better understand their craft. These interviews should uncover something about the origins of public poll results. Their answers will also provide a foundation for our investigations. This protostudy employs a social scientific method known as elite interviewing, mainly because we asked all the pollsters the same questions in the same order. Yet, the pollsters knew we were investigating their work, which raises issues with what social scientists term social desirability. The trouble is that people may act differently under observation—for example, by rationalizing their behavior. To ameliorate this potential problem, we decided to keep the pollster's comments anonymous. You can see the list of the pollsters we talked to in the acknowledgments section.

Data

This data—systematic observations—reflect twin decisions as to who to interview and what questions would prompt useful answers. We came up with 18 candidates representing the most prominent polling organizations in the United States, and then we tried to contact them via letter, email and phone. We could not establish communication with six, and three refused to take part, leaving nine interviewees. The participants were also given a chance to comment on a draft transcript in order to enhance this presentation's accuracy. Let me go through the highlights of their responses question by question. In the following section, the quoted words come from the transcripts save for grammatical corrections necessitated by the move from oral to written communication.

Results

Perhaps you could start by telling me where you went to school and what specialized training you had in polling?

Though there was some range in the interviewees' experience, they appear to bring ample training to their task. All are college-educated, usually in political science but also in English, history, and business. Three had advanced degrees involving substantial statistical training. Their earlier jobs were diverse, including news producer, historian, journalist, Washington staffer, and marketer. All entered the field as polling analysts and had at least 10 years in polling prior to reaching their current position.

What is your current role?

Eight attest to being the chief polling decision-maker at their organization (one was a deputy); all had tremendous influence, and probably ultimate discretion. over poll substance. Still, all acknowledge that their major decisions involve editors, journalists, or clients in a cooperative process, implying that they have less than absolute power. Two interviewees worked in standalone organizations; these proprietors claim less authorship of the polls, having to allocate more time to management and publicity, but their discretionary power matches pollsters enmeshed in media outlets, both report that they "sign off" on every poll their companies produce.

For the rest of the interview, please think only about polls with national samples designed for public release, How does your organization decide when to poll and what to poll on?

With this foundation, we come to the inquiry's core: how polling capacity turns into poll results. The best summary of these came from an interviewee who said, "What's going on in the world determines what you're going to poll." Polling staffs generally meet with editors (or clients) to determine timing and topic. We perceive that poll timing responds to three factors: the pace of events, available resources, and the competition between polling units, in that order. There was unanimous agreement that poll content, especially with national polls, depends on the news. Significantly, everyone intends that polls and questions are newsworthy and can be selected in an attempt to drive the news. One interviewee offers a typology that effectively organizes the relationship of polls to news into categories according to the proximity of polling to news.

Instant polls connect directly to breaking news. After a big event (the September 11, 2001 terrorist attacks serve as the example), pollsters "hit the field" to tap the public's reaction. The goal is to report as soon as possible. Several claim that instant polls seemed to be becoming less popular in favor of interest/investigative polls, maybe because the former are seen as clichéd, and the latter are "sexier" and more unique.

Interest/investigative polls correspond to feature stories—not so fixed to an event, but rather related to an ongoing story. Editors or clients often prompt these polls. Many interviewees explicitly regard them as "investigative journalism," implying that they dig into an aspect of public opinion. One interviewee adds that the topics often go beyond conventional political issues, encompassing health, work, and lifestyle, for instance. A third states that this kind of poll tends to be more expensive, being longer—sometimes tailored to specific populations—and consuming more staff time.

Archive polls contain a higher proportion of what our interviews referred to as "barometric" questions—probably to avoid the term *thermometer*, which recalls a specific format of question. Barometric questions are asked more regularly—examples cover presidential approval or the most important problem facing the United States. Likewise, during elections, voting questions become a fixture. Archive polls might delve into specifics but not with the depth of interest/investigative polls. Most interviewees also say that they try to poll frequently in order to provide regular readings. These polls also act as a kind of "grab bag," with reporters "tossing" in questions until space runs out.

After newsworthy events, available resources and other polling units' behavior emerged as the second and third most important factors behind topics and timing. Polls cost money, so only so much can be done. On top of that, proprietary pollsters hope to make a living, and media units, at some level, need to survive as businesses. Many respondents also cite the worth of spacing polls in time and forecasting future needs. Thus, though one presumes some flexibility, interviewees seem to avoid using too many resources at once or early in the budget cycle. They also hint that mirroring other units is undesirable. One respondent says, "If you thought, *I'm going to go this coming weekend*, and six polls are out the Monday before, you know your appetite isn't so great—it's a waste of your resources. You already sort of know what public opinion is, so you save your fire."

How long is the average poll, in terms of time—and, if you can say, roughly how much does it cost?

Moving on to financing and operations, our interviewees attested to determining the specifications for field houses, those who find and interview respondents—a typical one was proudly described as having, "90 terminals, 10 supervisors, over 160 interviewers, and 24 alternative language speakers." Field houses work largely on a contractual basis, unless organic to the polling unit. Some interviewees express a need for vigilance in case a house's procedures differs—one, for instance, reportedly follows "don't know" responses automatically with "there are no wrong answers," whereas others do not.

Today's typical national sample RDD survey, taking 30 minutes, costs between $25,000 and $60,000 dollars, not including staff salaries and other overhead. Field costs and staff salaries are polling's two main expenses. The range appears to be due in part to different organizational ethics. According to one, "[D]ifferent media polls use different approaches. Some are highly rigorous, others less so. I know of two that run their own field operations, and at least one other that's done entirely on omnibus. The choices fuel the cost."

Other factors affecting cost include the length of survey, expressed in minutes where 25 to 30 questions take around seven minutes. Larger samples or more specific sampling criteria, involving particular demographic groups, for instance, cost more. Finally, there seems to be a consensus that telephone interviews are the present standard in media polls. Although Internet, "blast" e-mail, and "robo" call methods were cheaper, at least one interviewee calls them "methodologically unsound" due to self-selection bias. Proprietors mention allowing clients to select from a menu of cost trade-offs, covering sampling quality and management, interviewer training, and respondent selection. Further, details concerning production of proprietary data and analyses are also customizable.

Knowing the rough cost of a given poll and the yearly budget of various polling units could provide an estimate of total polling capacity, but this subject brings some reserve to our interviewees' tongues. One says that their organization "does not release that information." Nevertheless, most claim that their units produce from 12 to 20 "full-scale" polls a year. At the same time, one respondent cautions that "this kind of accounting is not meaningful. One survey might be a brief check-in." Further, polling budgets display some elasticity; in this vein, many affirm that the presence of an election had a major impact on their annual budget—perhaps doubling in presidential election years. Polling partnerships also lower costs. Proprietors depend more on their clients, and one often waits for a "critical mass" before launching a particular survey.

Where do specific questions come from and how do you word them?

With a decision to poll on a topic made, we come to the critical question selection or formulation process, which one called "the hardest part of any survey." An interviewee sums up this process with the phrase "sift and winnow," which seems to match a proprietor's description of "a conversation followed by a set of memos by the clients, followed by conversations between the pollsters followed by drafts of the ideas that we generated followed by conversations, followed by redrafts followed by changes, minor corrections, etc." Another summary of this collaborative emphasis runs: "[A] lot of times, you're not sure what you're trying to get at. You sort of have to talk it through to figure out what it is, including drafting multiple question versions."

More concretely, questionnaire drafting involves the staffers joined by the journalists assigned to that area. The staff reviews previous polls on the topic, borrowing questions or language from relevant precedents and drafting new questions as needed. Drafting new questions can take substantial effort in order to make the question "measure the concept you think it measures." For new questions, the staff depends on journalists for a "guide to the terrain." Some interviewees say they consult with outside experts. These teams then try to remove bias, stemming from "parroting one side's language" or using "prejudicial" words. Some use pretests when breaking "uncharted ground." One interviewee, however, places less faith in pretests—"[A]a pretest is not going to find whether it's biased or not"—and more faith in "common sense, experience, and knowledge of the science of writing questions." Another appends two concrete rules: "[U]se only words understandable by someone with an eighth grade education" and "[B]egin with political questions . . . to keep these responses pure."

More generally, what do you think is the value of polling?

We wanted to give pollsters a chance to reflect on their political role. Overall, they impressed us as believers in the enterprise. Everyone reiterates Gallup's view of polls as a check on government and special interests. In the words of three, polls "verify the democratic process," "serve as an essential counter-element to all the manufactured data out there, which can be produced, by the way, not only by misinformation but as active disinformation for political or economic purpose," and "act as a check on the [kind of] stuff that Lyndon Johnson was saying about his popularity during the war in Vietnam."

What role do you think polling plays in democratic societies?

Interviewees also hold that "survey research informs our governance." More specifically, a different set of three said that it "brings in the public's view of issues and policies," "allows the voice and concerns of ordinary Americans to be heard in the newsroom," and "helps them [the elites] understand what people believe or where they're coming from." More concretely, they propose that polling is a politically useful tool. First, one thought it makes "policymakers say, *Well, maybe this is a problem—maybe we have to look at this further and change something.*"

In addition, polling was seen to help politicians: it "allows them to find ways to articulate their message so that the public understands it and buys into it," one said, adding that "that's a wonderful thing." From another: polling "allows leaders to know what kind of education or public relations needs to be done to sell people on it, or to neutralize opposition," and, in a third's words, it allows politicians to know "how to make strategic moves: what to say, when to say it, who to say it to." Some interviewees focused on elections, noting that "people are going to speculate about who is ahead, and we might as well tell you who actually is ahead," and that it plays a "role in terms of fundraising and what kind of coverage a candidate is going to get."

What role do you think polling should play in democratic societies?

All but two clearly endorsed polling in its guise as a provider of public knowledge. Almost all the interviewees alluded to the familiar Latin phrase *vox populi*, calling it a "reliable representation of public attitudes" and saying that "[in the] absence of reliable news polls, we would be left to the tender mercies of those other sources of purported information on public attitudes and information, and we'd be poorer for it." Furthermore, one says, "I am not a believer that public opinion should ever drive policy decisions, but I do think it's an important element in policy decisions . . . all from the standpoint that no leader can afford to be totally contemptuous of the public."

"I feel that polling can inform decisions so that they're made wisely by people in government. I am a firm believer in knowledge and knowing how people in the country feel—what they believe," concludes another. A third responds, "[O]n so many issues you find the public way ahead of the politicians, on what needs to be done and where things are. What it is and how it's done, the public really doesn't have a consensus. But it's providing that leveling base in decision making that becomes exceptionally helpful." The most skeptical two called polling a "crude" instrument, essentially warning not to rely too much on poll results in drafting policy.

What problems does polling face today?

Self-selection bias is the problem most interviewees mention. One states, "[T]he same kind of people doesn't want to talk to any of us. With the sample, we are all probably biased but we're all biased in the same way." Three repeat concerns over polling language, one saying "[P]eople are always more willing to not allow something then they are to prohibit it." One discusses agenda-setting: "There is a constant need for pollsters to be alert to emerging issues that aren't on the agenda yet . . . this problem will probably never be solved completely." Another alludes to a class issue: "[M]ost polls are conceived, designed, and executed by college graduates in places like New York, Washington, D.C., and Princeton."

In addition, they unanimously agree that poll reporting could mislead. One ascribes the problem to journalists' tendency to be "data-hungry but math-phobic." Another echoes this warning against "data mining to fit [a] poll's results into the larger story a journalist was telling." A third gives an anecdote: "[O]nce I found something that was totally opposite of what this reporter wanted to say. So I called him back, and I said, 'Look, your hypothesis is not right . . . he was so angry at me.'" A fourth emphasizes that "pollsters have the responsibility to explain how to look for good and bad polling and to understand what they should report and not report . . . in journalism school, there should be part of a course to understand how to read polls." One mentions bloggers' newfound role as a valuable counter to misleading reports: "[E]verything is public; we're all very good at making it easy to find our actual survey instrument. . . . I see a lot of chatter about question wording [and results], so it's useful."

CONCLUSIONS ON POLLSTERS

These interviews make me more comfortable with pollsters' power. They seem to bring the necessary background to their tasks, and their motivations do not seem particularly sinister. In our examination of the softer side of polling, we see that they work in a collaborative environment. Editors and clients have a great deal—perhaps too much—input into poll timing and topic, while reporters play some part in question selection or formulation. The interviewees worry about aspects of their practice, including self-selection bias, polling language, poll reporting, and the vetting of outside sample survey results. Still, all the interviewees believe in their work and point to the valuable political functions polling perform—checking special interests, helping politicians muster public support, and amplifying the people's voice, among other things. Now, we should know enough about polling (and have sufficiently deflected its critics) to move on.

Chapter 3

Gently Introducing Science, Starring the Median Voter Model and a Test of Citizens' Independence

In this chapter we will devote ourselves to the social science background that our investigations require. After a prelude that evaluates the state of political science, we will undertake an abbreviated but adequate—with any luck—crash course in social science. For those unfamiliar with science or those who need refreshing, this brief seminar explains how social science produces knowledge. We will focus on research's main components and how they work together. Afterward, we will delve into the American public's hearts and minds. These few essentials about the way Americans actually think and act build into the powerful Median Voter Model (MVM). Put bluntly, the MVM is the mother of all social scientific knowledge about Americans' political behavior. Not only does it summarize every important empirical discovery about our political behavior, it provides an unsurpassed framework for understanding public decisions.

The chapter concludes with some real science—an illustrative study that addresses one of our questions that the MVM emphasizes: *can information prompt the public to think independently?* This relatively simple research examines the relationship between media frames and citizens' attitudes toward partial birth abortion (PBA). It used an experiment to show that the *New York Times'* use of the words *baby* or *fetus* in describing PBA causally influenced, but did not fully determine, participants' judgments. So, this investigation hints that citizens do not automatically adopt the ways of thinking promoted by the media and other elites. In so doing, it begins to lay the issue of public competence to rest.

DOING SOCIAL SCIENCE

We must pause to acknowledge a sizable obstacle that gets in the way of understanding political behavior—namely, social science has barely emerged from its infancy. Compare political science to physics. As many know, two equations dominate the history of physics—Newton's $F = ma$ and Einstein's $E = mc^2$. Newton came up with the first one in the 1600s, after the falling of an apple. Einstein formulated the second almost 300 years later. Does that mean that 300 years of physics was wrong? No, certainly not. During that time, physics developed until Einstein achieved a more complete understanding. In addition, Newton's equation works well, for the most part; it supplies a good explanation of the relationship between force, mass, and acceleration at speeds that do not approach the speed of light. Of course, physics has moved on from Newton's insight. Political science, in my opinion, has just emerged from its $F = ma$ era; our equivalent of Einstein's famous formula is the Median Voter Model.

All science attempts to correctly portray the world we live in and explain this reality, normally to everyone's betterment. Anything that does not aspire to explain is not science, but description. In this sense, punditry or description is inferior to science. To the extent that pundits describe the world, they are doing journalism; to the extent that they analyze the world, they are doing science. However, although good descriptions are necessary, punditry is a poor form of science when it does not support analysis with proper evidence.

Political scientists also confront some unique problems. First, some people think political science is impossible. One particularly irritating exchange took place on *Hardball*, the MSNBC show aired on June 7, 2007. While interviewing actor Ben Affleck, host Chris Matthews asked Affleck about his political views. A modest Affleck hesitated, saying, "When they see me, you know, say, or some other actor, they don't mistake that person for a history professor or a political science analyst." Matthews then retorted, "I don't think there is such a thing as political science anyway . . . I don't know what this science is that they keeping talking about." He continued, "I keep asking kids who major in it in Ivy League schools. I say what is it—what courses do you take? How you can justify calling yourself a political scientist, when the whole thing is about art and personality and smart argument and circumstance," to wind up his tirade.

Matthews summarizes a widely held view that the label *political science* is an oxymoron; that there is no science in politics. After reading this chapter, I trust you will disagree. Nevertheless, this view underscores the difficulties. Unlike physical science, for instance, some social science findings become obsolete as society changes. Today, few worry about monarchs' claiming they rule by divine right. Humans' obvious complexity, including our self-awareness and capacity for change, makes social science still harder. People are far more varied, too. Two particles may be interchangeable, but identical twins are qualitatively different individuals. Finally, useful findings can be undone as they become public.

A favorite social science anecdote deals with shoplifting and mirrors. In the 1950s, psychologists stumbled on the fact that people confronted with their reflection tend to behave better. This discovery led to further studies, and notably to a test that put mirrors in drugstores. Sure enough, this experiment (which we will learn to perform) proved that stores with mirrors had less shoplifting. Enlightened shops began installing mirrors, and they worked—at first. Initial successes prompted stores to install more mirrors, and before long drugstores began to resemble Versailles. Alas, crime did not disappear. Criminals adapted, perhaps toughening their self-image, and shoplifting snapped back to previous levels. It is hard to envision a corresponding effect in the physical sciences.

As if that were not enough, people, particularly in politics, have goals, and they can misuse the findings of the best intended research. Candidates, for instance, tend to copy effective advertising techniques, reenacting the mirror story. In 1993, Richard Riordan won the Los Angeles mayoral election, and many pundits attributed his victory his campaign's "plan" for the city's future. (A political scientist would have gone farther, testing the hypothesis that candidates with plans get more votes.) As you might expect, in the next election, at least five candidates proudly offered plans.

Amazingly, and somewhat paradoxically given the obstacles, all of us would have a far easier time doing social science than physical science. The same amount of resources—money, time, or energy—buys a lot more cutting-edge social science than physical science. This situation arises from physical science's head start. Middle-class eighteenth-century Englishmen (women were typically, and wrongly, excluded) had access to state-of-the-art telescopes and successfully contributed to astronomy. Now, few, if any, can afford passable physical instruments, like particle accelerators or the Hubble Space Telescope. On the other hand, a group of energetic amateurs could effortlessly afford all the resources social science involves today.

Though some research was done prior to the World War II; contemporary social science got moving in the 1950s. So, on top of being tougher, we have spent considerably less time, money, and effort on social science. Social science, as a result, has made less progress, and many questions remain incompletely answered. At the same time, social science has actually become cheaper. In the 1950s, universities rationed access to giant central computers; today you can buy an enormously improved machine for your own desk or lap. Doing social science involves just two more ingredients—a dash of training and some structured observations of human behavior.

Naturally, we don't have to do social science to learn from it. But knowing what goes into knowledge eases application. Math teachers ask students to "show their work," meaning that full credit requires students to demonstrate the method for arriving at each answer. Being less certain than math, social science work benefits even more from showing one's work. No study is perfect, and no finding is utterly true; the passage of time can stress the sturdiest results. Seeing the work lets readers appraise a study's value and limits. To sum up, social science is tough but doable, and requires showing our work.

THE SCIENCE OF POLITICS

The earliest public opinion research closely followed polling's introduction. Much as pollsters were delighted to find a way of measuring public sentiment, scientists were thrilled to have a new tool for studying human behavior. However, their efforts revealed some unsettling facts about fellow citizens. We will go over these facts (which remain true today) by introducing ourselves to democracy's VIP: the average citizen. The Median Voter Model—political behavior research's crown jewel—then combines these facts into a memorable whole. MVM's value cannot be overstated; even most pundits use it, though, by and large, implicitly. Understanding MVM is tantamount to internalizing the bulk of what we know about Americans' political behavior.

The word average holds an important mini-lesson. The astounding variety associated with humanness forces social science to speak in generalities—stereotypes, to use Lippmann's word. Although many will recoil at the mention of stereotyping—justly so when, the method is misused—social science requires the use of stereotypes. We typically cannot predict any individual's actions, because humans are too complicated, but we can make decent predictions (with some work) about groups. Because predictions about groups mathematically equal predictions about that group's average member, social science always speaks in terms of averages. This practice also neatly dovetails with polling. So, although in some sense the average American does not exist, we speak of her (women outnumber men) as Ms. Average to summarize the behavior of Americans on the whole.

The American stereotype promulgated by Alexis de Tocqueville and enshrined in the great Frank Capra movies *Mr. Smith Goes to Washington* and *Meet John Doe* drove the first social scientific use of polling to study politics. Remember—Tocqueville came to America to observe how democracy worked. When he visited the frontier in the 1830s, he was gleefully shocked to discover farmers—at civilization's edge—debating political issues with the gravity of Parisian elites. Likewise, the heroic everymen portrayed by Jimmy Stewart and Gary Cooper personified the ideal linkage between national politics and ordinary people. Guided by this dream, Angus Campbell, Philip Converse, Warren Miller, and Donald Stokes, the pioneering political behavior researchers, expected their sample surveys to discover well-informed and engaged citizens. They were dismayed to find almost the opposite, publishing their results in the aptly named *The American Voter* (1960). This book demolished Tocqueville's stereotype.

Their discovery—that citizens of the United States have less political knowledge than anyone expected—has stretched into common knowledge. With little doubt, Americans tend to be ill informed about affairs of state. Many studies have replicated the first findings. One careful study, conducted in 1990, revealed, for instance, that more Americans were able to identify Judge Joseph A. Wapner of television's *The People's Court* than the Chief Justice of the Supreme Court, who (if we still don't know) was William H. Rehnquist (*What Americans Know about Politics,* by Michael X. Delli Carpini and Scott Keeter). Indeed, Ms. Average would have a hard time on *Jeopardy* if the category was American politics.

Less of us know the finding that really troubled early political scientists— their precious discovery concerning how Americans make political decisions. Keep in mind that explaining voting is at the center of political research. On one hand, votes are citizens' most observable political act; on the other, voting has unmatched consequence, as we discussed. Besides this prominence, an understanding of voting can be transferred to the public decisions that polling measures. The first major voting study used the presidential election of 1952, which pitted Dwight Eisenhower against Adlai Stevenson. Campbell and his colleagues, once more, expected to find deliberate creatures that knew about the issues as well as candidates and cast ballots accordingly. However, the discovery that the average voter knew little, particularly about where candidates stood on issues, dashed this hope. It raised the question: *how do voters decide who to favor?*

To explain voting, researchers wielded surveys like shotguns, peppering respondents with questions and then sifting the answers to see which questions most closely matched respondents' votes. This research strategy appears throughout social science and goes by the perhaps familiar name of correlational analysis. This kind of research, which stars in the next chapter, looks for associations between things as they ebb and flow in the universe, and then adopts the strongest association as an explanation. In the jargon, social scientists seek covariation, meaning behaviors that vary together: *every time people do or say this they also tend to do or say that*, implying that they have something to do with causing or being affected by each other.

Voting researchers hunt for poll questions that produce responses that correlate with the question "Who do you intend to vote for in the upcoming presidential election?" These pathfinders evaluated dozens of questions, and one stood out. The winner by a large margin, with a strong relationship with vote intentions in every election, goes by the name of partisan identification (or PID, probably the most widely used acronym in political research). Knowing someone's partisanship, merely whether they view themselves as a Republican or a Democrat, provides the best forecast of the average American's vote. We will talk more about the implications of party voting later on. For the moment, be content with the historical fact that these newfound truths spawned the MVM, the best summary of mass politics in the United States.

The Median Voter Model captures political science's view of American politics writ large; its elegant simplicity and tremendous explanatory power guarantees it a prominent place in any decent collegiate introduction. For those who haven't heard of it yet, spending a few paragraphs getting to know MVM is the single best investment any student of democratic politics can make.

MVM combines two (now obvious) insights: voters vote according to their partisan attachments, and candidates want to win elections. Of course, we correctly suspect that more than two factors influence elections (which is why MVM is called a model), but these two have the most power. Through purely deductive reasoning, they enable accurate predictions for the majority of American elections and offer an unsurpassed starting point for analyzing the rest. Moreover, the logic of MVM goes beyond elections to any public political decision. MVM construes the United States as a long street with the entire public living alongside. Accounting for our two-party system and the *American Voter* findings, MVM arrays citizens according to their party identification, with Democrats living on the left side of town and Republicans on the right; it further organizes the public using Rensis Likert's 1932 invention of scales.

Likert's idea should trigger instant recognition; he replaced yes and no answers with a point scale. Humans seem to intuitively appreciate scales; Bo Derek, in the eponymous movie, for example, was not just attractive; she was a perfect 10. I do not know whether analogous usages preceded Likert's, but they share the same ambition—to efficiently expand answerers' opportunity to express their opinions. Social science and polling depends on this technique to pack more information into each response. Saying "strongly agree, agree, neither, disagree, or strongly disagree" takes minimally more time than saying "agree or disagree" but provides significantly more info. We will use a scale in our experiment below; the MVM also depends on Likert's technique.

Academic pollsters ask not one but three nested questions to measure partisan identification, befitting its importance. First: "Generally speaking, do you usually think of yourself as a Republican, a Democrat, an Independent, or what?" Second, asked of partisans: "Would you call yourself a strong Democrat/Republican or a not very strong Democrat/Republican?" And third, asked of people who gave an "or what" to the first question: "Do you think of yourself as closer to the Republican Party or to the Democratic Party?" The three answers form a Likert scale that classifies respondents into seven categories: Strong Democrat, Weak Democrat, Independent-Democrat, Independent-Independent, Independent-Republican, Weak Republican, and Strong Republican. Yes, Independent-Independent seems redundant. This construction intentionally overlooks minor parties, which political science understands to have minimal significance in terms of the typical citizen's political orientations. The few respondents mentioning third parties usually count as Independent-Independent, not identifying with either major.

To see these questions' predictive power and whet our appetite for analysis, we can compare partisanship to vote intention and replicate *The American Voter's* central finding. We will use the 2004 American National Election Study (ANES)—the premiere academic electoral poll (it descended from *The American Voter's* surveys). Conveniently, anyone can google their website and examine or download this poll data for free. Our first analysis organizes answers to the partisan identification summary, gracefully labeled V043116, and vote intention, the stylish V043203. Social science prizes this particular question a great deal, though it appears simple enough: "Who do you think you will vote for in the election for President?" Putting the candidates—each represents a potential response to the voting question—across the top and the seven partisanship categories along the side produces a "crosstabulation." My friends call this form of analysis a crosstab; users of Microsoft Excel will know it as a PivotTable.

This crosstab makes it easy to see that the answers covary:

Category	Kerry	Bush
Strong Democrat	96.9%	2.6%
Weak Democrat	84.3%	14.5%
Independent-Democrat	78.5%	16.0%
Independent-Independent	39.8%	47.3%
Independent-Republican	14.1%	80.7%
Weak Republican	8.1%	90.6%
Strong Republican	1.1%	98.9%

Each number is the percentage intending to vote for that candidate in that partisan category. For example, in the upper left hand corner, 96.9 percent of the Strong Democrats plan to vote for John Kerry, while in the crosstab's middle, Independent-Independents split: George W. Bush wins 47.3 percent to Kerry's 39.8 percent. As we move down the crosstab from Strong Democrat to Strong Republican, the percentage supporting Kerry decreases. Please take your time to peruse this crosstab's analysis, noting how partisanship's tie to the vote stands out. Not coincidentally, winning among the Independent-Independents ensured George W. Bush's 2004 victory.

While we have this sample survey handy, let's look at another question that tells us where Americans live along MVM's street. This question taps ideology, which (unsurprisingly) covaries with partisan identification; it goes: "We hear a lot of talk these days about liberals and conservatives. Here is a seven-point scale on which the political views that people might hold are arranged from extremely liberal to extremely conservative. Where would you place yourself on this scale?"

In the 2004 ANES (V043085), respondents answered as follows:

In addition, 285 respondents said, "Haven't thought about it too much." These self-descriptions highlight a fundamental truth about Ms. Average. Out of the 1,105 respondents, 63 (about 5 percent) placed themselves at either extreme; in contrast, 297 placed themselves in the middle, and 285 did not place themselves at all. Though there are several ways to slice this data (why we show the work), they signal that Americans, when not eschewing ideology completely, tend to be moderates.

Adding candidates' desire to win to this brief analysis of partisanship completes our lesson. MVM's name tells candidates their precise goal. In the United States, the candidate who gets the most votes wins, so if one of two candidates nabs half the votes, then he or she at least ties. Thus, if someone gets half the votes plus one, triumph is certain! This target, 50 percent plus one, appears in MVM. The first M stands for median, a statistical term. As

Category	Percent
Extremely liberal	27
Liberal	112
Slightly liberal	102
Moderate/Middle-of-the-road	297
Slightly conservative	145
Conservative	201
Extremely conservative	36

we know, averages express a central point in numeric series; in baseball, the batting average is the number of hits divided by the number of at bats. Medians are another centrality expression. If you rank a series of numbers from lowest to highest, then the median is the exact middle, the number with half below and half above. Statisticians use medians when numbers have a skew; economists always chart median home prices, for instance, because while homes can be super-expensive, they cannot cost less than zero.

When MVM arrays voters by partisan strength, it ranks every voter, putting extreme Democrats and Republicans at each end. To employ some stereotypes, the right is anchored by flag-waving, shotgun-wielding, pickup-driving rednecks (before you get angry: I have been sunburned, own a pickup, and wave flags). The left, in contrast, features a quiche-eating, Birkenstock-wearing hippie, probably smoking something illegal (no comment). As we move toward the middle, partisanship, not to mention the stereotype, is less pronounced. Given that extremity translates to loyal party voting, MVM models all the lefties as voting Democrat and the rest as voting Republican, or vice versa, if you prefer. This construction also captures the party voting heuristic that we discussed in the first chapter.

Here is the payoff—and MVM's most important lesson—whichever candidate wins the median's vote wins the election. To verify this, adding the people to the left or right of the median yields 50 percent of the electorate, which means the median's one vote chooses the winner. Observe also that polarization, a popular topic in current political science research, does not affect the median's pivotal position. Even if Republicans and Democrats become more extreme in their positions, the median stays quietly in the middle. On the other hand, if the entire country moves to the right or the left, the median follows. It makes sense to say, for instance, that Americans became more conservative in the 1980s. The median, to be precise, accurately represents the entire electorate. When the median speaks, everyone listens.

In this way, MVM exposes the golden path to winning American elections: mobilize your base and attract the moderates. A corollary holds that extremism, while entertaining and personally rewarding, never wins. Look up the elections of 1964 and 1972, which featured so-called extremists: first Barry Goldwater on the right and then George McGovern on the left. Both lost in landslides, only getting the few votes at the ends. In contrast, self-proclaimed moderates, like Bill Clinton the "new Democrat," or George W. Bush the "compassionate conservative," succeed—although their parties, above all activists and donors, keep them from reaching the exact center.

MVM shows why third-party candidates rarely win elections, as well. They tend not to have a base, so they need to steal voters from one party or the other. More often than not, the major party candidate that the third party steals from loses too, like Al Gore did in 2000. Simple math and a bit of reasoned speculation shows that Ralph Nader caused Gore's defeat. Wikipedia states that 2,883,105 people, or 2.74 percent of the electorate, voted for Nader. How would they have voted had Nader not run? Some may have stayed home; certainly few would have voted for Bush. Perhaps just 1 in 10 would have voted for Gore. With this slim proportion—above all in the swing states—Gore would have easily won.

The most important MVM lesson underlines the relative unimportance of most votes in democracy's grand scheme and spotlights the humongous exception—the vote of Ms. Average. As we might know, many elections are barely contests; over 90 percent of congressional incumbents are reelected in landslides, for instance. As elections get closer and closer, however, more and more votes essentially cancel out. In the closest elections all but a few votes cancel out, and Ms. Average selects the winner. Thus, instead of worrying about each voter, we need only focus on those near the center. Politicians and their campaign managers know this lesson well and use it whenever they talk about "swing voters." The stereotypes "soccer moms" and "NASCAR dads" embody candidates' attempts to get a handle on the most important group in mass politics. Still, one should also discern that by voting you pull the median voter fractionally toward your position, whereas nonvoters do not affect the median position one whit.

Voting research often addresses what makes moderates swing. We know that party does not do it for this group; by definition, they are independent. They lack the partisan loyalty that makes explaining most votes so easy. If we can answer this question, it will go a long way to resolving our issue: can the public benefit from education? Let's start studying some real citizens. In the ANES data we saw a smidgen of correlational work—one of two major research strategies—that support the party voting hypothesis. Now we'll take a detailed look at the other basic social research procedure and experiment with experiments. Our experiment assesses how people respond to information. The risks are high. The more certain messages influence political attitudes, the better things look for Lippmann, and the worse for Dewey.

STUDY NUMERO DOS: INVESTIGATING THE MEDIA'S IMPACT ON CITIZENS' POLITICAL JUDGMENTS

This living and breathing piece of research employs an experimental design. It has all of experimentation's merits—entirely lacking subtlety, we will easily master the short, sweet setup and analysis. This experiment forms part of a larger study of the public's attitudes toward partial birth abortion (PBA) that carries into the next chapter. The portion below constitutes about a third of the PBA study; nevertheless it has all the standard parts of any scientific project: question/hypotheses, data, and analysis. We will discuss these as we go to fill in important aspects that actual scientific reports skip for the sake of efficiency. Those interested in seeing a more formulaic presentation of the same experiment may look to an article that appears in the *Journal of Communication* (2007, 254–271); I am proud to announce that this work won the International Communication Association's award for best political communication article in 2007.

Our research question is: *do media reports determine citizens' judgments?* Despite its diminutive size, this question allows the study to address a vital characteristic of public capabilities. Remember also that we ought to place less value on public opinion to the extent it displays a lack of competence. This experiment investigates one aspect of competence—independence. We want to find out if the media tells citizens what to think, or whether they act independently. Equivalently, we ask whether citizens are more than parrots. Talking birds—think "Polly want a cracker"—do no more than repeat what they are told, so we tend not to take their amusing expressions seriously. If the same is true of our fellow citizens, we might as well give up now. Given that this is only the third chapter, you can be assured that the experiment produces optimistic results. We are going to go over it thoroughly to show the work, and to bolster our scientific acumen. Those with ample science training may want to skim the next section.

Every study begins with a question, the first of three study building blocks. Questions open the heart of scientific practice. First, questions mark a study's focus and scope for all to see; we, for instance, are interested in information and judgment. Scientists are not mystery writers—the mystery lies in the subject, not the research design. Scientific reports want to convince the reader, so clarity takes precedence over good storytelling. Second, good questions, called *well-formed*, automatically generate a hypothesis—again, the guess that propels the research. Question and hypotheses go hand in hand, which is why I consider them the same research element. Proper questions are falsifiable, like our question: they lead straight to a yes or no. In our case, we can hypothesize that no, the media does not determine citizens' judgments or, yes, it does. While the question isolates focal concepts, the hypothesis pretty much repeats the question.

Studies proceed by trying not to disconfirm the hypotheses. Thanks largely to Karl Popper, the exponent of falsifiability's import; science demonstrates a truth by failing to prove it false (for further details, pick up *The Open Society and Its Enemies*). This notion forces science to march in a clumsy fashion that may seem to be self-defeating. Nevertheless, science follows this rule invariably, and will continue to until someone proves Popper false. Hypotheses accomplish their mission by identifying a presumptive causal relationship. Causality is the watchword of science, and researchers generally mix up the words *causality* and *explanation*, as most do. Think of a hypothesis as an arrow linking two things. The arrow stands for causality, emanating from suspected causes like the media to effects like citizens' judgments.

Scientists call the things within question/hypotheses variables. The word variable reinforces an early statistics lesson: no one studies constants. Constants, by definition, do not change and cannot explain anything. Their dogged fixedness leaves nothing in them to explain. Constants are boring. Causality lives solely within changing things, or variables. Therefore, science deals in variables and relegates constants to the margins. Scientists love to watch their variables hop around, and struggle to use other variables to explain these hops. Within a hypothesis, the cause is the independent variable and the effect is the dependent variable.

Given a question/hypothesis, you would think we could doff our Fedoras and rush off Indiana Jones style, looking for an answer. Nope. We first have to figure out what to observe. This underappreciated task goes by the name *operationalization* (a great word for parties). To operationalize a variable, we select what to monitor in order to chart a variable's ebbs and flows. Good measures require careful thought and creativity. The book *Unobtrusive Measures* (Webb, Campbell, Stanley & Sechrest, 1966) tells of a clever researcher who operationalized museums exhibits' popularity by counting the number of times the floor tiles had to be replaced. Mahzarin Banaji and her colleagues developed another great measure. She measures racial prejudice, which as you might expect, can not be discerned with the question "Are you prejudiced?" Instead, she uses the Implicit Association Test to get at attitudes of people. Their website describes some truly brilliant social science.

More to the point, bad operational measures devastate a study. When you think you are measuring one thing and are actually measuring something else, or nothing at all, you are not doing good science. So we need a good measure to observe independent judgment. Regrettably, an easy way to measure it does not exist. We might fantasize about a magical gauge—a super MRI that scans citizens and rates their independence. But in the absence of a far more developed neuroscience than we currently practice, we must rely on comparison and create situations designed to give independence an opportunity to appear.

Science always requires some comparison. Let me offer my son (figuratively) to show comparison's inestimable worth. I would happily report that he possesses uncommon genius, mastering walking and talking in such a short time. Yet an inner scientist compels me to consider my point of view:

to me he is unique, literally without compare. I know other kids, but not with the same depth. His teachers or doctors have a far better estimate of his ability, if only because they evaluate so many more children. The same reasoning dictates colleges' reliance on the SAT test for admissions. This test aims to deliver a perfect comparison despite the fact that it covers less than four hours of the roughly 15,000 hours a typical applicant has lived.

BACKGROUND:
INDEPENDENT JUDGMENT AND MEDIA FRAMING

To develop a comparison to track independent judgment, we need to probe the meaning of independence. My thinking points to the proposition that independent reason requires disproportionate response. To illustrate, if someone hears two equal arguments and compromises by splitting the difference between the two, we haven't seen much reasoning, because they basically agree with both. Further, let one arguer whisper and the other scream (taking things to the extreme). Should someone endorse the scream, we conclude that they had been bludgeoned into acceptance. But should they endorse the whisper, our astonishment might suggest the use of reason. Harking back to the first chapter, this intuition—selecting a whisper over a scream requires reason—seems to secure Habermas's previously mentioned idea of reason as the "unforced force" that overcomes coercion. By extension, someone would also be using reason in choosing between equally loud arguments.

We also want our study to resemble reality; it wouldn't do to have participants subjected to whispers and screams, so we need the media's workings to guide our implementation. As we will discuss at the book's end, our media system stresses the appearance of fairness. With due respect to those who believe in media bias, this emphasis generally forestalls blatant advocacy in journalism. So, in thinking about the comparisons we create, we cannot just present arguments; we must limit ourselves to more subtle differences. Fortunately, as in most pertinent areas, existing social scientific research provides a good pattern for our study.

The label "framing" applies to the study of subtle communication differences. Scholars credit Erving Goffman with coining this use of the term, which covers as well the way in which the presentation of messages affect reactions. Optical illusions exemplify his premise. Depending on the viewer's perspective, one famous shape appears to be either two faces or a vase. Similarly, I consider basketball's seven-foot-five Yao Ming huge, but he seems less gigantic when standing next to the Empire State Building. Neither the shape nor Yao have changed, but what audiences take away varies radically with its frame. Being such a neat and relatively intuitive idea, framing plays a large role in media studies.

The psychologists Daniel Kahneman, Amos Tversky, and Paul Slovic produced the most famous framing study. This research, detailed in the book *Judgment under Uncertainty: Heuristics and Biases*, was so spectacular that it won a psychologist the Nobel Prize in Economics! Essentially, they used framing to test the principle of "descriptive invariance." This principle, a tenet of rational choice, states that if the essentials of a decision remain fixed, then the decision will be stable. In other words, if anyone changes their mind in response to different descriptions of the same choice, they are irrational. They used a standard experimental design, which we will discuss to become familiar with experimentation and lay a foundation for our study.

Whether they deal with humans, drugs, or anything else, two related features define experimentation. First, experimenters randomly assign participants to different groups, called *conditions*. Random assignment might actually mean rolling a die as a participant arrives. This use of chance yields enormous returns. Random assignment equalizes groups to overcome the obstacle of heterogeneity; it guarantees that the conditions will be statistically equivalent with only chance differences between them. Say we put men in one condition and women in another, or even that we put the people to arrive first in one and the rest in another. Indeed, if we divide participants in any way other than by random assignment, this mistake would doom the experiment, because the conditions would not be the same statistically. Furthermore, experimenters go to great lengths to treat all the participants alike after they are assigned. (Our experiment on PBA framing and judgment was conducted at the same time every day, in case people judge differently in the morning than in the afternoon.)

Second, experiments feature a *manipulation*, the solitary exception to the identical treatment rule. The experimenter changes one condition in an exceedingly precise way. Also known as the *treatment*, this intervention embodies the attempt to give life to the sought-after comparison. The manipulation becomes an experiment's independent variable; with a proper setup and execution, it alone is the cause of any observed effect, a difference between the conditions, after the treatment.

In their famous framing experiment, Kahneman and his colleagues manipulated the description of a medical decision. After randomly assigning participants to two groups, the first group read the following:

> Imagine the United States is preparing for the outbreak of an unusual Asian disease, which is expected to kill 600 people. Two alternative programs to combat the disease have been proposed. Assume the exact scientific estimates of the

consequences of the program are as follows: If program A is adopted, 200 people will be saved. If program B is adopted there is a one-third probability that 600 people will be saved, and two-thirds probability that no people would be saved.

Another group, otherwise identically cared for, read a different description:

Imagine the United States is preparing for the outbreak of an unusual Asian disease, which is expected to kill 600 people. Two alternative programs to combat the disease have been proposed. Assume the exact scientific estimates of the consequences of the program are as follows: If program C is adopted, 400 people will die. If program D is adopted, there is a one-third probability that no one will die, and a two-thirds probability that 600 people will die.

According to the laws of probability (which boil down to multiplication and division) these descriptions present the same choice. To double-check: program A will save 200 people, and B will save an average of 200 people (600 people one-third of the time); it is most likely that 400 people will die. In the second, C will allow 400 people to die, and D will allow an average of 400 people to die; it is most likely that 200 people will live. In their experiment, Kahneman and Tversky have artfully manipulated the framing of the choice.

Which programs did participants choose? Undergrads randomly assigned to the first description favored A to B by 72 to 28 percent. In contrast, as the mention of the Nobel Prize foreshadows, undergrads treated to the second description favored D to C by 78 to 22 percent. Amazing! Indeed, these heroes demonstrated their participants' irrationality.

In general, experimental designs, like this, alleviate objections as the structured comparison and painstaking procedure make causality apparent. Yet, we should always question an experimental conclusion's applicability. Perhaps, these undergrads were weird—scientifically speaking, not representative of "normal" people. So Kahneman repeated the design many times on math majors, economists, and doctors, among others. Obviously, they succeeded in convincing the scientific world, and the Nobel Prize people, that humans can be irrational in this way. We will talk more about framing and some limits on the effect later on.

OUR EXPERIMENT

We want to know whether the media determines peoples' attitudes toward banning PBA or whether they can exercise independent judgment. To find out, we will conduct an experiment allowing us to compare participants' reactions to simulated newspaper articles that feature manipulated frames. These otherwise identical articles operationalize framing by using the word *baby* or *fetus* in detailing this procedure. Thus, our framing experiment follows the standard pattern, changing the format and manipulation to suit our interest.

Before going into detail, we ought to acknowledge that political controversy surrounds the term PBA itself. We will discuss this, as well as the historical details of its political evolution, in the next chapter. What should be clear is that I selected this topic with an eye to maximizing our chances to closely observe a framing effect. We expect these two specific words—*fetus* and *baby*—to tap into something essential about the way people think about PBA, and to change judgments accordingly. More precisely, we predict that people exposed to the word *baby* will display more support for banning the PBA procedure. This expectation stems from research into political decisions laid out in the next chapter; for the time being, it's an educated guess. The next chapter's analysis of Supreme Court and Congressional discourse also shows that political players echoed this word choice.

To create the treatment, we located a *New York Times* article that described PBA and reported on a pending Congressional ban. Shortening it to roughly 300 words produced the version that appears in Figure 3.1. (Before the experiment started, we also asked several experts to approve its look. We interviewed the first participants, as well, happily finding that they did not doubt the article's authenticity.) The four conditions are "fetus," where the article was left alone and that word appeared 14 times; "baby," where that word was substituted for all 14 appearances of fetus; "competitive," where the word baby was substituted for every other appearance of fetus, producing seven appearances for each term; and "control," where participants did not read any article. Given this recipe, anyone who wishes could faithfully repeat this design.

To collect data, we recruited people to participate, randomly assigned (can't say that enough) each to a condition, allowed them to read the correct article, and then asked them questions (see Figure 3.2 for a diagram). The uniqueness of this study stems from the timing, location and identities of the participants. The data came from New Haven, Connecticut, in the summer of 2001. To avoid certain objections, we sought out adults as well as undergraduates, ending up with 185 people—roughly 50 were in each condition except the control, which had 35. Later rechecks of our random assignment luckily (literally) found no statistical differences in age, education, or political partisanship across conditions. Upon completion, participants were debriefed and paid according to American Psychological Association guidelines.

Congress, Nation Still Divided Over Partial-Birth Abortion

WASHINGTON DC, February 27— Congress passed a bill in its last session that would have banned the abortion technique, which is known technically as "intact dilation and evacuation" (D&E). The debate was graphic and contentious, with some longtime abortion rights supporters in Congress voting to ban the procedure. President Clinton vetoed the bill, saying the measure failed to include exceptions to protect the health of the women involved. Officials expect that bills to ban it will be reintroduced soon.

Intact D&E is used by some physicians to remove a relatively large **fetus** from the womb in one piece. The feet of the **fetus** are removed first, then the brain is removed by puncturing the back of the head. By doing so, the **fetus'** skull is partially collapsed for easy removal through the cervix, the narrowest part of the birth canal. Often the **fetus** is dead before the procedure begins, although occasionally it is alive. Sometimes the procedure is done at a stage in gestation when the **fetus** has no chance of surviving outside the womb were it born alive. Sometimes it is done later, when the chance of survival, albeit small, exists. The moment in development when that transition to "viability" occurs is not fixed. However, after about 25 weeks of gestation, many premature **fetuses** survive.

The most common alternative to intact D&E is "dismemberment dilation and evacuation," in which the **fetus** is removed in pieces. Some physicians believe the intact technique is safer because it is less physically traumatic to the pregnant woman. There are no statistics on the number of intact D&E procedures performed on **fetuses** in the United States each year. Reporting by several newspapers suggests that at least 2,000 are performed. That research

also suggests that at least half, and possibly the great majority, of intact D&Es are done on healthy **fetuses** carried by women who are themselves healthy. That last impression contrasts with statements made by most pro-choice organizations and their spokesmen. In general, they say that in most cases the procedure is done only when the **fetuses** have severe abnormalities, or when the woman is so ill that ending her pregnancy is imperative.

The mixed reaction to the bill can be found in the most surprising of sources. For example, a representative from the National Coalition of Abortion Providers, stated in an interview that when the bill to ban intact D&Es was introduced, he called many abortion clinics in his organization and asked how common the procedure was and on what condition of babies it was generally performed. Although he is a staunch abortion rights supporter and usually aligns with the views represented by the pro-choice party line, he was surprised to learn that the procedure is typically performed on healthy **fetuses** rather than malformed **fetuses**, as pro-choice backers had previously believed.

These findings have affected his response to the bill. "I felt very uneasy about it, knowing what I knew...I just decided not to interject myself into the debate," he said. Pro-choice and anti-abortion groups will continue to face-off over the highly debated issue of D&E abortion procedures, and the legality of aborting not only malformed but also healthy **fetuses** late in pregnancy. One anti-abortion supporter reemphasized the party line: "This is murder, plain and simple."

Figure 3.1. Simulated Newspaper Article Used as the Experimental Manipulation. (Fetus is bolded for emphasis.)

The independent variable is the condition—what article they read—and the dependent variable is their attitude toward banning PBA, which we observe with a Likert question (for the reasons given earlier). This key question went "indicate your support or opposition for partial birth abortion where a one indicates strong support for legalizing partial birth abortion and a seven indicates strong opposition to legalizing partial birth abortion." Our experiment took about three weeks to recruit and administer to 186 participants. We meticulously transcribed our observations of each participant into a single computer spreadsheet—our data.

Defending the sanctity of the relationship between our participants' behavior and the computerized data they yield requires constant vigilance. Technology tends to disguise the connection between the two, perhaps giving rise to the erroneous view of science as sterile. When we mortals examine a data set, we typically see a spreadsheet full of numbers; the good analyst, like

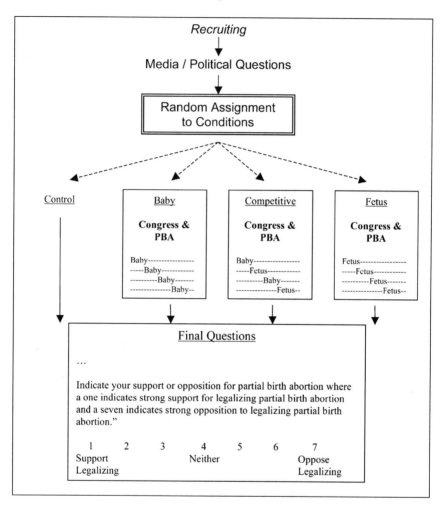

Figure 3.2.   Our PBA Experiment's Procedure and Conditions.

Superman with his X-ray vision, peers through these numbers to the humanity beneath. In this case, each number faithfully represents exactly what our participants read and the judgments they made.

So now that we have paid the price demanded by an experimental design in terms of set up and data collection, we can cash in and breeze through the analysis. Contrary to some expectations, analysis can be exceedingly simple. An analysis performs the comparisons built into the data. The design sets the path that the analysis follows; astonishingly, there are only two basic types of research design, and we have met both—experimental and correlational.

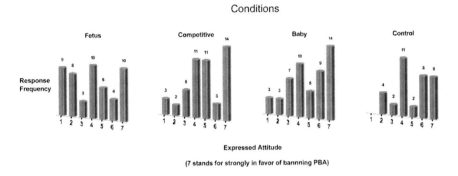

Figure 3.3. Judgments Concerning Banning Partial Birth Abortion by Condition

With an experiment like ours, we look at the data to see if a change in the dependent variable accompanies the manipulation of the independent variable. Recall that we only care about one thing: the attitudes participants display toward banning PBA. Figure 3.3 shows every answer participants gave to this question by condition with the taller columns indicating more responses. We can summarize the answers by averaging, producing four numbers, one for each condition. Now the result!

RESULTS

In the fetus condition, participants express an average support of 3.96. The participants in the rest of the conditions express a level of average support of around 4.8. More precisely, ban support averaged 4.84 in the competitive condition, 4.84 in the baby condition and 4.91 in the control condition. It appears that the manipulation had the expected effect; the final step checks whether the difference is due to chance or whether it is real in the sense of being statistically significant.

Significance testing closely tracks the mathematics of survey sample error detailed in the second chapter. Recall that sampling error is a way of describing the level of vagary within a survey result due to the workings of chance in sampling from a population. Similarly, we can look at the workings of chance within our experimental results. We compare the differences in the averages we observed, given the range that the participants' answers display (this range leads to the calculation of a statistic known as the *standard error*) as well as the number of participants. If the difference between two averages is due to chance, it is tagged as insignificant (either statistically or in any other way).

To do the test, we form a ratio that compares the differences in the variation within in each condition to the variation between the conditions. This statistical technique goes by the name of ANOVA, which stems from its origins as an acronym for *analysis of variance*. Most researchers turn to the computer to do the work; it calculates the needed ratio and looks up its value on a statistical table. But we need some background.

Computers generously shovel out responses to any request. Statistical expertise lay in making the right request and then translating the output into meaningful English. Experiments make entering the right request easy. After loading the data, we ask our computer to run an ANOVA comparing all conditions and another one comparing the fetus condition to the rest. Our computer tells us that F (3, 181) $= 2.73; p \leq .05$ for the former and that F (1, 183) $= 8.25; p < .01$ for the latter. What are F and p? Well, they mean the same thing. F is a ratio of variances that tells the computer what to look up on what we call a p table. The p table represents all the values associated with a standardized set of outcomes. Thus p, referred to as the p value, captures the likelihood that a particular difference is due to chance.

Our second F of 8.25 and our p value of less than .01 mean that the difference we saw has less than a one in a hundred chance of being due to pure luck. In the jargon, our results attain statistical significance. To give the canonical interpretation, we would have to run the experiment over a hundred times to observe this result once by chance alone. Most researchers consider 20 times enough, so by convention, a p value of less than .05 is sufficient for statistical significance. Given our question/hypothesis, data, and analysis, we have now failed to disconfirm the claim that the manipulation caused participants exposed to the word *fetus* to express different attitudes than the rest.

DISCUSSION; OR, WHAT HAVE WE LEARNED?

We can now draw some conclusions about these results and try to generalize to all citizens' behavior. Starting with the simplest result, we see that people in the control group, who read no article, express support for the ban that is statistically indistinguishable from those in the baby condition. What does this suggest? The control group received no new information, so had to work from what they knew when the came in. Therefore, this similarity indicates that peoples' existing notions of PBA closely match those prompted by the baby article. We will expand upon this finding in the next chapter in the rest of the PBA study.

Next, we see that using the word *fetus* changed peoples' attitudes. Substituting this one word 16 times moved the average response by almost a full point on a 7-point scale. The scale's size is arbitrary; for instance, if we used a million point scales, we would see a bigger gross movement. Instead, we embrace the comparison; the relative change. Now we know: if newspapers replaced the word *fetus* with *baby*, readers would be more likely to oppose banning PBA.

Finally, we come to the competitive condition, our foremost interest. Two conclusions stem from the similarity between judgments evoked by the competitive and baby frames. Initially, we might imagine a conversation between a newspaper reporter and editor about our findings. An editor could question the appropriateness of a given term. Imagine this grilling: "Using *fetus* has political implications," says the editor. "But," the reporter would respond, "every word does." How can these journalists avoid the political implications of word choice? The most intuitive solution, alternating *baby* and *fetus* in each article, will not work. According to our result, readers faced with alternate wordings will judge as if they were exposed to just one.

This observation takes us to the lesson about citizens' judgments. The people who saw the word *baby* and the word *fetus* in the same article behaved as if they made a selection. In their judgments, we observe only the presence of *baby* and none of the presence of *fetus*. This outcome suggests that the media—in the form of the competitive article—did not fully determine respondents' judgments. Instead, something inside the participants' minds also guided their determination. Indeed, this evidence is consistent with the claim that these citizens used a kind of reason that allowed them to choose one frame and ignore the other.

The fact that we have run only one experiment mandates some caution. The Kahneman design has been run dozens, if not hundreds, of times. More importantly, the Kahneman trials used different settings and kinds of people, always with the same result. Nevertheless, in our opening encounter with public opinion research, we have an optimistic result. At least the 49 citizens randomly assigned to the competitive condition of our study demonstrated independence in a simple but rigorous test. Scientists call this type of finding an "existence" result: it implies that the public can make independent judgments in some circumstances.

Knowing more about science, and inspired by some additional faith in our fellow humans, we can proceed to more complex questions, research, and findings

Chapter 4

Why Do Americans Favor Some Things yet Oppose Others? and Explaining Republican Success against Partial Birth Abortion

This chapter concentrates on the forces, which we will now call *variables*, hiding behind Americans' responses to poll questions. In the appropriate lingo, whether people say yes or no, support or oppose, and vote for or against becomes this chapter's *primary dependent variable*. We want to uncover the independent variables that drive these responses. Putting these two types of variables together creates a theory of survey response. This theory fills in the citizens' part of our overall portrayal of public judgment. Remember that broader theory covers how politicians, the media, and citizens interact to produce the public judgments that polling measures.

Before delving into survey response theory, let me reiterate its democratic significance by recalling Walter Lippmann. His theory holds that stereotypes drive citizens' judgments, implying that we should not value these kneejerk responses to political events. This instance emphasizes survey response theory's tie to democratic faith. The more good characteristics—genuine, informed, thoughtful, and the like—a theory indicates that responses possess, the better for democracy. History bears witness to the steady progression of our understanding of survey response, but I must report that these hypotheses, evidence, and analyses make the public look pretty bad. We will expand on this work in the next chapter; here we return to the *American Voter*.

We must elaborate upon the link between partisan identification and voting—the biggest finding in political behavior research. I suspect that many intelligent readers will not realize the full significance of early voting behavior research. For this reason, let us talk about the Michigan researchers' leading competitor. Michigan's rivals happened to work at Columbia University, so we can frame their competition in athletic terms. While Michigan might trounce Columbia in most popular sports (I shudder to think about them playing football), their social science contest was fair. Sample survey data provides the arena for this replay, and the team that produces the best explanation of voting behavior wins. This tale of political behavior research's beginnings also introduces correlational analysis.

To score this game we will use the correlation coefficient. The name of this wondrous statistic denotes that investigations like this leave the relatively safe world of experimentation and enter the correlational research jungle—cue Guns N' Roses for some antique musical accompaniment. Correlation coefficients emerge from our friend the crosstab; they provide a statistic (read: number) to describe the strength of the link between the variables. Do not let the word *coefficient* make you anxious; as we will discuss next chapter, *coefficient* is another word for *slope* or *multiplier*. Computers do the heavy lifting in almost all statistical analysis; they remember formulas and do the necessary calculations. We just need to know what correlation coefficients do; with them, we can compare the analytic results that crosstabs present.

The chapter concludes with another helping of actual research, using the Zaller model to complete our investigation of the public's judgments on partial birth abortion. After adding correlational analysis to our statistical kit and replaying the game, this chapter shows how the *American Voter* research led directly to the way that political science sees public opinion today. In particular, we will meet Phillip Converse and John Zaller, perhaps the two most prominent names in public opinion studies, and probe their work on survey response. Each offers a model that attempts to capture the essence of public opinion. The first of these, Converse's Black and White model, shaped nearly all subsequent polling studies. The second, handily known as the Zaller model, represents the most advanced thinking political science has on public opinion.

We will also consider these models' normative implications and discuss a few of their shortcomings in line with science's neverending quest for perfection. Then we will complete our study of partial birth abortion attitudes. First, we shall locate the term's origin and then chart how this label, accompanied by the use of the word *baby*, passed through the Supreme Court, the United States Congress, and the *New York Times* to shape the public's attitude toward this medical procedure. We have a lot of ground to cover, so be warned—this is a hefty chapter!

A WORD ABOUT VALIDITY, THE VALUE OF SCIENCE

Why do we need correlational research? Experiments offer social scientists a precision instrument. Like a surgeon's scalpel, they painstakingly slice into particular human activities by putting potential connections under the microscope to test suspected causal linkages. Correlational research, in contrast, is less exacting. (In the last chapter, I likened it to a shotgun.) Given these descriptions and the stereotype of scientific fastidiousness, one might wonder about the utility of correlational techniques. Why would social scientists wander through human affairs and blast whatever suits their interest with questions? The reasons relate to experimentation's limits. First, one cannot always run an experiment. Second, experiments are not perfect (gasp!); they, too, have problems. The concept of validity helps us identify these limits; put too simply, good science is valid, whereas bad science is not.

An illustration shows some of experimentation's shortcomings. Take the hypothesis that democracy causes less war than other governmental forms. We need not delve into the reasoning behind this guess of Immanuel Kant's to attest to an experimental investigation's impossibility. Observe that each country counts as a case and that we need to manipulate each one's form of governance. A proper experiment would randomly assign governments, some democratic and some not, to countries. We would then sit back and count the number of wars they started. In principle, this design meets all of experimentation's requirements; indeed, it would confirm or deny the hypothesis. But it is utterly unrealistic. Even if we had resources to buy land, set up countries, and choose governments, human research guidelines rule out this kind of tampering. Many would-be political studies confront this problem. We cannot randomly assign party loyalty to research participants, so our central concept—PID—remains somewhat immune to experimental study. Still, I maintain that thinking about a research question in experimental terms often does wonders to clarify a problem, even if you eventually resort to correlational techniques.

Second, a built-in vulnerability attends all experimental results. This limitation falls under the heading of external validity, which asks whether the findings apply to everyday life. (The adjective *external* hints that validity has another major component.) Upon completion, experiments produce a finding—namely, things cause something else, or they don't. However, this finding is bound to that research's particular time, setting, and population. Any application requires interpretation or extrapolation. This requirement translates to a standard—for experimental findings to be externally valid, they must generalize to other situations.

We saw one instance of questionable external validity in Kahneman and Tversky's framing experiment. The first criticisms of their study targeted their undergraduate participants. Perhaps college students are not as smart or sophisticated as "real" people; hence the critics propose that the results would not generalize. Kahneman and Tversky had to repeat their experiment on doctors and statisticians in order to respond. Correlational studies also raise the external validity concerns—look at V. O. Key's criticism of *The American Voter* below, for instance; experiments, which requires manipulation, tend to be more vulnerable in this area.

As you might guess, there is another kind of validity which bestows experiments' raison d'être (French for *justification*). The structure of experiments makes them uniquely gifted at identifying causality. This kind of validity—*does the study support the conclusion?*—falls under the heading of internal. As opposed to its external cousin, internal validity addresses the relationship between the design—the question/hypothesis, data, and analysis—and the findings. Good experimental designs tend to breeze by internal validity concerns. Unless a mistake is made—which veteran researchers often spot quickly—experimental designs support only one conclusion. Notice this strength comes from the way experiments put a phenomenon under control, trading reality for power. In perfect science, which we strive toward, research would be valid in both senses, internal and external. In fact, some methodologies blend experimental and correlational designs to achieve that goal—but I skip ahead. Correlational research tends to be strong in external validity and weak in internal validity—the opposite of its experimental sibling.

A CORRELATIONAL RESEARCH PRIMER

Correlational studies scan the world for things that go together—a job not as easy as it sounds. The world teems with complexity—the grounds for alluding to the jungle. Our interests, theories, and expectations steer our observations, but correlational research constantly faces unique dangers: not observing enough, not observing enough of the right things, observing the right things in the wrong way. These problems arise from the fact that correlational researchers rarely reach a clear stop. This difficulty gives rise to correlation's intrinsic internal validity disadvantage. Nearly anyone can think of just one more thing to look at in any research area. Despite this, the more data we collect and the more analysis we do, the greater—hopefully—will be the knowledge generated.

The magic word in correlational research is *association*—or, technically, *covariation*. Evolutionary psychologists generally see associational thinking like this as adaptive—a sign of intelligence. With apologies to cave folk, the association between fire and lightning prompted early humans to look for fire after lightning storms. It may have promoted the investigation of other sparking mechanisms, as well. Some psychologists even think of brains as correlation detection machines, adept at finding patterns in observations. Like any good thing, we can take correlation detection too far. I, like others, am tempted to anthropomorphize my computer, to attribute a special kind of causality called *intentionality* to an inanimate object. As cute as it may be to give the computer a nice hat, this tendency does little good when I try to blame it for hiding my files.

The leap from correlation to causality can cause misunderstanding; hence the well-known statistical dictum: *correlation does not imply causation.* Anyone surveying the world sees an association between crime and ice cream purchases. In other words—and this is the right way to view all correlations—when ice cream sales go up, crime goes up; when crime goes down, so do ice cream sales. They *go together, covary,* or *correlate*—all synonyms. This example's correlation does not imply causation; further study does not show that ice cream provides criminals extra energy, or that criminals celebrate by buying ice crime. Although these hypotheses are not bad speculation, evidence shows that ice cream sales as well as criminal activity correlate with warm weather. Analyses of multiple variables, of which we will see more, reveal that hot weather causes both crime and ice cream sales. We do need to keep in mind that the dictum has an oft-missed corollary: *without correlation, there cannot be causation.* The dictum encourages us to look carefully before we leap. In this light, correlation, what goes with what, can best be seen as a step to understanding what causes what.

CORRELATION COEFFICIENT: SPEARMAN'S FAMOUS RHO

The most widely used measure of correlation is the Pearson product-moment coefficient, usually called Spearman's Rho (pronounced row, as in your boat), or simply rho. A correlation coefficient is a single number that registers the strength of the relationship between two variables. Spearman's Rho, which, inexplicably, Francis Galton reportedly invented, provides one formula for calculating that statistic. Good statisticians will geekily recount other formulas such as Kendall's Tau and Gamma; each gives a better (or worse) way of calculating correlation, depending on the circumstances. This variety reinforces our lesson that analysis boils down to asking computers the necessary questions to compare observations. Computers, in the form of statistical programs or Microsoft Excel, store the formulas and instantaneously and cheerfully (oops, shouldn't say that) deploy whichever you prefer. The popularity of rho arises because it seems to fit most circumstances best.

The same principle underlying crosstabs, the prime analytic tool, extends to rho—organize the data to see how well the variables relate. Harking back to the last chapter, the more a crosstab's observations fall along the main diagonal—the line between the top right and the bottom left corner—the

	Well	*Sick*
Eat broccoli	None	Several
No broccoli	All the rest	Nearly none

stronger the relationship between two variables is. To illustrate: My son regularly claims that he gets sick when he eats broccoli. Suspending my disbelief, we can probe his claim: that broccoli associates with sickness. Glance at this crosstab showing my son's fanciful broccoli data:

This crosstab portrays a near perfect relationship: the cases either fall in the upper right cell (sick with broccoli) or the lower left (well without broccoli). These cases on the diagonal fit the hypotheses; the cases off the diagonal do not.

Rho is a number between −1 and 1 that precisely describes a relationship's strength. The broccoli data specify that number would be close to 1, a near-perfect correlation. When rho reaches 1, it announces that every time you see one variable change, you see the other change the same way. As relationships weaken, rho decreases toward 0. At 0, rho signifies that two variables have no relation; in technical parlance, they are independent. A negative sign in front of rho does not add much meaning, signifying only that the relationship runs the opposite way; when the other variable rises, the one falls. (To be complete, computers calculate rho by dividing the covariance of the two variables by the product of their standard deviations. If this abridged explanation fails to satisfy your interest, please turn to any number of free tutorials on the Internet.) Now, we have the tool to score a Michigan-Columbia survey research rematch.

POLITICAL BEHAVIOR RESEARCH SUPERBOWL I

The Wolverines of the University of Michigan battled the Columbia University Lions to explain votes in three presidential elections, 1948, 1952, and 1956. This may seem like ancient history, but those presidential elections closely resemble our own. In other words, the variables that explained the outcome then work more or less as well today. 1948 pitted incumbent Democrat Harry Truman against Republican Thomas Dewey, in 1952 Democrat Adlai Stevenson faced Republican Dwight Eisenhower, and 1956 featured a Stevenson-Eisenhower rematch. Not to spoil, but we already know the Wolverines won, undoubtedly pleasing X-Men and/or Red Dawn aficionados. Their *American Voter* findings form the Median Voter Model's foundation. As sociologists headed Columbia's effort and psychology informed the Michigan effort, this competition represents a victory of psychology over sociology, as well. I want us to use polling data from the 2004 national election to replay their contest, make several points regarding voting and segue to the prevailing Michigan approach to political attitudes.

Both teams sought an explanation for why Americans prefer one candidate to another. We know from previous discussion that survey researchers generally study voting behavior with the poll question, "Who do you think you will vote for in the election for president?" In the correlation game, then, researchers try out questions, and the team that produces the best questions wins by obtaining the highest correlation. The pivotal presumption is that questions with the highest correlation provide the best "explanation." A few reasons sustain the use of the word explanation; I particularly like two. First, we can stretch the idea that without correlation there can be no causation to say that stronger correlations are more likely to indicate a causal tie. Second, strong correlations lead to sensible predictions. Consequently, when we learn which factors strongly correlate with votes, we can predict electoral outcomes.

The ultimate irony in 50 years of political behavior research is that Michigan won even though their game plan was almost entirely wrong. I attribute their victory to persistence, as we shall momentarily see. The Columbia playbook comes straight from sociology, whereas the Wolverines relied on now obsolete psychology. Sociological studies examine people in groups. In their book *The People's Choice*, Bernard Berelson, Paul Lazarsfeld, William McPhee, and Hazel Gaudet reveal that they believe that "voting is essentially a group experience. People who live, work, or play together tend to vote for the same candidates" (137). Most pollsters group these characteristics under the heading of *demographics*, a common word in survey or market research.

Demographics—from the Greek "picture of people"—consist of descriptors, such as race, age, income and educational attainment. They form the independent variables in many studies, perhaps because researches can measure them quickly and easily. The Columbia researchers put these characteristics together to create the Index of Political Participation (IPP). Survey researchers often use indices that combine several responses to capitalize on the hunch that more questions contain more information. Each individual's IPP score, then, summarizes a range of demographic details predicting whether that respondent would favor the Democrat or Republican.

We often spot sociological thinking in political analysis. Union members are solid Democrats, and southern white Baptists vote Republican. More refined sociopolitical thinking creates an index by putting several characteristics together to target a specific group. In the 2000 election, for example, pundits blustered about soccer moms. In part their view rests on the MVM; they tried to identify swing voters who could tip the balance. That part is fine; the rest of their thinking comes from a failed hypothesis. These pundits followed the same path as the Columbia researchers, hoping that a few demographics, specifically suburban females with kids, determine voters' decisions.

We turn again to ANES survey data from the 2004 election to reenact the epic struggle, starting with Columbia. This replication is quite simple; pick a few questions, combine their responses, and see how well the resulting index correlates with the intended vote—it *is* that easy. The stickiness manifests in choosing the right questions; we need to sift for those few that successfully operationalize (remember that word) Columbia's hypothesis. These steps describe survey research in a nutshell. We carefully transform or develop ideas and concepts into poll questions whose responses enter analysis as variables. In this study the dependent variable is fairly clear: its question V043203, suitably recoded (like last time) into John Kerry or George Bush.

The independent variable's questions should match Columbia's thinking. The ANES stopped asking some of their questions, because their theory did not work. Nevertheless, *The People's Choice* (a limited preview is available on Google Books) says that the IPP contains things like religious affiliation, economic status, and urban or rural residence. Luckily, the 2004 ANES has those things; if it did not, we would have to find another survey, pay for our own, or give up. I choose three questions—V043299, V043247a, and V042043—that cover race, religion, and some geography, respectively. This data resides on their free website, meaning that you can choose your other questions and see if you can do better than me (I hope you do!).

We start with V042043, which observes the "urbanicity" of the respondent's residence. Rural area, small town, suburb, large city, and inner city form the set of possible responses. First, Microsoft Excel or its equivalents gives the frequencies—the observations within this variable:

This frequency chart shows that most of the 1,144 respondents who answered come from the suburbs (372, or 30.7 percent), and the least come from the inner city (74, or 6 percent). Step 2 uses a friendly crosstab to confirm our guess that urbanicity relates to voting. Like the earlier partisanship voting crosstab, this one puts the vote intention along the top, urbanicity

	Respondents	*Percentage*
Rural area	184	15.2%
Small town	270	22.3%
Suburb	372	30.7%
Large city	244	20.1%
Inner city	74	6.1%

	Kerry	Bush
Rural area	33.2%	57.1%
Small town	43.3%	48.1%
Suburb	44.4%	48.4%
Large city	56.1%	33.2%
Inner city	64.9%	20.3%

down the side and the percent voting for each candidate by locale within each cell. (Some rows do not sum to 100 percent.)

This crosstab reveals a pattern; large city and inner city respondents tend to favor Kerry; the rest tend toward Bush. The third step reorganizes urbanicity to better reflect this pattern. There are several ways to do this (show your work!); I place the large city and inner city respondents into one new category and the rural into another, given that small-towners and suburbanites are too close to call—recall the sampling error in these data. This produces a clearer crosstab that shows the urbanicity vote relationship.

How strong is the relationship in this crosstab? The correlation coefficient knows! My computer calculates this crosstab's rho as .18—not that strong, but not zero, either. Now we repeat these three steps for the other two questions in our neo-IPP (which I will not show, to save space).

You may wonder why I only use three questions. Generally, the more questions the better the prediction, so to keep the contest fair, I limit the Lions to the same number of questions that the Wolverines use to measure partisanship. Finally, I sum the three questions to form an index, a 2004 IPP. The payoff lay in this crosstab.

Our neo-IPP has seven categories (I cleverly built it that way), just like Michigan's measure of partisanship. However, it uses numbers, because I was not clever enough to think up catchy labels. In addition, no respondent fell into the top category, boringly named "–3". We should confirm that this index relates to the vote: as we move down the crosstab, Bush does better. Now look at the score; the crosstab's rho (drumroll!) equals .29—greater than zero, but not too good. If we thumb back to the partisanship vote crosstab (page 69), it seems to show a stronger pattern. Indeed, that crosstab produces a correlation of .75—a very strong relationship. So this analysis shows that

	Kerry	Bush
Democratic locales	58.2%	30.2%
Republican locales	33.2%	57.1%

	Kerry	*Bush*
−3	N/A	N/A
−2	75.0%	0%
−1	69.9%	19.9%
0	55.7%	33.0%
1	39.1%	53.7%
2	27.5%	64.3%
3	12.5%	87.5%

partisanship—the Michigan way of thinking—beats the IPP by a score of .75 to .29. The Wolverines win!

The post game wrap-up features a few quick items. Aside from showing that psychology dominates sociology in the study of political behavior, this contest underlines scientific pragmatism. The theory that predicts best wins. Had Columbia's measures done better, we might see public opinion quite differently now. You might respond that social factors play a role in determining an individual's party, and you would be right, but party question still correlates more closely with vote. We will soon talk more about the nature of individuals' partisan attachments. Second, this exercise emphasizes the inventiveness of the Michigan researchers. This discussion began with the irony that Michigan's game plan went totally awry; only their persistence saved them. Their stubborn march to explain voting behavior led to a novel concept, an invention named *partisanship*. That failed game plan also influenced the way we think of survey response today.

THE WOLVERINES' GAME PLAN

The Michigan researchers we met in chapter 3, Angus Campbell, Philip Converse, Warren Miller, and Donald Stokes, practiced psychology, studying individual behaviors and attendant thoughts and feelings. The Wolverines start with the notion of attitudes. To speed through some basic psych, mental constructs fall into at least three categories—beliefs, attitudes, and values. Most research overlooks beliefs, simple thoughts like *the Sun rises in the east*, to study attitudes. Next, nearly everyone applies Gordon Allport's 1935 definition: *an attitude is a belief plus an evaluation.* Thus, adding "I like that" to "the sun rises in the east," forms an attitude: "I like the sun's rising in the east." This statement expresses a positive attitude toward the sunrise's location. The evaluative dimension of attitudes allows them to drive our behavior and, not coincidentally, trumpets attitudes' inextricable connection to judgment. But certain attitudes are so central that they affect other attitudes. These super attitudes are values. In some sense, values delineate our identity. If I value the sun, I may like the color yellow, call summer my favorite season, and want to live in Florida.

With this focus on attitudes and values comes the desire to know how people acquire attitudes, and how these attitudes change. Like the rest of social science, these studies got going after World War II, and balance theory, the first coherent way of explaining attitude change, arrived in time to influence the Michigan researchers. In retrospect, balance theory seems too simplistic; indeed, it has been shown not to work very well. Nevertheless, balance theory and cognitive consistency theory, its more formidable descendant, begat all attitudinal research; they spawned the Michigan researchers' initial thinking about political attitudes.

Fritz Heider, balance theory's auteur, thinks that some need to maintain mental balance causes people's attitudes to form and change. He also suggests that attitudes come in sets of three, so that any two attitudes influence the third. Friendship illustrates Heider's thinking. Imagine that you like Eric and he likes John; Heider predicts that you would like John, too. Your attitude plus Eric's attitude determines the third. This hypothesis extends smoothly to politics. For instance, I do not like Communism, and Eisenhower does not like Communism, so I like (read: vote for) Ike—Eisenhower's famed nickname. Balance theory developed into cognitive consistency theory, which postulates that a kind of psychological consistency pervades human thought (*cognition* is psych jargon for thought). The accumulation of evidence, including some from *The American Voter*, eventually forced psychology to abandon consistency theory. Nevertheless, the Wolverines expected to find consistent attitudes in politically well informed and engaged citizens, at least when their studies began.

THE DEMISE OF CONSISTENCY THEORY

How do Campbell, Converse, Miller and Stokes operationalize consistency in survey research? We saw one way last chapter—what is called "issue voting." Under issue voting, citizens vote by selecting the candidate who best matches their stances. This hypothesis brings balance theory into politics, as the Eisenhower/Communism illustration shows. Yet, as we learned in discussing MVM, the Michigan researchers gave up on issue voting as an explanation for political behavior. Their respondents, representing the citizenry, knew little about candidates' issue stances. The respondents did, however, seem to be able to deduce (if that word suffices) some positions from the candidate's political party—a clue that led to the investigation of partisanship.

In retrospect, the Michigan researchers seem a tad obsessed with consistency; perhaps their vision of democracy was too compelling. Their work takes three solid swings at demonstrating Americans that had consistent political attitudes. By 1964, when Phillip Converse published a fairly compact article, "The nature of belief systems in mass publics," they had given up. This article, public opinion research's most hallowed text (it appears in *Ideology and Discontent*, a notoriously hard-to-find book), details consistency theory's three failures. In going over them, we learn three lessons. First, it shows how to use sample surveys scientifically. These researchers have a hypothesis, develop questions, poll, and then, when the analysis disconfirms their guess, try twice more. This sheer stick-to-itiveness wins them the status of the field's founders. Moreover, their intellectual honesty—their willingness to let the data judge the correct answer—spawns today's view of political behavior. Second, knowing that most individual's attitudes lack consistency is a very important fact/finding. Third, retracing their research and its critiques marks where our investigation must go.

Their first two designs rely on values. In politics we call core values *ideologies*—coherent ways of organizing political thought and behavior. Communism serves as the prototypical ideology. One joins the party (sounds kind of fun, not), signaling the adoption of communist values. Good communists make political judgments consistent with their ideology: more precisely, the ideology determines answers to political questions. The Michigan researchers guess that their investigation will uncover American ideological drivers. Their word "constraint" names the causal relationship between ideology and attitudes. Specifically, they think that one ideology would constrain the political attitudes of each individual. The Wolverines also thought two familiar terms—*liberal* and *conservative*—would best describe the ideologies that all Americans use.

Offhand, their idea may seem unintuitive to us ideologically confused Americans, but it certainly comports with stereotypes. When you read environmentalist, someone with the political ideology of environmentalism pops to mind. That person lives life according to principles consistent with helping Earth. In that sense, environmentalism constrains their thoughts and behavior; we would not expect them to drive a big SUV or work for an oil company. We would expect them to support green fuels and vote for, say, Ralph Nader. The Wolverines thought all Americans ought to behave the same way. This normative undertone—the insistent *should*—runs beside consistency theory in their expectations. In their view, when democracy works properly, then ideology, like being liberal, causes mass attitudes, like supporting social welfare, higher taxes, and more public education.

The Michigan researchers devise a fairly simple, almost descriptive, first test for ideological constraint. In the 1952 and 1956 ANES surveys, they ask eight open-ended questions (their website offers this data). Questions 520018 to 520021 run, "What is good/bad about the Democrats/Republicans?" and questions 520027 to 520030 run, "Why vote/not vote for Stevenson/Eisenhower?" The Wolverines put the responses together to assess their ideological content. They create four categories—the "levels of conceptualization." They dropped the respondents who were considered most sophisticated—those who used ideological reasoning—in the highest category, "Ideology and Near-Ideology." Notice the unmistakable normative presumption. The "Group Benefits" category follows on the next rung. These respondents use their memberships to talk about political outcomes: "Republicans are good for farmers," for instance. The "Nature of the Times" responses stand on the third rung. Their answers refer to how well someone, their family, or the country was doing. References to a bad economy sit here. Finally, at the bottom of the pile—the responses the Wolverines think are least sophisticated—fall in the "No Issue Content" category; here, respondents avoid abstraction, groups, and issues to comment directly on the candidates or parties: "I like Ike's temperament."

The Wolverines, in essence, test respondents, representing the American public (have to remember that), and assign grades based on their use of ideology. How did we do? Only 12.5 percent of all responses merit a seal of approval (see *The American Voter*, 144). Even this small number reflects some generosity; originally the researchers divided the highest category into "Ideologues" and "Near-Ideologues"; then, only 2.5 percent pass, with the near-ideological 10 percent getting partial credit. The next main category holds the largest numbers: 42 percent of the respondents draw on group benefits. The bottom categories each have about a fifth of the respondents: 24 and 22.5 percent, respectively. In short, 88.5 percent of *American Voters* fail the first Michigan consistency test.

Their second try subtly applies consistency theory to political attitudes. The Wolverines came up with a test that did not require respondents to be aware of an overriding value; it sees instead whether some ideology constrains attitudes behind the scenes. Logically, constrained attitudes should display strong correlations with each other. For comparison, they also tested this hypothesis on candidates in the 1958 congressional elections, asking them roughly the same questions. They expected that the candidates' attitudes would reflect ideological constraint and set the standard for the public's attitudes; this additional data also confirmed the researchers' beliefs about the content of liberal and conservative views. As expected, the elite congressional candidates did rather well, scoring an average correlation of .53 among five standard domestic issues, for example. The public, in contrast, disappoints, scoring a .23 on the same measure (Belief Systems, 229).

With two strikes, our steadfast researchers give consistency theory a last chance, examining constraint across the passage of time. They ask the same survey respondents questions on nine political issues in 1958 and again in 1960 and 1962. Pollsters call this kind of survey a panel study; this particular one tells us whether individuals' responses change over time or whether they remain the same—nice and stable. You should anticipate that the sample did not do too well. If responses are perfectly consistent, we should see a correlation of one. Actual analysis uncovers low correlations. With two exceptions, the correlations between time 1 and time 2 on the nine attitudes fall roughly between .3 and .4—nowhere near perfect. Only one response has a correlation above .7—partisanship, another clue to its political import! A question concerning school desegregation did pretty well too, with a correlation near .5. On balance, respondents are unlikely to give the same answer to a political question two years later.

Looking at these same respondents in 1962 put the final nail in consistency's coffin and allows Converse to develop the first model of survey response. Once again, 1960's responses bear little relationship to 1962's. Even worse, the responses from time 1, 1958, correlate to time 3, 1962, just as well as the responses from time 2, in 1960. To Converse, this data demonstrates that people effectively flip back and forth at random. He encodes this finding in the "Black and White" model, which holds that other than a tiny core group with crystallized attitudes, respondents answer survey questions randomly.

Let's inspect this momentous model and its claim. Its name reflects Converse's view that there are no grey areas in survey response theory. A citizen either has an attitude or does not. Those few with attitudes earn the sobriquet *crystallized*; these ideologues inhabit the highest level of conceptualization, possessing the political sophistication to avoid flip-flops. The bulk of the public, at least 80 percent, displays a qualitatively different level of political sophistication. These citizens have no ideology that organizes their attitudes, fail to vote in a stable ideological way, and, worst of all (from the perspective of polling), respond randomly to survey questions. By now, we ought to automatically translate the Black and White model's implications. If respondents flip a mental coin, saying yes for heads and no for tails, who should care about these responses? In light of this view, survey researchers call these random expressions "non-attitudes," implying that nothing stands behind them. Elitists, like Lippmann, may well chime, "I told you so."

Some quick comments end our review of the Wolverines' contributions. The Michigan data does not say what proportion of the responses are truly random; in fact, Converse says the Black and White model merely fits the data best, leaving space for further investigation. Later scholars, as the next chapter discusses, propose that the random responses cancel out, leaving aggregate poll results to reflect just the crystallized (read: genuine) views. Other scholars, Zaller in particular, suggest that the randomness within individuals may reflect the information citizens receive, endowing responses with some meaning. And finally, as we have discussed, partisanship (and other dispositions) may be a reasonable guide for citizens' political choices.

PARTISANSHIP AS THE PRIMARY EXPLANATION OF POLITICAL BEHAVIOR

The Michigan research unambiguously reveals the status of partisanship (PID) as the prime correlate of Americans' political expressions, such as survey responses and votes. This finding immediately elevates the question *what is partisanship?* At first glance, partisanship equals the answers to three survey questions—no more and no less—wherein respondents express the strength of their identification with the Democrats or Republicans. The Wolverines appear to think that PID taps some kind of emotional attachment, much like being a sports fan. I like the Democrats or Republicans just akin to the way I like the Yankees or the Red Sox (actually, I like the Dodgers); I root for them and want them to succeed. Put this way, the use of PID seems to be at odds with how we might hope citizens should behave.

Other scholars give PID interpretations that open up more pleasing normative interpretations. V. O. Key suggests that PID corresponds to an individual's "standing decision" with regard to the two parties. Citizens, in his view, vote for their party unless something disturbs them. For example, kids ought to be in bed by eight o'clock, except on special days like Halloween. This revision makes the use of PID more palatable. Similarly, Morris Fiorina proposes that PID is a "running tally," a report summarizing someone's past votes. If I always vote one way, then identifying with that party appears reasonable. Both scholars emphasize that PID is a tendency and not an unsophisticated attachment.

Fiorina, in particular, uses his running tally idea to develop a hypothesis: namely, that people use a retrospective heuristic when they vote. Heuristics, which we bumped into in the first chapter, are simple rules that let us easily make complex political decisions. Under retrospective voting, whenever something obvious and bad happens, like a war or a depression, citizens respond by overriding or updating their tally and voting against the incumbent. As said, this mechanism keeps officeholders on their toes, trying to avoid war and economic downturns. Less obviously, Fiorina's idea lets the

nature-of-the-times voters, in the middle of the Michigan levels of conceptualization, fulfill their democratic duty, suggesting that they may not be so
derelict after all.

To this moment, we have only examined correlational evidence linking
PID to political attitudes and behavior; we need more to assign PID a causal
role. Aware of this need, researchers use logic and auxiliary studies to confirm PID's standing as the pilot, and not merely another passenger. Converse
draws one inference from PID's stability; if it remains stable and unchanging,
like a constant, then presumably it cannot be an effect. PID also precedes the
vote in time (more on this soon), hinting strongly at PID's causal nature.

Later studies examine the origins of PID. The most rigorous might be
Kent Jennings and Richard Niemi's *Generations and Politics*—a panel study
that follows participants from birth until adulthood. They find that your PID
generally comes from your parents. Parents who share the same PID typically produce matching offspring, whereas kids from mixed-PID marriages
tend not to inherit a PID. In addition, Republicans and Democrats usually
marry others of the same party. So, somewhat paradoxically, a socialization
process—cultural inheritance—configures the Wolverines' most important
variable. The key departure from Columbia's thought is that this socialization
focuses on PID to the exclusion of demographics.

The Michigan researchers and their followers use PID to create a convincing explanation for how most Americans vote; political scientists refer to this
portrait as the "funnel of casualty." In this funnel, voting—the outcome or
dependent variable—waits at the narrow end. The independent variables, all
the forces that impinge on votes, spread back from the outcome. The funnel
also arrays the factors by time, which moves backward from election day.
PID, the most potent force, sits smack in the funnel's middle. PID's position
also marks a critical distinction between long- and short-term forces. All the
things we think of as the campaign—the candidates and the issues—count as
short-term forces, because most researchers agree that political campaigns
really begin around Labor Day, 10 weeks or so before the election. In this
setup, PID is the last long-term force to affect votes, and its potency has an
enormous consequence. Long-term forces decide roughly 80 percent of all
votes before the campaign even starts, long before most citizens even know
the candidates' names.

The funnel of causality implies that campaigns may not be very important,
only affecting roughly 20 percent of the electorate—a good reason for us to
appreciate attempts to link PID to good governance. On the other hand, we do
not want to push this logic too far. The MVM teaches that a single vote can be
decisive, so any electoral victory may depend on the decisions a few people
make. Moreover, these few are independents, without a PID, an emotional

attachment, standing decision or running tally that nudges them to vote one way or the other. Another reason that campaigns may seem not to matter lies in that close elections tend to see evenly balanced campaign efforts. If both candidates use equal skill and comparable resources to push and pull the median voter in their direction, we may not see much overall movement. Then again, if one candidate dominates the campaign, we will almost certainly see the campaign affect on the outcome. This insight brings up propaganda, one-sided campaigns that we will resume discussing later.

ROBERT LANE AND V. O. KEY RESPOND TO THE WOLVERINE VIEW

Knowing the Wolverines' discoveries, we can weigh two important critiques, begin to solidify our own views, and identify new avenues for investigation. The Michigan findings land on students of political behavior with both feet, and their thinking still affects every serious work. We, as non-experts, may not find ideological constraint and response stability all that appealing; a friend recommends Pizza Hut for dinner once, but someone who demands Pizza Hut time after time gets irritating. This brings Ralph Waldo Emerson's quip about foolish consistency, the hobgoblin of little minds, to mind. Nonetheless, it does not add up when someone loudly professes "I am liberal" and opposes Social Security, or a self-proclaimed conservative wants to increase government regulation. The Michigan data and analysis prove that nearly all Americans are not ideological sophisticates, and that many, if not most, of us seem to answer survey questions randomly.

Robert Lane thinks that the Michigan researchers measure ideology incorrectly, and faults *The American Voter's* internal validity. Lane proposes that all but a few individuals have an ideology, which he defines as coherent justifications for political views. Lane implies that the vocabulary of individuals' justifications may employ different vocabularies, meaning that the Wolverines' tests may not use the right words to capture respondent's thoughts. To translate, Lane suggests that asking everyone the same question hides Americans' rich but idiosyncratic ideological depth. His operationalization follows his hypothesis; instead of constructing a poll, Lane chats with his participants in person. During this interview, he sits, has some coffee, and engages in political conversation. According to plan, every so often he drops an ANES-like question into the discussion: *what do you think about Communism (or free trade)?*

When responses to these political inquiries seem inconsistent, Lane probes further. His book, *Political Ideology*, recounts his finding—nearly every person could present an internally consistent justification for their view—the polar opposite of the Wolverine's conclusion! What should we believe? This is more than a question of faith; it demands that we reconcile two scientific studies, two views of truth. I trust you can see how their methods and definitions differ. In some sense, which I suspect they would admit, they call different things ideology, as well. Thus, in this sense, both are right.

According to Converse, no common ideologies organize most American's political attitudes, but to Lane, nearly everyone can justify their views reasonably. On the other hand, given our interest in polls and public opinion, Converse's technique beats Lane's on the grounds of efficiency. Imagine trying to sit with each of a thousand people discussing politics for a few weeks. In my view, Lane offers another existence result, saying *my people meet this standard, so others can, too.* We will try to keep Lane's demonstration of citizens' abilities, as well as the importance of political language, in mind during our investigations.

The prolific V. O. Key questions the Michigan results' external validity. His spark of genius recommends that we move our attention away from citizens in isolation and toward the interaction between citizens and the messages they receive. Simply put, he thinks that the sophistication of citizens depends on the information in the political environment around them. We call this the *echo chamber hypothesis.* As he states in his book *The Responsible Electorate,* "the people's verdict can be no more than a selective reflection of the alternatives and outlooks presented to them" (2). This guess yields a prediction: specifically, citizens' sophistication increases in highly charged political years, but in slack times, they become ideological dunces. In validity terms, he accepts the Wolverines' result for the 1950s but claims that it would not apply to more politicized eras.

In the 1930s, to pad Key's scenario, American citizens frequently heard strong opinions regarding the New Deal, because politics had such prominence during the Great Depression. Key thinks that this polarized discourse would weave its way into citizens' attitudes, and that surveys would therefore show more constraint. Thus respondents would define themselves as liberal, supporting Franklin Delano Roosevelt and his polices, or as conservative, opposing them—increasing the level of correlation between any two attitudes. By the 1950s, Key's story has ideology disappear from the American scene. He maintains that Eisenhower and Stevenson agreed too much for citizens to use ideology. Both supported Social Security and opposed Communism, for instance. Key thought that the 1950s were an aberration, and that the *American Voter* results reflected this weirdness.

It would be nice if Key tested his guess with survey data. At the time, he could not; no ANES-type surveys were conducted during the 1930s. So

Key and everyone else had to wait for ideology to resurface in American politics. The opportunity came in the psychedelic sixties. Prehistoric history for many of us, this era featured a real party, the infamous sex, drugs, and rock 'n' roll, as well as an upswing in political conflict. This decade's Civil Rights movement and Viet Nam conflict came with protests and massive news coverage that riveted public attention. Equally important for Key, politics became ideologically polarized. Liberals supported hippies and civil rights and opposed the Viet Nam conflict—unambiguous stances that conservatives unambiguously opposed. Sixties citizens also took part in the two most polarized presidential elections in American history (ones that largely prove the MVM). In 1964, extreme conservative Barry Goldwater, whom some accused of advocating nuclear war, ran against liberal Lyndon Johnson. In 1972, the extremely liberal George McGovern, with the support of the flower children, ran against the more conservative Richard Nixon.

At last, political science had the perfect circumstances to check Key's guess; researchers just had to compare levels of ideological constraint in the 1960s' surveys to those in the 1950s'. Sure enough, later ANES surveys show an upswing in ideological constraint relative to the 1950s. But—and it is a big but—the ANES changed questions in 1964! This change creates an internal validity problem—the early and later questions were not comparable. John Sullivan, James Piereson and George Marcus argue (in the *American Journal of Political Science*) that the ANES change was good thing, and that the new questions give a more accurate reading of public sentiment, because in the old questions the alternatives were unclear. Take a look at the old version, and responses from 1956:

> The government in Washington ought to see to it that everybody who wants to work can find a job. Now would you have an opinion on this or not? (If yes): Do you think the government should do this? ($N = 1,587$)
> 48%   Agree strongly; govt. definitely should
> 14.7   Agree, but not very strongly
> 7.6   Not sure; it depends
> 11.5   Disagree, but not very strongly
> 18.2   Disagree strongly; govt. definitely should not

Now the newer version from 1964:

> In general, some people feel that the government in Washington should see to it that every person has a job and a good standard of living. Others think the government should just let each person get ahead on his own. Have you been interested enough in this to favor one side over the other? (If Yes): Do you think

that the government should see to it that every person has a job and a good standard of living or should it let each person get ahead on his own? (N = 1338)
36.4% Govt. should see to it that every person has a job a good standard of living
13.0 Other, depends
50.6 Govt. should let each person get ahead on his own

Initially, everyone should see that support for government seeing to it that every person has a job fell markedly, from 48 to 36 percent. Why did it fall 12 percent? Some thought produces no less than five hypotheses as to why responses changed.

First, the Black and White model logic suggests that responses may randomly vary, so the change may be due to chance, in which case the fall doesn't really matter.

Second, there may have been a real shift in people's attitudes; people may have grown more opposed to this kind of government intervention between 1956 and 1964.

Now, although the untutored may see these questions as synonymous, we should be able to spot more differences that increase the difficulty of pinpointing the reason for the drop.

Third, the presentation of the other side of the argument in 1964, "others think the government should just let each person get ahead" clarifies the question and produced more accurate responses, as Sullivan and his colleagues argue; alternatively, the addition of this argument sways responses in an inauthentic way.

Fourth, the response options are reduced from five to three, possibly changing the substance of the responses.

Fifth, the eagle-eyed should spot the addition of the phrase "standard of living" in 1964, which suggests that respondents may be willing to give jobs but not more.

Besides illustrating a topic that we will devour in the next chapter (how hard it can be to interpret poll results), this sifting shows that this test of Key's hypothesis is less than perfect.

The real problems with this test are time and money. We cannot go back to the 1950s and ask the new questions, and for reasons of expense the old questions were never asked after 1960. Sullivan, Piereson, and Marcus did run an experiment comparing constraint across the question formats, and their results support the idea that the new format prompts increases in the appearance of ideological constraint (in their participants). I believe that this evidence, as well as some reflection, leads most survey researchers to agree with points four and five and prefer the 1964 version. Still it is fair to say that this test of Key's idea was not good enough to eliminate doubt. At the same time,

Key's external validity critique and his hypothesis concerning the importance of political information remains so plausibly intuitive that nearly everyone suspects that the information available to voters in the political environment affects survey responses. See how tough social science is?

THE ZALLER MODEL

In my experience, John Zaller's effort, which he calls the RAS model, provides the best theory of survey response available. This model tackles the question of how the political environment's information combines with the desiderata of respondents' minds to cause public opinion. Perhaps the most amazing part of this research lay in its empirical inventiveness; by categorizing respondents according their political knowledge, Zaller can use static surveys to investigate dynamic effects. If this sounds complex, it is; I do not know of any more intricate piece of social science model. Physical scientists may scoff at this posturing, alluding to the convoluted Krebs cycle, which describes how cells turn sugar into energy, or Maxwell's labyrinth equations, which cover electromagnetism—and they may be right to spurn an early science's progress. Still, doing Zaller's ideas justice requires a level of discussion that goes beyond whatever else the political world offers. I promise to convey its essence as best I can to expose the knowledge it encapsulates and interpret its bearing on the Lippmann–Dewey debate. I urge those with motivation to pull up Amazon and order his book, *The Nature and Origins of Mass Opinion.*

Without doubt, Zaller's masterpiece merits the word *model*, as it specifies how a set of inputs produces a precise output. In comparison, Converse's idea is more of a hypothesis—a simpler guess about how people respond to poll questions. Zaller goes beyond hypothesis to talk about what must be taken into account when predicting a respondent's yes or no—a true theory of survey response. As a result, if we observe these factors, then we can actually calculate the exact percentage of respondents that we expect to say yes. The Michigan findings do provide the foundation for Zaller's work—in my reading, he never contests their results. Still, he expands Converse's Black and White model by adjusting the random response with political information. In so doing, he fundamentally reshapes Converse's interpretation of public opinion. His model of individual response highlights this insight.

Zaller uses the metaphor of an urn to replicate what goes on inside people's heads. For those who avoid gambling, urns are fancy buckets that take center stage in games of chance, like bingo or the lottery; they hold balls. In his metaphor, these balls stand for the political information filling citizens' heads, and response entails drawing a ball from the urn. Critically, each ball has a valence (read: good or bad flavor), so when you draw a good ball, you say yes (or the equivalent), while a bad ball prompts a no. The key words *receive*, *accept*, and *sample* mark the three stages that he proposes underlie the process of filling up the urn and drawing a ball.

In the first stage, citizens receive political information from *elites*, Zaller's word for members of the political class—politicians, experts, and the media—that send public messages. This flow of information passes bits of good news and bad news to citizens' ears. Critically, the more attuned someone is to politics, the more information they receive—the first stage—so political junkies hear lots while the politically inattentive get much less. The acceptance stage comes second; here one's dispositions (read: the tendencies that stem from knowledge or experience) filter incoming information before storing it in the urn, figuratively letting some balls in and blocking others. One's dispositions, of which PID is the strongest, govern the process of rejecting objectionable information. Think about presidential approval: under Republican administrations, an individual Republican's loyalty keeps much of the bad news about the president from reaching the urn, whereas Democrats tend to filter out the good news.

The first two stages occur prior to the time of the poll's interview, signifying that citizens bring a head more or less full of political tidbits to that table. Zaller goes on to give a precise guess; in his view, two variables determine the mix of good and bad balls in a respondent's urn—the amount of good news, relative to bad, in the information flow, and the strength of dispositional filtering. The third stage, sample, completes the process. When faced with a question, respondents metaphorically reach into the urn and draw a random ball that dictates the response as described above.

This setup's payoff comes in the form of a prediction that links survey response to the two variables governing the urn's contents. First, the higher the proportion of good messages in the information flow, the more likely respondents are to draw positive balls when asked. As the relative amount of bad messages increases, larger numbers of people draw negative balls, increasing opposition. Mathematically, the Zaller model holds that the likelihood of agreement equals the amount of positive messages divided by the total number of messages. Dispositional filtering then shifts this expected value in the direction that they bias the urn's content. To illustrate, envision a world where elites send 10 messages regarding a Democratic president. If 9 of the 10 say nice things—the president is smart, doing a good job, and the like—we would expect 90 percent of the independents, who do not filter, to express approval, Democratic identifiers to be even more positive, given their tendency to reject the negative message, and Republican identifiers' approval to come in below 90 percent, because they accept the negative message but block some positive news.

Zaller then steps from this model of individual response to a portrayal of collective poll results. He, a loyal survey researcher, views public opinion as the aggregate of individual responses. Thus, his best prediction of poll results is the sum of all the individual predictions. More math shows that Zaller believes that the relative percentage of good information in everyone's urn's after accounting for the population's dispositional biases best predicts aggregate response. Zaller reasonably suggests that nearly every political message originates with a major party. This observation leads to a hypothesis—the proportion of positive messages in the information flow depends on whether prominent Republicans and Democrats agree or disagree. Put simply, when both parties support a program, the lion's share of the messages will be supportive.

On the other hand, party elites send conflicting messages when they disagree. Republicans may support something that Democrats oppose, ensuring that the number of good and bad messages will be closer to even. Due to citizens' filtering certain messages and sources, these elite stances affect public opinion. When the parties agree, Americans on the whole move to support the consensus (he calls this a "mainstream" effect); when they disagree, public opinion polarizes—Democratic identifiers head one way and Republicans the other. This completes my sketch of his model; review the preceding paragraphs as necessary before continuing.

ZALLER'S TEST

A model essentially organizes a set of hypotheses. Like any hypothesis it needs an empirical test that combines data and analysis. Zaller offers some potent tests, but before inspecting one, we should step back and consider what such tests of public opinion dynamics require. Following an earlier lesson, I want to outline an experimental design first. This method would demand assembling groups with a variety of dispositions and bombarding them with messages such that we would manipulate the proportion of good news and its senders in this information flow. Such an experiment would have two obvious external validity drawbacks. First, the participants may not represent the citizenry as a whole. Second, these participants would be placed in an artificial realm, removed from the real political messages. Correlational designs and sample surveys provide an alternative, of course, but this method is difficult too.

What kind of correlational design would best assess Zaller's model, or any similar take on response dynamics? An optimal design requires polling representative samples of the population at regular intervals, perhaps week by week or month by month. These polls need not look at the same people, like a panel study; instead, they track representative responses—hence pollsters call this setup a *tracking poll*. Tracking polls are phenomenally pricey; each poll costs as much as a regular poll. The total price multiplies the unit cost by the number of intervals. If we want to look three times, for instance, our design would be three times the price of a single poll. Tracking polls face another more subtle hurdle. If we want to asses the impact of altering information flows, we need our polls to bracket the message change precisely, ideally right before the message changes and soon after. Lacking crystal balls, it is tough to get the timing right and ask questions that address the change.

Elections are the only political events that have high enough stakes to regularly warrant tracking polls. Moreover, only major candidates have the resources to pay for them. To candidates, they make economic sense—you may as well spend a few million dollars monitoring a half a billion dollars worth of advertising's impact. Candidates jealously guard their data and rarely make it available to prying academics. Kathleen Hall Jamieson has raised the money to fund the recent National Annenberg Election Survey, which tracks presidential elections, and make it publicly available (google it for a look). Still, even this expensive study asks only a few questions—around 40—compared to the hundreds of questions in the massive ANES. Finally, elections rarely offer the right situation to fully test the RAS model, because the candidates' messages are so intense, and of equal volume. So what does Zaller do?

Zaller invented an empirically ingenious way to use the observations from a single survey to examine the dynamics of survey response. His trick uses political knowledge as a proxy for time. In plainer words, ANES surveys regularly ask knowledge questions such as "Who is the chief justice of the Supreme Court?" and "Which party has a majority in the Senate?" Zaller reasons that the most politically engaged answer these questions correctly. Consequently, these questions identify respondents with high political knowledge who receive political messages first as well as those with minimal knowledge who get them last (if at all). Thus a political knowledge index organizes respondents by time of message reception. This insight allows Zaller to use past ANES data in a way that the surveys' creators never imagined! At the same time, the ANES survey's question range covers many issues. His most impressive study investigates how respondents' attitudes during the Viet Nam conflict change in concert with their dispositions and the information they receive.

Zaller describes the elites' Vietnam messages—the main independent variable in his study—this way: "Liberal opinion leaders overwhelmingly supported the war in 1964, but mainly opposed it in 1970. Conservative elites, by contrast, continued to support the war throughout the period of American involvement." Accordingly, Zaller expects this information flow to show "how the mainstream and polarization patterns form and change over time in response to changes in the intensities of competing messages in a two-sided information flow" (187). Zaller then uses four ANES surveys, from 1964, 1966, 1968, and 1970, to chart the messages' impact using the question "Which of the following do you think we should do now in Vietnam: pull out of Vietnam entirely, keep our soldiers in Vietnam but try to end the fighting, or take a stronger stand even if it means invading North Vietnam." Within each survey, he divides the respondents into five political knowledge categories—a second independent variable, placing the most informed on the right and the least on the left. The arrangement allows everyone to see the march of time in each snapshot; the most informed live close to the political present while the least reside in the past, because messages require more time to reach them. He also separates respondents into two groups according to their dispositional filter—a third independent variable, tagging the peace-loving liberals as doves and the warmongering conservatives as hawks.

Sure enough, in 1964, hawks and doves display similar patterns. More political knowledge correlates with increasing support for the war—the dependent variable. Presumably this pattern reflects the propagandistic environment that led to the United States' involvement in Viet Nam. These messages echo those before World War I and foreshadow those associated with Iraq. First, engaged citizens heard of the Gulf of Tonkin incident, in which North Vietnamese patrol boats shot at American ships. Next they receive messages associating Ho Chi Minh, the North Vietnamese leader, with Communism. Finally come the justifications for sending American troops; pundits publicize the domino theory, which argues that when South Viet Nam falls to Communism, other counties will follow. Perhaps these arguments sound far-fetched, perhaps not—either way, the survey data show that engaged citizens, hawks and doves alike, support war. At the same time, the least informed citizens did not—again, hawks and doves alike. Zaller suspects that these inattentive citizens had yet to hear of Viet Nam.

Through the intervening years to 1970, the pattern of public support radically changes—due, Zaller claims, to the shift in the elites' message. As he states, the liberal elites turned against the war. This new stance gave rise to demonstrations, protests, and riots—the whole nine yards. In response, conservative elites heightened their rhetoric, most maintaining staunch support. In the data, doves, starting with the most informed in 1966, begin to oppose the war. By 1970, all but the least informed doves expressed some opposition. In short, Zaller analyzes data from four surveys to show that changes in public opinion mirror developments at the elite level. Thus, as the propagandistic consensus transforms into a liberal–conservative conflict, dovish respondents swing to oppose the war, while the hawkish stay supportive.

EVALUATING ZALLER'S WORK

In discussing this work, let me first say that Zaller does a remarkable job given correlational research's inherent difficulty with internal validity; I find no fault in the way he deploys and carefully marshals NES data to support his hypotheses. His model offers a lucid view of survey response, public opinion, and the relationship between political elites and ordinary citizens. Nevertheless, all models demand choices in their simplifications. Any researcher must decide the relative worth of including any factor in the model, keeping in mind each additional factor's cost in increased complexity. Zaller's RAS model offers a lot of meat to chew while maintaining *parsimony*—the scientific value of explanatory economy. Recognizing this necessity, I believe some important phenomena fail to make his cut; chief among these is the impact of question wording.

As we have mentioned, and as we will discuss in the next chapter, choosing the wording for questions is the toughest part of a pollster's job. At the same time, finding unambiguous ways to interpret poll results offers the best way to unlock their democratic utility. By taking questions one at time, like the other projects we examined, Zaller's model avoids this thicket. His Viet Nam study, for example, depends on one question. But this spotlight has a price. His model never engages effects such as framing. Similarly, it sees a deterministic relationship between urns (read: memory) and news. For example, the model takes elite messages to be either good or bad, leaving little room for ambiguity or interpretation.

My main criticism of Zaller's model, data, and analytic technique is the trouble it has dealing with independents. He appears to inherit this tendency from the Wolverines, and possibly for a pragmatic reason. Independents do not possess the political backgrounds and inclinations that make it easy to predict or explain their attitudes. Some may also argue that independents are too few, too tuned out, or too wishy-washy to be consequential; as we know, MVM supplies a sufficient response to this critique—whenever major parties fight to a draw, independents break the tie. My remark may resonate with Lane's; consequently, I will use different data and analysis, as we shall see, to assess the linkage between political discourse and citizens' attitudes.

In Viet Nam, for instance, many credit an ostensible independent, the newscaster Walter Cronkite, with turning the public against the war.

Wikipedia reports that when Cronkite stated that the Vietnam War was unwinnable, President Johnson said, "If I've lost Cronkite, I've lost the American people." To take another Viet Nam example: Richard Nixon promised "peace with honor" in the 1968 campaign; such a message (read: clever political rhetoric) is hard to categorize as either good or bad. Yet it is safe to say this slogan was effective. Both the Wolverines and Zaller give us little appreciation for the pivotal role that political independents play. Moreover, what understanding they do generate gives little hope to Dewey's adherents.

I am also obliged to point out that Zaller has a great deal in common with Lippmann. The optimistic me recoils when I look at his work on the whole. In his model, citizens exercise little judgment apart from dogmatically rejecting selected messages. Each response results from the mix of elite messages as well as the chance element retained from Converse. Put bluntly, his citizens essentially parrot the messages they receive from elites. This empirical view does not keep Zaller from believing in democracy, but in his vision, as in Lippmann's, elites do the thinking. Zaller believes that five conditions can reconcile the elite domination of public opinion with democracy (314). The conditions follow, paraphrased:

- Experts' dispositions parallel the public's, so experts consider all viewpoints.
- Experts have incentives to develop effective solutions.
- The press covers all experts sufficiently.
- Politicians keep within the parameters of expert opinion.
- Citizens align with elites who share their dispositions in case of disagreement.

You might examine your recollections of Iraq or reexamine the World War I story to see whether either episode meets these criteria—I do not think they do. You may also discern that they spill past the bounds of public opinion research. These criteria do highlight the value that Zaller places on expertise, which coincides with Lippmann's technocratic vision for good government But the major difference separating Zaller from Lippmann is Zaller's notion that citizens resolve fights between experts. On the other hand, these citizens do not stand as reasoning or deliberate judges choosing between experts. Instead, they join a game of tug of war, so poll results reflect experts' and their followers' pulling one way or the other. Still, I reiterate, Zaller's model works insofar as it explains his data. I would like to conclude by deploying his model to complete our investigation of elite discourse and the public's attitudes toward partial birth abortion. In so doing, I believe we can carve out a space for the existence of independent judgment that we saw in the last chapter.

STUDY NUMERO TRES: EXPLAINING REPUBLICAN SUCCESS AGAINST PARTIAL BIRTH ABORTION

The conclusion of our study of public opinion toward banning partial birth abortion (PBA) builds on the experimental results from the last chapter; essentially,basically I plan to take the finding concerning the effects of using the word *baby* into actual political discourse—the jargon for "talk," and examine how the messages elites sent led the public to oppose the procedure. This study has two parts. In part 1, we look at the origin of the term PBA in political discourse. More of an anecdote than a study, this tale suggests that the media helped abortion foes by adopting and publicizing this label. This part also examines a specific instance of political discourse in the Supreme Court and Congress to confirm our suspicion that the ban's supporters use the word *baby*, while opponents opt for *fetus*, when discussing PBA.

The second part tracks the usage of *baby* and *fetus* in Congress and the media (in particular the *New York Times*), and the public's response to these messages. We shall see that the congressional Republicans did a much better job with their rhetoric than their Democratic rivals. This study then uses time series analysis, a more sophisticated form of correlational, to show that usage of the word *baby* preceded public support for banning the procedure. Although this research affirms the Zaller model, we need to keep in mind the fact that these results depend on two contingencies. First, the media and politicians continuously used a laden term, *partial birth abortion*, to the exclusion of more clinical terms, like dilation and extraction (DAE). Second, the experimental results from last chapter indicate that the concept of *baby* dominates the concept of *fetus* in citizens' reactions to PBA. Without these effects, the Republicans may have failed. I believe these contingencies offer Dewey some ammunition in his fight with Lippmann over the public's competence. Once again, these results appear in the *Journal of Communication* (2007, 254–271).

THE POLITICS OF ABORTION AND THE ORIGINS OF THE PBA LABEL

Most scholars, like Lawrence Tribe, trace the emergence of abortion as a national political issue to *Roe v. Wade*, the 1973 Supreme Court case that generally legalized the procedure throughout the United States. Abortion proponents see that decision as a landmark victory, indeed, it overturned several state laws that criminalized abortion and closed many avenues for future regulation. Yet *Roe* also mobilized abortion's opponents. E.E. Schattschneider discusses this pattern in his wonderful book *The Semisovereign People*. As he puts it, democratic politics always features a battle between a relatively complacent majority that accepts the status quo and a passionate minority that favors change. To succeed, the minority must build a new majority, either by converting members of the existing majority or by bringing neutral citizens to its side. Hence, *Roe* created a new status quo in 1973 that simultaneously ignited abortion's opponents.

The familiar designation "pro-life" appeared as a self-descriptive name for the movement that evolved to oppose legal abortion. Soon after, abortion supporters coined the term "pro-choice" to describe their position. We can easily detect these terms' propagandistic thrust, the way they invite support or acquiescence—perhaps getting past one's filters by appearing reasonable—while putting opponents in the precarious position of opposing either life or choice. (Some academics go farther, saying that this kind of linguistic battle gets to the heart of mass politics; I disagree, but we will defer this debate to chapter 6.) So far, at least, rhetorical war surrounding abortion seems relatively even. Around 1995, however, that battle appears to have shifted when abortion opponents introduced the term *partial birth abortion* to the fray.

PBA describes a relatively rare form of abortion that became the focus of efforts to impose a nationwide ban. At first glance, we might be willing to see this as a stroke of propagandistic genius; certainly few doubt that this term reshaped the rhetorical conflict to the opponents' advantage. Yet, as you should expect, I want to analyze this term's origins more closely. I attribute these words' appearance to sheer persistence. At least one prior attempt to label the procedure failed. The term "brain suction abortion" (BSA) made its first media appearance in February of 1995 in an Ohio newspaper report on a proposed state ban. A variant, "brain sucking abortion," appears in the *Congressional Record* seven times from 1995 to 2000. These aside, there is no further trace of BSA's use. This search suggests that the term did not catch on. It might be that the media rejected this term because it felt it was too graphic; if so, the media enjoys some discretion in coverage.

The PBA label did appear, however, and a cursory search would uncover thousands of uses of this term in the media and public records. We also would discover that an attempt to relabel the procedure later in the saga also failed. Abortion supporters as well as members of the medical community recognized the term's negative connotations and proposed the more clinical term *dilation and extraction (DAE)* in its place. Even with some public discussion of the terms' relative merits—DAE, for instance, has more standing in the medical community—PBA was the dominant term. In the content analysis of the *Washington Post*, presented below, PBA saw 14 times more use than DAE. In other words, for every hundred times either term appeared, 94 featured PBA. This anecdote hints at PBA's staying power after its adoption.

In tandem with this discursive competition, a struggle to ban PBA took place in governance's formal institutions. From 1995 to 2000, Congress passed laws banning PBA three times, in 1995, 1997, and 1999/2000. President Clinton vetoed the first two acts, and the Supreme Court overturned the third in *Stenberg v. Carhart*. During this time, public support for banning PBA rose substantially, as charted below. It is important to be aware that as public opposition increased, the Centers for Disease Control report (2002) that the number of procedures performed declined, from around 18,000 in 1990 to around 15,000 in 2000. This decrease in procedures undermines one potential alternative hypothesis—namely, that public opposition's rise directly related to increases in the number of procedures. With this background, we can begin some more formal analysis.

EXAMINING WORD CHOICE AMONG COMPETING ELITES IN PBA RHETORIC

Our first portion investigates word choice among members of the elite; our question: *did elites use different vocabularies in articulating their support or opposition to partial birth abortion?* As we should see, this question is entirely falsifiable; either yes, they did, or no, they did not. Our expectation, of course, is that they did. Stenberg v. Carhart, the leading PBA Supreme Court cases offers the observations necessary to create the data. This case arose when the state of Nebraska fired physician Leroy Carhart for performing a PBA in violation of a state law. Don Stenberg was the Attorney General of Nebraska; he appealed to the Supreme Court a lower court order to rehire Carhart. So, Stenberg opposed PBA while Carhart supported it.

One nice advantage that studying Supreme Court cases offers is the easy availability of written records. Our first look at PBA discourse examines the 34 amicus briefs filed in Stenberg. For those who don't know, amicus comes from the Latin phrase for *friend* and is used to decribe legal documents given to the court by those otherwise not involved in a case. Of the 34 briefs, 22 supported Stenberg and 11 supported Carhart (I excluded the 1 neutral brief from the analysis). Some quick Internet work, then, allows us to download a set of arguments produced by sophisticated communicators who formally identified themselves as for or against banning PBA.

The next step subjects the briefs to a technique that researchers call *content analysis*. A great deal of communication research uses content analysis, which puts messages into categories for further investigation. For example, the *American Voter* Wolverines perform a content analysis when they place survey respondents into ideology usage categories. The bottom line of any content analysis lies in the utility of its categories; the researches must devise a scheme that will provide enlightening results. Better sets of categories also have clear definitions to separate categories and smooth the categorization process. Once the categories are setup, content analysis follows one explicit rule: treat every message consistently. This rule ensures that similar messages end up in the same category, a kind of internal validity. One internal validity diagnostic examines how many messages did not fit a category—obviously, the smaller this number, the better.

The actual work of content analysis can be quite tedious, possibly involving a number of human coders trained in the scheme, but the amicus content analysis employs computer coding. Computer coding tends to be more reliable, so long as the program has no bugs, but it can only tackle relatively simple messages or schemes. Our question only demands that we categorize and count the words in the briefs. The hard part lay in accounting for synonyms. Computers seem up to this task; any numbers of text analyzers come with thesauri and counters. These results stem from a program called Simstat. After deleting nonsubstantive words such as "the" and "of," all but roughly 3 percent of the words fit into one of 15 categories that try to capture the meaning of each word: *Baby/Child, Birth, Death, Partial, Life, Procedure, Abortion, D & E, Physician, Pregnancy, Fetus, Health, Woman, Religious,* and *Choice.*

Here are the results, organized (as always) into a crosstab. Down the side are the 15 categories, and across the top are the total number of words in that category, the words used by the Stenberg side (pro-ban and against PBA), and the percentage of the total used by those on Stenberg's side.

We can take a few seconds to examine this analysis. First, there are a total of 18,832 words. Perhaps not surprisingly, the most used words dealt with abortion, and the least with the DAE label. Further scrutiny shows both sides used the 1,176 words referring to pregnancy almost equally. On the other hand, the crosstab tells us that the most disparate categories were *Baby/Child, Birth, Choice,* and *Religious.* The ban side uses the first two more and the last two less. Of these *Baby/Child* appears as the foremost difference; ban proponents used this term six times as often as opponents, with the root *baby* accounting for 98 percent of that use. This key difference supports our use of *baby* in the experimental design.

Let's take a look a closer look at arguments in Stenberg and focus on whether the use of *baby* or *fetus* advocates related to the advocate's position on abortion. Our next crosstab focuses on the competitive use of *baby* or *fetus* in the briefs and the oral arguments as well.

Category:	Total Words	Pro Ban Use	Percent Pro
Baby/Child	716	832	86
Birth	625	807	77
Death	642	841	76
Partial	985	1301	75
Life	636	1009	63
Procedure	946	1539	61
Abortion	1821	3183	57
D&E	72	125	57
Physician	1185	2137	55
Pregnancy	585	1123	52
Fetus	550	1176	46
Health	462	1272	36
Woman	728	2245	32
Religious	230	840	27
Choice	95	402	23

The first row shows that the pro-ban side used the word *baby* three times as often as the word *fetus* in the briefs, yet the side against banning PBA used the word *baby* less than half the time. Further, in the oral arguments, the attorneys representing the pro-ban side used the word *baby* 80 percent of the time (though there were few uses of either word). On the other hand, the attorneys representing the anti-ban side only used *baby* 16 percent of the time. This analysis seems to show a strong preference for using *baby* or *fetus* that depends on one's political position.

We turn to speeches in the U.S. House of Representatives to replicate this analysis, where a similar but less dramatic pattern can be found. Specifically, the text of all the House's floor remarks and extensions mentioning PBA were subjected to the same kind of analysis performed above. From 1995 to 2000, Republicans tended to use *baby* more often, and this gap grew over time. In

	For Ban		Against Ban	
	Total Baby and Fetus	Percent Baby	Total Baby and Fetus	Percent Baby
Amicus Briefs	1654	76%	579	40%
Oral Arguments	5	80	24	16

the Congresses of 1995–1996, 1997–1998, and 1999–2000, Republicans used the word *baby* relative to *fetus* 85, 92, and 94 percent of the time while the Democrats used it 86, 85, and 84 percent of the time, respectively. The reason for the high Democratic usage of baby remains unclear, perhaps it relates to the loss of every PBA floor vote; nevertheless Republicans display a clear correlation between vocabulary and political position.

THE RELATIONSHIP BETWEEN POLITICAL TALK, THE MEDIA, AND PBA ATTITUDES

We now come to the last part of the PBA story. Knowing something of the messages politicians sent and the influence of the PBA label as well as the word *baby*, we want to demonstrate that these messages pushed the public toward favoring a ban. On top of that, we can examine the media's role in transferring messages from politicians to the public. Once more, the goal is relatively simple; we expect to find two correlations, first between politicians' talk and the media's coverage, and second between the media coverage and public opinion. Yet—as always—the path leading to these answers twists and turns. In the first place, relative to the data available on political talk, there is little public opinion data on PBA. Next, because we want to make a causal statement about the relationship between politicians and the media, we need a more complicated statistical technique, known as *time series analysis* (TSA).

Because this is not a statistical text, we won't go into TSA in detail; there are many free statistics primers on the web. Suffice to say that repeated observations, typically at regular intervals, constitute a time series. For example, when meteorologists record the temperature each day, they create a time series that highlights the weather's variation. If you look ahead to Figure 4.1, for instance, the grey line charts the *New York Times's* use of the word *baby* in PBA articles by week from 1995 to 2000.

TSA is a form of regression that allows researchers to estimate a correlation between time series. Many of you may have heard of regression, as well you should; it is the most powerful statistical tool available. We will learn more about regression in the next chapter, when we use it to study question wording effects. I like to think about regression as a way of overcoming problems in the data. As we know, experiments generally require little sophisticated analysis, because they strip away obstacles to leave clear comparisons. Correlational studies, in contrast, demand more complicated techniques to help sort the mess. Using regression allows researchers to simulate combinations of independent variables that may never appear in the real world; it also allows us estimate the impact on the dependent variable of each variable in the combination.

TSA attempts to sort out the messiness of observations collected over time; the main problem it solves is called autocorrelation. Usually the best prediction (read: explanation) of any observation in a time series its immediate predecessor. Think about your height: as you grow, and even after you stop, how tall you are today depends on how tall were yesterday. Thus, time series data nearly always displays autocorrelation—a correlation with itself. When you compare two time series, the autocorrelation can lead you to overestimate the strength of their relationship, because they both may have autocorrelation. If this explanation does not make sense, do not worry; as with other kinds of statistics, if we know how to organize the data properly, ask the computer the right question, and interpret the results, we will be fine. For now, I will do the interpretation.

Three time series compose our PBA data. Each focuses on the usage of *baby* relative to *fetus* by particular speakers in a specific venue. My coauthor, Jennifer Jerit, fed the content of every text mentioning PBA into a computer program (Simstat) that marked and counted the number of times *baby* or its cognates, and *fetus* or its cognates, were used in a given week. The observations convert to proportions that chart the use of *baby*. As the study spanned 1996 to 2000, each series consists of 386 weekly observations. The first location is the House of Representatives; these messages made by members of Congress include floor remarks, committee reports, and some other documents found in Thomas, the Library of Congress's legislative database. The second two series came from the *New York Times*; after downloading every one of their articles mentioning PBA from Lexis-Nexis, the articles were divided into editorial and news coverage. Again, the computer produced 386 observations of the proportional use of baby in these two areas of the paper.

Without explaining some technical terms, a TSA assesses the "Granger causality" between the three time series. Granger causality, invented by Nobel Prize winner Clive Granger, sees whether using an additional time series provides a better forecast of a given times series than just that series alone. Here, our TSA shows that the proportional usage of *baby* in the Congressional time series Granger causes the usage in the *New York Times*' news coverage. Thus, if we want to predict the *Times's* use of baby in a given week of PBA coverage, we would do best by looking at Congress's usage as well as at previous *Times* articles. On the other hand, knowing what the *New York Times* has done would not help us forecast Congressional speech. Thus, we say that Congressional usage influences media coverage but media coverage does not influence Congressional usage. Indeed, this analysis shows that the media acts as a faithful transmitter: the Granger causal path runs from congressional rhetoric to news and editorial content. I should add that a similar analysis produced the same result with the *Atlanta Journal Constitution*.

This study's finale may seem sadly anticlimactic due to the lack of data on national attitudes toward banning PBA. Polling organizations asked relatively few national questions regarding PBA, making it impossible to include public opinion in the time series analysis. I also do not want to delve into individual data like Zaller; we will make do with the 12 national survey questions dealing with attitudes toward banning PBA that can be found from 1996–2000. These questions by Gallup and Princeton Survey Research Associates, with the following wordings, were charted (each asked respondents to indicate their level of support for a PBA ban):

Gallup: "[D]o you favor or oppose the following proposal: A law which would make it illegal to perform a specific abortion procedure conducted in the last six months of pregnancy known as a 'partial birth abortion,' except in cases necessary to save the life of the mother?"

Princeton: "Do you think there should be a law making illegal 'partial birth' abortions, that is, one form of late-term abortion performed after the fetus is able to live outside the mother's womb, except when necessary to save the life of the mother?"

Thus, we have 386 observations of media coverage and only 12 observations of public opinion. Given this situation, Figure 4.1 shows the aggregate support for banning PBA with squares (for Gallup) and triangles (for

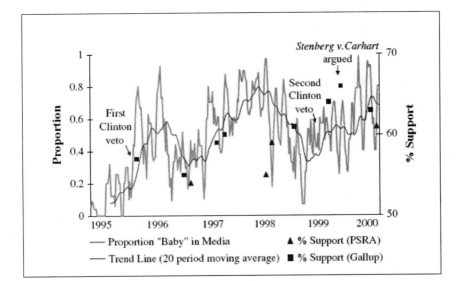

Figure 4.1. Baby Usage in Media Coverage of Partial Birth Abortion and Public Opinion.

Princeton) from 1996 to 2000. The grey line charts the proportional use of the word baby in New York Times by week. Finally, the black line represents a "smoothed" version of the grey line, which was created using a 20-week moving average.

With a bit of squinting, I think that the marks representing the public's attitudes ward banning PBA seems to rise and fall in tandem with the proportion of usage of baby in the *New York Times*'s news stories. In short, I believe that these data and analyses on the relationship between political discourse (the flow of information), media coverage, and public opinion generally support the Zaller model. This part of the investigation suggests that in the case of PBA, politicians generally led the public and that the media seems to take their cue from political discourse, rather than communicating independently.

On the other hand, I want to repeat the two findings that point toward a more optimistic view. The experimental results support the idea that citizens can be a more active factor in the democratic equation. Participants in the competitive condition chose, in some sense, to support a ban—a power that presumably could have gone the other way under the right prompting—in the face of two messages. That result suggests that citizens do more than probabilistically choose between competing messages and may use more sophisticated filters than Zaller proposes. We might expect that in more complicated situations, the variety and content of messages in public discourse, rather than its sheer proportion, would determine citizens' views. In addition, although the media data and analysis portray media as faithful transmitters of elite/expert messages, the PBA story reveals that the media rejected the earlier BSA label, implying that they play a role in an issue's development. What remains, of course, is an examination of other subject areas to test these findings and to elaborate upon a more general theory of the relationship between elites, media, and the public.

Chapter 5

Questions Are Just as Important as Answers, Particularly in a Study of Public Opinion on the Iraq Invasion

This chapter spotlights, and then tries to solve, the principle problem facing public opinion polling—one that hinders the use of polls to guide governance. Polling confronts any number of problems, as we outlined; some experienced readers may suppose I am speaking about reaching people. Cell phones and the Internet have left fewer people with home telephones to answer, and polling's main resource—readily accessible respondents—is fading away. This is a pressing problem, but it concerns economics and technology more than intellect. Citizens still live, though they are harder to reach. Pollsters have gotten used to relatively cheap answers. Little of the money for a national telephone sample survey is spent on phoning or paying respondents. Sample survey information, as I argue, is priceless to democracy, but that does not preclude paying respondents or allocating more money to get in touch with them. More generous financing, including sufficient incentives for the citizen-participants, would fix this problem. Money, in contrast, will not solve the principle polling problem—question wording effects.

Returning to the fateful 2003 decision to invade Iraq, Lippmann zombies often use hindsight to highlight poll results that indicate widespread public support for taking military action. For example, 86 percent of a national sample agreed that "If the United States were able to present evidence that convinced you that ... Iraq has ties to Osama bin Laden's terrorist organization know as al Qaeda ... it would be justified in using military action against Iraq" (Gallup 2/2/03, sponsored by CNN). This datum seems to justify public blame; before accepting that blame, however, we should look at other results; let me point one out. Only 41 percent said "favor" to the question, "Would you favor or oppose taking military action in Iraq to end Saddam Hussein's rule, even if it meant that United States forces might suffer thousands of casualties" (Princeton Survey Research Associates 1/12/03, sponsored by the Pew Research Center).

This near contradiction suggests that using polls to pinpoint the public's desires is not so straightforward, raising the most critical issue—interpretation. In particular, what should we do when the results offered by representative samples of American citizens seem to disagree? Perhaps we should dismiss the earlier question, arguing it is out of date. That does not work, because investigation (see Figure 5.1) shows no clear trend in support for military action. We must acknowledge the fact that public support depends on the wording. The two Iraq questions attach distinct scenarios to the common "taking military action" thread. Were the aggregate responses identical, we might conclude support remained constant, but they do not. Should we average responses, calculating support at roughly 60 percent? This solution is haphazard, particularly when different question versions have strongly diverging answers. Perhaps, we can create a "superquestion" that combines these two, but that approach would grow to be unwieldy. We need a way to deal with what researchers call *wording effects*.

In general, a wording effect crops up whenever comparable samples provide different responses to poll questions targeted at the same attitude. Our study of framing, wherein a shift in the background changed participants' judgments, parallels this phenomenon. Like framing effects, wording effects call the responders' competence into question. Refer back to the example of public gullibility in the first chapter, where respondents endorsed the fake 1975 Public Affairs Act. Incongruous results at least give public opinion interpreters too much wiggle room, as seems to be case with Iraq. At a deeper level, the viability of multiple interpretations lends credence to the false but widespread misconception that public opinion is easy to manipulate. At worst, these effects lead reasonable observers to conclude the public is moronic or that something is wrong with polling. Our task, then, is to reconcile the toughest instances, where a change in the wording of poll questions produces seemingly conflicting results.

Again, let me reiterate the stakes. Apparent contradictions in citizens' responses challenge the public's competence and polling's ability to pinpoint collective preference—the concerns that lay at the heart of our investigation. Like the Chinese pictograph for crisis, which combines the characters for danger and opportunity, I trust that by this chapter's end our resolution of the question wording problem will uncover public opinion's hidden quality. In reviewing past research, we shall talk about split-half designs, a kind of experimentation that allows researchers to unambiguously attribute response change to question wording. While methodologically unassailable; I assert that split-half findings have ambiguous implications; a review of split-half findings does little to settle the Dewey–Lippmann argument over the public's wisdom.

After that, we shall go over the ways that pollsters and researchers deal with the specter of question wording. In keeping faith with Dewey, we shall dismiss the first—turning to experts. The second path, standardization, or trend analysis, plays a critical role in polling and sample survey research. Research from Benjamin Page and Robert Shapiro illustrates this method; furthermore, their highly relevant book *The Rational Public* argues that public opinion responds sensibly to political developments over the long haul. We will also, naturally, talk about some of standardization's limits. The third route, looking for associations (read: correlations) within sample survey data, dominates academic public opinion research. We have already discussed correlational research, and have seen the preeminent use of this method in John Zaller's study.

This chapter backs a fourth method; a new approach that uses the statistical tool of regression to systematically interpret poll results and investigate related issues like public competence. Regression analysis is the most potent statistical tool available to social science. While our crosstab friend lets us examine the relationship between two, maybe three factors, regression allows us to pin down the relative effects of many variables. Rather than trying to standardize questions or looking solely at between question correlations, regression will let us account for question wording effects in the public's attitudes toward taking military action in Iraq. Our analysis of 250 national poll questions indicates that any public support was highly nuanced and narrowly tailored. I take this evidence to mean that the public has no—say again, no—responsibility for the war. More broadly, the regression method can resolve question wording problems in current treatments of poll results, translating into clearer interpretations, better understandings, and an affirmation of our faith in the public.

POLLING'S BIGGEST PROBLEM: QUESTIONS AND INTERPRETATION

In thinking about three ingredients of polling—sampling, aggregation, and interviewing—two should come across as undemanding by now. Sampling effectively reduces to the simple (if tedious) listing of the population and random picks. Nothing more than high school algebra may go into weighting the sample to match some norm. The process is routine enough that samples have become commodities; anyone can hire a firm to create a proper sample for a specific population. They would generate a list of phone numbers or e-mail

addresses from your criteria and hand you a bill. One irony in public opinion texts is the amount of time they spend on sampling theory. Every book,
including mine, presents the same facts. The need to firmly establish the
representational value of random samples could be the reason for this over-
emphasis. In practice, pollsters rarely fuss with sampling once the population
is defined. Beyond metaphysical doubts, aggregation, the second ingredient,
is even simpler than sampling, requiring no more than arithmetic.

Now we come to the third ingredient, interviewing, which combines questions and answers. After buying a sample, the same firm will find respondents
and conduct interviewees for an extra fee. They only need one thing; producing that thing—a list of questions (often called the *instrument*), is polling's
most demanding aspect. George Gallup, pollsters' patron saint, started his
discussion of interviewing with a claim that "you really can find out people's
opinions simply by asking them" We want to agree, but we need to think
about some alternatives

Let's explore the difficulty of constructing poll questions with a simple
situation —you have met an attractive other and want a date. Fulfilling this
wish entails posing a question; what should you ask? To take one dimension,
you could say something specific: "Would you join me for a movie on Tuesday?" in place of a more general "Would you go out with me?" Comparing
them, we should concur that a "no" to the first question does not hurt quite so
much as one to the second. This kind of reasoning leads high school students
everywhere to spend hours mulling this choice. We try to get the language
just right while summoning our courage. Pollsters face an analogous challenge. To get the biggest bang from expensive questions, they have to make
them meaningful. Complicating things, they recognize the potential effect of
hundreds of factors, such people's ability to dissemble. What does "I can't
make it Tuesday" mean? Perhaps Wednesday is a better day—or perhaps the
object of desire does not want a date at all.

Signaling game theorists exist to analyze these situations, which they dub
strategic interactions. In the jargon, they attempt to infer someone's sincere
preferences from what they say and do. They have realized that outside
observers can always imagine a strategic (read: inauthentic) explanation for
any statement. Take the silly question that tries to measure the strength of your
marital commitment: "Would you cheat on your spouse, if you knew no one
would find out?" A "no" could either equal "I would not cheat" or "I am telling you I would not cheat" (nevertheless, I would still cheat). In the extreme,
we need some kind of lie detector to spot strategic behavior. Clichéd lie
detectors rely on connecting the accused to wires that observe heart rate and
galvanic skin response, read sweating, to measure the truth. These machines
are fairly unreliable. Recently neuroscience, as discussed in the next chapter,

has tried to improve lie detection. In science fiction, this problem has been solved—witness Frank Herbert's Bene Gesserit "truthsayers"—but needless to say, neuroscience still has a ways to go.

There is one arguably pleasing solution; instead of spending time analyzing one answer, we ask more questions: "What are you doing Wednesday or Thursday?" More data initially tests for consistency, where an extra no makes it less likely that our invitation will be accepted. The truly brave ask, "Why not," trying to get to the underlying cause. Pollsters follow the same strategy, using multiple questions to dig at respondent's attitudes. George Gallup advocates a "quintamensional" (fivefold) technique that probes all aspects of opinion: (1) awareness and general knowledge, (2) overall opinion, (3) reasoning behind the views, (4) specific problem aspects, and (5) attitudinal intensity. Capturing all five aspects requires a lot of questions; on the other hand, such thorough questioning should lead to suitable comprehension, if we care enough about public judgment.

I definitely endorse this view. However, if more questions generate a wording effect, it reduces comprehension, not to mention respect. Recall our discussion of Habermas's claim about self-executing or "performative" speech acts. When respondents answer yes to "Do you support X?" the lone plausible reading is that at the time, they support X. After dismissing most trustworthiness concerns (surveys are anonymous), this view implies that we can ask enough questions to figure out what everyone believes. Trouble raises its unsightly head when respondents appear to support X in one question, and then seem to say the opposite—in the very same survey. An unsurpassed work—*Questions and Answers in Attitude Surveys*—that sits on most pollsters' shelves begins unwrapping the problem with this comment:

> Many of us tend to speak of public issues at a fairly high level of abstraction: the gun control issue, the abortion issue, and so forth. Yet it is clear that the general public, at least in the aggregate form represented by question marginals, often responds in terms of more concrete phrasing of issues, as indeed it should on an intelligent basis. (11)

Accordingly, Howard Schuman and Stanley Presser, the scientist authors, believe that more abstract questions, such as "Do you think we should invade Iraq," are too vague. Conversely, risks emerge when we move toward precise inquiries—particularly, that poll questions do not capture the public's holistic or genuine preferences. In this vein, the Iraq commentators cited above, among others, can be accused of cherrypicking questions to support their arguments.

Given our reading of Phillip Converse's work, we know that individual responses may be scattershot, but there is more consistency after aggregation. Our hopes for aggregate behavior—a hypothesis—should be clear. Following Schuman and Presser's presumption that "indeed it should on an intelligent basis," we crave similar answers to alternative versions up to the point at which questions seriously diverge. This expectation also matches chapter 3's framing research. There we hoped participants would ignore minor (read: stylistic) changes and react to major (read: substantive) revisions. We would be perplexed if someone refused to go out on Tuesday but agreed to go out tomorrow, were tomorrow the same Tuesday. Likewise, we see no problem if tomorrow is Thursday.

From another angle, Schuman and Presser express skepticism regarding the existence of "perfect" questions:

> When scrutinized, almost every survey question is subject to criticism. Both in our presentations and those of others, we have noted time and again the reaction that results should not be taken too seriously because the questions are flawed. Sometimes terms are ambiguous, sometimes the wording seems biased—there is no end to problems when one looks carefully at questionnaire items. (12)

To take an entertaining example, comedian Stephen Colbert often inquires "George W. Bush, a great President or the greatest President?" One need not search hard to find bad questions, such as the Reichstag exemplar of chapter 2. This notion might apply to push polls that employ known false premises. With respect to Iraq, for instance, it could be argued that a question erroneously linking Saddam Hussein and terrorism falls into this class; we will save that conversation for later.

HERE COMES THE SPLIT-HALF EXPERIMENT

Empirical question wording research, Schuman and Presser's included, nearly always employs a method known as a split-half design. This method sticks to the experimental paradigm depicted in chapter 3. Using questions as stimuli, manipulation, or treatment (synonyms all) is a split-half experiment's identifying feature. Researchers randomly assign two (or more, as in split-thirds) question versions to groups. The random assignment logic and careful experimental procedure—we have to handle the groups identically—guarantee that whatever words separate the questions causes any difference in response between groups.

Pollsters often used split-half experiments in surveys, essentially ensuring that representative sub-samples supply the answers for comparison. In one technology—CATI—interviewers read respondents questions from a computer screen; CATI stands for Computer Assisted Telephone Interview. The pollster programs different question versions into the computer, and it randomizes the questions to ask respondents. Thus, the respondents never realize that other participants in the same survey are answering different questions. In general, split-half designs let pollsters accurately measure the effect of whatever changes they want.

Example 1: Ambiguity in Sending Troops

Let me give an extended example of this method and the challenge split-half results pose. In 1974, Schuman and Presser embedded a split-half design within a national sample survey. A random half of the respondents heard "if a situation like Vietnam were to develop in another part of the world, do you think the United States should or should not send troops?" The other half (also random) heard the same question with the words "to stop a communist takeover" added to the end. You should see our researcher heroes intended to assess the impact of that phrase in the question. The Vietnam situation, then and now, conjures the idea of an oppressive quagmire, so few respondents agreed to send troops. Just 18 percent of them said yes to the first version. What about the second? 33 percent said yes there. Adding the phrase unquestionably increased support for sending troops by a whopping 15 percent! This effect is highly statistically significant and has been replicated several times since.

The extra 15 percent finding (as well as many other studies) appears to dash our hopes. On the other hand, such findings often raise as many new questions as they resolve. We need to invoke the spirits of Walter Lippmann and John Dewey for guidance. What sense would they give this finding? We speculate that Lippmann would discern support for his stereotype hypothesis. We still shudder when evil communists threaten takeover, so he could justifiably claim that the extras reflexively reacted to an emotional buzzword. As we know, that reaction telegraphs idiocy. Dewey might reach the opposite conclusion. Intelligent people would not send the Marines without a motive, and stopping communism is a great reason. Consequently, Dewey might applaud watching a good rationale produce more public support. The contradicting results also have contradictory interpretations.

A third kind of interpretation gets at the rest of the matter—many readings of this type of finding split the difference between Lippmann and Dewey. Imagine an interpreter scans the results and concludes that reminding citizens that Vietnam involved communism is appropriate. This presumption resolves any apparent contradiction and eases its application. Now, 33 percent of Americans (plus or minus 3 percent) performatively favor sending troops. We must, however, ask what warrants this assumption. Or restated, what is the correct language? The sole answer is nothing beyond the interpreter's opinion. This sketch, then, speaks to the wording problem's heart: a multitude of split-half results requires choosing one formulation by fiat or essentially giving up on polling as the definitive measure of public opinion.

In practice, the range of possible questions aggravates the difficulty of choosing the "right" version. Poll items regularly include background facts, argumentative frames, and consequences. Continuing with the Vietnam item, for example, we could preface the equation with information: "As you may know, the United States fought in Vietnam." We could also try to spotlight the point of contention: "Some people say that sending American troops to Vietnam was a mistake." Last, we could do what Schuman and Presser did and add a consequence cum justification: "Suppose sending troops would stop a communist takeover." Further, a range of options inhabit each broad category. Many facts could be construed as relevant, anything from "on average, communist insurgencies succeed" to "a brigade from the 82nd Airborne can be there by tomorrow night." We can even debate each word: are we stopping communists, Sandinistas, rebels, freedom fighters, or what? Altogether, the permutations are infinite.

Our acquaintance with framing effects suggests that any alteration or combination thereof has the potential to affect response. Then, if the amendment does induce change, anyone can claim that the alteration produces superior results—perhaps it clarifies the question or captures elite debate more faithfully. Naturally, such claims can be met with skepticism, and others could criticize what they perceive as manipulation. Accordingly, our interviewed pollsters maintain that coming up with good questions is the hardest part of their job. What can be done? I can come up with four prospects: experts, standardization, shifting focus, and regression.

I trust that previous discussion of expertise will help quickly discharge the first. If there are no perfect questions, then specialists could determine the best version. Indeed, several pollster interviewees report occasionally seeking expert help. Two deductions reached in chapter 1 keep this route from cracking the question wording problem. First, in light of partisanship and other motivations, a diverse group of specialists is unlikely to reach any consensus. Alternatively, a homogenous expert group could reach the wrong conclusions about the public's underlying desires (as possible with Iraq). Second, political competition could prompt cherry-picking pundits to argue publicly that less advantageous wordings are biased or manipulative, thereby diminishing polling's credibility. In short, if we do not want to trust public judgment to experts, we should not leave its interpretation to them, either.

Route #2: Standardizing Poll Questions

A second path involves standardization, a common habit in polling and research. With a variety of versions, the most used wordings typically evolve into accepted versions that garner respect and to an extent understanding. Pollsters promote this process by reusing old questions. So long as the purpose stays the same, no one needs to reinvent the wheel. The presidential approval question, for instance, nearly always runs, "Do you approve or disapprove of the way X is handling his job as president?" All the organizations that poll on approval use this established version. Other phrases have achieved this status as well, notably the words "if the election were held today" that appear in sample survey trial heats. There are too many ways to ask about voters' preferences, and settling on one sweeps the wording problem away.

One rule that our interviewed pollsters report following stems from split-half research. Specifically, Schuman and Presser, again in 1975, tested the influence of the word "forbid." In one experiment they asked a random half "do you think the government should forbid public speech against democracy?" The other half faced the same question except the words "not allow" was substituted for "forbid." After calculating responses correctly, they compared the percent who would "forbid" such speeches to the percent who would not "allow" them. Sure enough, only 28 percent fell in the former category while 44 percent fell in the later. Thus, moving from forbid to allow caused a statistically significant 16 percent change. We might have seen these as synonymous; evidently, they are not. Knowing this finding, pollsters steer clear of the word forbid in poll questions—a simple rule that eliminates the problem. Would all problems were so easily solved! We shall raise objections when we detail the rest of this research.

TREND ANALYSIS AND THE RATIONAL PUBLIC

The logic of standardization expands into trend analysis—an indispensable part of polling and public opinion research. The analysis of trends entails exploring answers to the same question asked at intervals, so history makes sense of today's responses. Take presidential approval, for example; a CBS/ *New York Times* poll ending on July 14, 2008 recorded a rating of 28 percent for George W. Bush. This number has little import in isolation. Comparing it to past observations, however, shows that it is historically quite low and that it has not moved significantly in some time. Researchers also see patterns when looking over approval ratings for many presidents, noticing phenomena like the "honeymoon" period, a time when all presidents garner high ratings—their first months in office.

Many see Benjamin Page and Robert Y. Shapiro's 1992 book *The Rational Public* as the most noteworthy set of trend analyses conducted. Their conclusion that long-term trends in public opinion sensibly reflect political developments also bears on our investigation. On the very first page, they define *rational* (read: good), saying:

> We propose to show in this book that the American people, as a collectivity, holds a number of real, stable, and sensible opinions about public policy and that these opinions develop and change in a reasonable fashion, responding to changing circumstances and to new information. (1)

Notice the emphasis on stability, which flows from the black and white model (chapter 4). Recall that model, which also influenced John Zaller, holds that the bulk of sampled individuals give virtually random replies whereas responses at the aggregate (whole sample) level remain steady. Page and Shapiro correctly take Converse's findings to mean that aggregation "cancels out" the individual randomness. Imagine a wide highway where drivers randomly change lanes. Randomness implies that the number moving left roughly equals the number moving right, so overall lane position remains constant. Critically, canceling out implies that poll results reflect the core respondents, who supply "real" opinions.

They, like the Michigan researchers, start with taking another whack at Colombia's Index of Political Participation. They demonstrate that groups identified by demographic variables, such as gender, form "parallel publics" whose attitudes move in tandem over time. For instance, though women are more likely to favor gun control than men are, this gender gap stays roughly constant year-in and year-out. In analyzing the same gun control question from 1972 to 1990, the two groups display the matching trends. In other words, their lines correlate. Corresponding trend analyses of these attitudes produce virtually identical paths across race (black or white), wealth (rich or poor) and age (young or old).

Their work pointedly suggests that public opinion is not very dynamic, meaning that it rarely shifts dramatically. Only 18 percent of 1,128 poll question pairs in their entire dataset have results that differ from one time to the next by more than sampling error. Of these changes, less than half were greater than 10 percent. They then argue that big changes originate in political reality. For instance, between 1942 and 1985 answers to "do you favor negro and white students attending the same schools?" gradually move from around 30 percent to over 90 percent, mirroring the liberalization of national politics. They also compare trends in economic attitudes to economic indicators. One chart shows ups and downs in collective response to the question "should government do more to expand employment" and the unemployment rate from 1966 to 1992. These two lines loosely correlate; when national unemployment rises, more people support government action and vice versa.

In all, Page and Shapiro reach nine conclusions about public opinion. Permit me to comment on each to finish the appraisal:

1. Collective policy preferences are real, rational, and coherent.
   This one justly refocuses the empirical tradition spawned by the black and white model on aggregate preferences.
2. Collective policy preferences are generally stable.
   Number two will require extensive further discussion.
3. Citizens are not incapable of knowing their own interests or the public good.
   Numero tres (for our Spanish speakers) restates the Aristotelian-Deweyian view from chapter 1.
4. Public opinion generally reacts to new situations in sensible and reasonable ways.
5. Collective deliberation often works well.
   There is nothing disagreeable with these two statements, though to my mind their research proves neither. My hesitation traces back to the adage: *correlation is not causation.* When their trend analyses embrace real-world events, like the unemployment rate, they can discuss the nature of public reactions with some confidence. On the other hand, showing matching trends in public opinion can never isolate the underlying forces. As a point of comparison, Zaller's work is superior in this regard.
6. Political education in the United States could be improved.
7. Lack of information may facilitate government nonresponsiveness.
   These two speculations are likely to be true.
8. Elites sometimes mislead the public or manipulate policy preferences.
9. The marketplace of ideas cannot be counted upon to reveal political truth.
   We will deal with claims 8 and 9 in the next chapter.

The most pertinent objection to Page and Shapiro follows from their focus on stability and gradual change in claim two, which chafes against conventional notions of judgment. *Ceteris paribus* (Latin for *all else equal*), who would want an umpire who steadily judged more and more pitches to be strikes? We expect them to judge each ball as it crosses the plate. Thus, we expect dynamism; the calls should change to match the pitches. With public opinion, Page and Shapiro's long view and their dependence on trend analysis suppresses the dynamics. Trend analysis, by definition, precludes looking at questions with different wordings, squelching potential wording effects. This practice has advantages; for one, interpretation is less controversial—any observer can agree that the trend has moved, changed direction, or remained relatively stable. Nevertheless, trend analysis flushes a lot of data for easy interpretation.

Exact wording: "Would you favor or oppose having U.S. (United States) forces take military action against Iraq to force Saddam Hussein from power?" from ABC News and ABC News/*Washington Post*.

Looking at all the questions can offer a better way to assess public judgment. To convince, we will perform a quick trend analysis. In the national sample survey questions concerning taking military action in Iraq (detailed below), ABC News asked, "Would you favor or oppose having U.S. forces take military action against Iraq to force Saddam Hussein from power?" 19 times. This, the most asked item in our 250-question dataset is the best traditional trend analysis candidate. Figure 5.1 presents the responses.

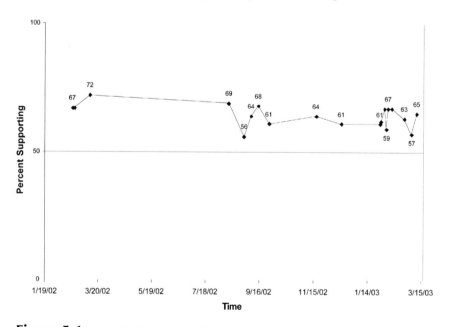

Figure 5.1 Trend in Support for Military Action to "Force Saddam from Power"

Examining this chart shows that support oscillates between 72 and 59 percent, with no clear trend toward or away from war. The absence of a trend suggests that any propaganda campaign, defined in the next chapter, did not work. Still, the 64 percent average support across all responses strongly suggests that a majority approved of military action throughout the period. These conclusions ring true within the purview of trend analysis, but our study of a wider range of questions will show them to be false.

What do Page and Shapiro think of question wording effects? Their view matches their parallel public notion—namely, responses to alternative questions move in tandem. For evidence they offer five national sample survey questions regarding racism asked between 1963 and 1990. Like the trend in favor of school integration, these items reveal less racism over time. Concentrating on two items: "no right to a segregated neighborhood" moves from around 40 percent to almost 80 percent, while "can't discriminate in home sale" starts at 30 percent (in 1972) and increases to roughly 60 percent. Thus, they follow the same course, supporting Page and Shapiro's argument.

Even if trends in responses to alternative questions are always parallel (and I have my doubts), I chose these two items to bring out another predicament emerging whenever trend analysis meets wording effects. This type of analysis can never locate when a majority of Americans gave up racism. Initially, the question is too abstract, as Schuman and Presser claimed. At the same time, the two specific trends—neighborhood desegregation and real estate discrimination—show that the majority barrier was broken at different times. A majority opposed segregated neighborhoods by 1972, while it took until 1987 before a majority opposed restrictive real estate dealings. This comment raises the quandary of absolute public preferences, which we will inspect when discussing route three—looking to correlations—in a moment.

Example 2: Forbid/Allow Continued: a Conundrum

To complete the standardization story, we pick up the forbid/allow discussion. Although Schuman and Presser discovered an effect regarding public speech, this finding failed to generalize in other split-half experiments. For instance, "Do you think the government should forbid the showing of X-rated movies?" produced 41 percent support while "Do you think the government should allow the showing of X-rated movies?" suggested 46 percent were unwilling to allow such showings. Likewise, 50 percent would "forbid cigarette advertisements on television," but 54 percent would not allow them. Neither of these differences came close to the magnitude of the first effect.

The three experiments—public speech, X-rated movies, and cigarette advertisements—show some oddness in response. For instance, to manipulate the answers, we could use the word "allow" if we want agreement or "forbid" if we do not. The wording effect raises the specter that respondents attend to pollsters whims. But the inconsistency in the effect quickly quashes that specter. Consider a Deweyian inference that imagines respondents possess some innate first amendment scholar. Respondents are unwilling to forbid constitutionally protected political speech, but they care less about commercial communication. This explanation is plainly far-fetched; nevertheless, nothing in the results disproves it.

Schuman and Presser remark:

> It seems that the forbid-allow effect can best be attributed to a subtle interaction between words and subject matter.... But these interpretations are too much after the fact to be offered with great confidence, and given the large size and uncertain scope of the effect, further work on it would be desirable. Indeed, its non-obvious nature offers a challenge to students of survey research. (283)

In a sense, these heroic researchers met their (and anyone's) match. Bear in mind that the three experiments on "forbid" and "allow" stem from one quite simple substitution. Given all the permutations and the continuous arrival of new situations standardization yields but a partial answer to the wording the problem.

Route Three: Looking to Correlations

Having definitively illustrated the problem, Schuman and Presser suggest a third approach to question wording. Their research leads them to conclude:

> Absolute marginal proportions are to be greatly distrusted ... . The basic problem is not that every wording change shifts proportions—far from it—but that is extraordinarily difficult to know in advance which changes will alter marginals. (311)

In other words, the question wording problem is too erratic to pin down, let alone crack with a set of fixed rules. Combined with their view that there are no perfect questions, they contend that we can never trust poll results in isolation. They believe that the aggregate response to any one question—what they call the marginal proportions—always contains an unknowable amount of uncertainty.

Schuman and Presser advocate that researchers focus on correlations between responses rather than using individual responses by themselves.

This practice bypasses the absolute in favor of the relative. More precisely, a correlation between two items isolates the strength of relationship between them (as we know), while the level of support on any one question disappears. For example, we recognize that self-identified Democrats tend to vote for Democratic candidates; this relationship holds without regard to the average support any candidate receives. Bill Clinton won more Democratic votes than less successful candidates, such as Michael Dukakis, even as the association between PID and the vote remains steady. For this reason, Schuman and Presser regard correlations as the sole basis for meaningful public opinion research.

Of course, this resolution does little to make poll results useful outside of academia. Put bluntly, we care about the absolute values of polling's marginals. As with the racism illustration, we seek facts. Only the responses to single questions offer decisive clues. This logic applies to any political situation. Should 70 percent of a representative sample express a favorable opinion, we want to regard that with more esteem than 55 percent approval, whether or not that support is highly correlated with some other factor. Thus, while looking to correlations is vital, Schuman and Presser's proposal does not address the issue of correct wording, which is central to uncovering true preferences (insofar as they exist).

Route Four: Using Regression to Interpret Poll Results.

I propose turning to regression as a fourth way to deal with wording concerns. This approach shares split-half research's spirit in that it seeks to determine the effect of alternative wordings, the chief difference being that it puts a larger number of questions and changes under simultaneous examination. The idea is to exhaustively catalog every modification in a set of poll questions, and see how these changes affect aggregate response. In so doing, we shall statistically "remove" the modifications' impact, coping with the uncertainty in Schuman and Presser's otherwise untrustworthy marginal proportions. This technique also suits the growing amount of public opinion data available. The University of Connecticut's Roper Center (described in a moment) has nearly a half a million national survey items in its iPOLL databank. However, to use regression to interpret multiple, or even conflicting questions; we need to learn about the most powerful statistical tool available today.

Warning! This brief lesson requires some algebra, particularly the equation of a line: $y = m * x + b$, or y equals m times x plus b in English. If you are uncomfortable with this math or the discussion of regression, please google lessons as needed while you read the next sections.

A QUICK GUIDE TO REGRESSION

Regression is a statistical technique that expands on the correlation coefficient we discussed last chapter. In fact, with two variables, one independent and one dependent (called *bivariate regression*), regression and correlation coefficients are mathematically identical. Regression's utility stems from its ability to deal with more than one independent variable. Moreover, in assessing the effect of each possible cause, it estimates the distinctive effect of that variable on the dependent variable. Thus, regression lets researchers make predictions and test hypotheses. This potent genie stands ready to help analyze any data we collect. You can read about regression in many excellent web tutorials; their pictures and sample data are especially helpful. Here I will provide a quick overview to put us on the same page. As usual, the mainstay of statistical competence entails learning what to ask the computer and how to interpret its output.

Understanding regression begins with lines; to refresh our memories, a line is shortest distance between two points on a chart with two axes. When we graph lines, the mathematical equation is $y = m * x + b$. X is the independent variable on the horizontal axis and y, the dependent, on the vertical axis. B is the intercept or constant—the value of y when x equals zero or where the line crosses the y axis. The critical value is m—the slope or the amount y changes in response to a one unit change in x. Indeed, coefficient is another word for slope.

To illustrate, say we oversee street pavers who promise to pave 10 miles a day. We can use the line equation to calculate their results. Here, the constant is zero and the slope is 10. Consequently, total paving, y, goes up by 10 for each day, x, that they work—so far, so good. What if wanted to verify their work from observations, which is the same as not knowing the value of m? Regression allows us to do that; a regression would estimate the average amount of work the company does per day from the data we collect.

The key in this move from math to statistics is the error term, which is called epsilon (a Greek e). Statisticians think of error as the noise inherent in observations of a variable. For example, say our pavers do worse when it rains, or that we were sloppy in our measures of their paving. If the weather or sloppiness is random (over the long run), these dips and bumps enter our data as error. Specifically, this error, positive or negative, resides in each observation. Statistics seeks to account for that error in order to get to the underlying structure, in this case the value of m. Formally, error is required to sum to zero—statisticians invented Page and Shapiro's use of canceling out. Thus, if our observations' error is truly random, regression successfully estimates the average amount of paving done each day. Computer regression produces the estimate of *m* with the "best fit." Typically, this uses an algorithm known as *ordinary least squares* that minimizes the sum of the squared errors.

With a data set, the computer happily churns out estimates and calculates other measures. Incongruously, statisticians call these regression estimates *b* instead of *m*; we shall refer to them as *regression coefficients* or *coefficients*. There is one coefficient for each independent variable, and each is the best (usually least squares) estimate of the relationship between that variable and the dependent variable. Like a correlation, a coefficient of zero suggests there is no relationship. Unlike a correlation, coefficients can range to astronomical positive and negative values, telling us exactly how much *y* is likely to change in response to a one unit increase in *x*, the independent variable. An additional number comes with each coefficient, the standard error of the coefficient estimate, or SE. The SE works like the sampling error in a poll result. Computers calculate SE from the variation in the observations; it denotes the interval around the coefficient in which the true value is likely to fall. Thus, smaller SE (relative to a coefficient) means more precision.

Scientists divide the coefficient by the SE to form a ratio to test hypotheses (look back at the lesson in chapter 3). Generally, we want to know whether there is a relationship between the independent and dependent variables or not, whether the true coefficient is zero. Again, as with sampling error, the rule of thumb states if the coefficient is twice as big as the SE (or bigger) then there is a 95 percent chance that the true value is not zero. Stats jocks refer to this as the "conventional" level—the cutoff at which a regression coefficient is statistically significant. Likewise, if the coefficient is small relative to the SE, you can be pretty sure that sure that there is no relationship between the variables—the true value is zero. When this happens, statisticians say that they cannot distinguish between a "real" effect and changes due to chance, the noise in the data.

The main advantage of regression arises from its ability to deal with more than one independent variable. Recall that any data set consists of a number of observations for each case. Now some jargon: we *regress* the dependent variable against the rest to estimate the strength of their relationship with the dependent variable. The regression algorithm statistically *removes* the effects of the other variables in producing each coefficient estimate. Variables in the regression are *controlled* for with respect to the other variables. (Note: Regression does nothing with unobserved factors, or with variables left out of the equation.) In all, Spearman's rho can only envy this feat. Only the number of cases limits the number of independent variables; officially, you can enter one independent variable for each case but one. Generally; it is better to have far more cases then independent variables, because that decreases the SE, generating more precise estimates.

To do regression, we issue the right command, which identifies the dependent and independent variables in the data. The computer generates a coefficient and SE for each independent variable, among a host of other numbers. The most important number in this output is the constant; it represents the predicted value of the dependent variable if all the independent variables are set to zero. The constant is analogous to the intercept in the equation of a line. The constant plays a key part in interpreting coefficients, as we shall see; it sets a baseline against with other values can be compared.

You can spend your life studying other "diagnostic" numbers, which tap into regression's nuances; I believe we only need to know one more, the statistic that covers the model's fit, known as the adjusted R squared. The computer calculates this number for every regression; it ranges from zero to one like the correlation coefficient (the word *adjustment* is related to the number of variables). An adjusted R squared charts the percentage of the variance in the dependent variable accounted for or "explained" by the independent variables. Hence, with an R squared of 1, all fluctuations in the dependent variable are accounted for, giving perfect predictive accuracy. Naturally, this rarely happens. We always prefer regression results with higher R squares, all else equal. In our research, we will see an R squared of around 0.9, which implies that the observations (the question wording) statistically explain all but 10 percent of the ups and downs in public support for taking military action in Iraq. At the same time, it indicates that the other tenth remains mysterious.

Regression yields many substantive benefits as a means for understand wording effects and public opinion. In terms of public competence, our expectations remain the same—we hope respondents' reactions change in the face of substantial changes while their answers stay put with minor alterations. To be precise, we want to see statistically significant coefficients accompany changes in meaning; otherwise, we hope they are statistically indistinguishable from zero. To the extent that the data in the analysis violate this expectation, our esteem for public opinion wanes. On the other hand, regression lets us examine many more wording changes than the one or two most split-half designs take on. Furthermore, if aggregate survey responses behave systematically (producing a good fit), the coefficients will reflect the nuances in the public's desires. In using this method on poll results stemming from the Iraq war, we will see a concrete example of regression in action that reveals the public's wisdom, which other methods cannot detect.

STUDY NUMERO CUATRO: QUESTION WORDING EFFECTS, PUBLIC COMPETENCE, AND THE DECISION TO INVADE IRAQ

Perspectives on Public Opinion before the Iraq War's Start

Many of us are too familiar with the United States' involvement in Iraq; but I should outline how pundits have presented the public's judgment regarding going to war. These works repeatedly claim that the public supported an invasion—to list a few: Demetrios Caraley's *American Hegemony: Preventive War, Iraq, and Imposing Democracy*, Wesley Clark's *Winning Modern Wars: Iraq, Terrorism, and the American Empire*, and Ian S. Lustick's *Trapped in the War on Terror*. Interestingly these authors span the ideological continuum, from left to right. This allegation has even started to appear in public opinion texts, such as Oskamp and Schultz's *Attitudes and Opinions*.

Pundits also generally agree that the Bush administration's messages played the decisive role in motivating public opinion. To be sure, research has documented that the Bush administration's sales pitch turned on linking Iraqi dictator Saddam Hussein to the 9/11/2001 terrorist attacks and on his possession of weapons of mass destruction (for example, Steven Kull. Clay Ramsey and Evan Lewis's "Misperceptions, the Media, and the Iraq War" in *Political Science Quarterly*). When combined, these two premises—the administration's message and presumed public support, lead to deductions that perfectly match those of World War I. Kevin Phillips (2004), for example, declares:

> Bush officials beat their new public relations war drum: "We must strike because Iraq and Al Qaeda are connected, and Saddam has arsenals of weapons of mass destruction that he could make available to terrorist groups." Experts were unsure on both points ... the public, however, was won over. (311)

With different names, this passage would easily slip into the writings of Walter Lippmann.

This case raises two interrelated issues that we can pose as research questions: First, a question of public competence: why did the public support such a fiasco (the title of Thomas Ricks' bestseller)? The question requires evidence about the public's desires. The pundits cited uniformly point to one or two poll results like the 86 percent quoted at the start of the chapter. Given our reading, we should suspect that choosing among poll questions is not the best way to understanding public desires. As we argued, a better way to interpret the sample survey results is needed. We shall use regression to investigate and document the true state of public opinion. Our research strategy, then, entails reexamining public preferences via multiple poll results and alternative wordings to show that the public did not unequivocally or enthusi-astically support taking military action. This evidence will fatally undermine the first claim that public support led to a fiasco. The next chapter tackles propaganda and public education, our last important issue.

Data

The regression method works best with lots of questions (to increase precision) and lots of variety in question wording (to gauge the dynamics underlying the expressions). All the public opinion data—questions, results, and times—needed to analyze public support for going to war in Iraq comes from iPOLL, the databank of poll questions and answers at the University of Connecticut's Roper Center. Their website claims iPOLL contains "half a million national survey questions" from "70 years of U.S. national public opinion survey data" that "covers over 150 survey organizations, including all the major academic, commercial and media survey organizations in the US." Currently, iPOLL is the most accessible source of survey items; along with question wordings and answers, each databank record contains methodologi-cal details such as the dates, population, and conducting organization.

At the same time, we need commonality, or some way to screen questions to ensure that they tap the relevant attitude. Exploratory analysis of the iPOLL records related to the Iraq invasion indicated that pollsters used the term "military action" most frequently; therefore, this iPOLL databank search used the Boolean (computer syntax for connectors such as "or") "military action" and "Iraq" between the dates 3/17/2002 and 3/17/2003, the year before the start of military action. This search returned 620 poll question records asked of national samples. If you follow this recipe, anyone should be able to repro-duce this data set exactly. I would hope the more enterprising would try out the method on aspects of public opinion that pique your interest.

Before we start, many of the 620 questions iPOLL served were unaccept-able from the standpoint of this analysis (not their fault). The major reason for discarding questions (298 in all) was that they do not tap attitudes, whose definition as a belief with an evaluative element by Gordon Allport was discussed in chapter 3. For example, eight questions deal with emotions, like "If the United States does take military action against Iraq ... Do you think you would feel ... excited?" Other non-attitudinal questions ask about political leaders or possible Iraqi responses or incorporate concepts such as importance: "Please tell me how important you think it is that ..." obstructed comparison to the rest. Further questions require excessive conversion. These questions oversample (17 questions), have more than 10 response categories (9), assess factual information (12), or depend on other items in the survey (34), such as "you just said you favor military action, do you think we should use ground troops?" Finally, two questions came from in person exit polls.

The rectangular dataset for this analysis, then, contains six observations for each of the remaining 250 questions. To reiterate, all 250 questions contain the phrase "military action" (almost always prefaced by the word "taking") and the word "Iraq," so they hit the attitude toward that action. Going over each observation helps us picture the dataset—the questions that we will use to probe public opinion—and quash some alternative hypotheses, which attribute attitude change to something other then wording.

After the first observation—the literal wording—we have, second, the date the survey ends (all took between two and four days). These dates indicate that the items cluster around the year's end and just before the invasion: April 2002 had 4 questions; June, 2; July, 2; August, 12; September, 33; October, 37; November, 11; December, 16. January 2003 had 37; February, 55; March, 40. The impact of question timing is assessed precisely below. Third, 14 organizations or partnerships conducted all the surveys in which the questions appear. By order of volume: Princeton Survey Research is responsible for 89 questions; CBS News/*New York Times*, 34; CBS News, 29; Hart and Teeter Research, 21; Harris Interactive, 16; Gallup Organization, 15; ABC News, 11; ABC News/*Washington Post*, 11; Opinion Dynamics, 11; *Los Angeles Times*, 7; Quinnipiac University, 2; Greenberg Quinlan, 1; Techno Metrica, 1; *Washington Post*, 1. No systematic change in effects was detected across organizations.

Fourth, the survey populations fell into three categories: national adult, 232; national likely voters, 4; national registered voters, 13. Excluding the latter 17 items from analysis produces no substantive change in results. Fifth, the sample size ranges from 506 to 1867, with a mean of 1018 and a standard deviation of 218. The percentage of people responding "don't know," "not sure," and the like spans 1 to 17 percent, with an average of 7 percent and a standard deviation of 3 percent. These responses are not correlated with the level of support.

The sixth and final observation requires calculation; it encompasses the percentage of respondents supporting the war, reflecting our central concern. A single observation, "support for taking military action," sums the aggregate support for that policy in each question. It totals respondents who "favor," "approve," "support," and the like without regard to whether an adverb, such as "strongly," modifies the answer. In questions that make timing distinctions, the percentage only includes those who favor action "sooner" or "immediately," or who favor not "waiting." This observation also holds those who support military action contingently, so long as that contingency can be analyzed as part of the question. Overall, this observation summarizes those endorsing military action, and, in the context of a given question, sooner or with certain conditions.

To illustrate, all those who favor taking military action "right now," if "Iraq does not allow the inspections to continue" count as supporters, and that combination of phrases enters the analysis according to the rule laid out below. Overall, support for taking military action sooner averaged 55.5 percent with a standard deviation of 13.9 percent. Across questions, support was roughly normally distributed in the famous bell curve; this kind of distribution of the dependent variable is optimal for any regression analysis because there is a range of outcomes to be analyzed yet no outcome is particularly deviant (read: extreme or inexplicable) at the outset.

IDENTIFYING QUESTION VARIATIONS

The toughest step in the construction of this analysis requires carefully identifying alternative question versions as they exist in a given set of poll questions. As with most correlational studies, relying on a real-world data set means that we have to take the polling as is. This fact has several implications. First, we lack random assignment, which increases the hazards attached to attributions of causality. In contrast to Page and Shapiro, however, we are not dealing with an extended time span, so the opportunities for causality to move back and forth are limited. We still need to be cautious. Next, the analysis is limited to the ideas pollsters introduce into the data. We will not be able to investigate areas without coverage. Fortunately, these organizations used plenty of versions regarding Iraq. The most delicate issue concerns the covariation of phrases within questions. If one phrase is always there whenever a second is present, they are perfectly correlated. In these few cases, regression estimates the joint effect of the both phrases because it cannot compute them separately.

The call for care in this situation translates to having a process of identifying versions that anyone can follow and endorse. Jonathan Gordon and I use the principle of interchangeability, which we believe is the best way to isolate pollsters' changes and addendums. The 250 questions on military action in Iraq feature 77 unique wordings—an average 3.2 repetitions per question (with a standard deviation of 3.4). We examined each unique question wording to chart the alterations across questions. This process consisted of two steps. First, we stripped all the nonsubstantive phrases common in all poll questions, such as "I am going to read a list" and "Do you favor or oppose." The remaining material was examined to find interchangeable phrases.

To illustrate this process, the exact phrase "as part of the war on terrorism" appear in two questions, ". . . to try to remove Saddam Hussein from power in Iraq as part of the war against terrorism" and ". . . to end Saddam Hussein's rule as part of the war on terrorism." (The ellipses always represent the phrase "taking military action"). Hence, "as part of the war on terrorism" is interchangeable. Likewise, the complementary phrases "to try to remove Saddam Hussein from power" and "to end Saddam Hussein's rule" are also interchangeable. While all questions had the phrase "military action" and the word "Iraq," only 49 questions had two other phrases, and 201 had only one more phrase. No question had more than two phrases. Altogether, 76 phrases exhaust the interchangeability criterion and completely account for the substantive meaning of the 250 questions.

Here they are—the 76 phrases in their exact wording that capture all the wordings necessary to build the 250 questions. This list also numbers each phrase for discussion, reports their frequency (the total number of appearances in the questions), and groups the phrases into five categories: rationales for war; mentions of Saddam Hussein; allies, the UN, and other countries; timing; methods and tactics; costs; as well as a miscellaneous category with one item. These categories emerged after the phrases were identified to aid later comparisons. Some items could have been placed in multiple categories, but the categories are mutually exclusive for clarity.

There are a lot of phrases, but exactly this number was required to span the content pollsters put into their questions. You can see that the number of questions and variants dwarfs even ambitious split-half experiments.

Rationales for War

The first category, rationales for war, includes 26 reasons for taking military action in Iraq. All of the phrases center on the UN weapons inspection process findings, or on supposed evidence in the hands of the United States and the Bush Administration, and are sorted by frequency (in parentheses):

1. Bush administration has made a convincing case about the need (4).
2. Bush administration might not move quickly enough (4).
3. Iraq allows inspections at some sites, but prevents UN weapons inspectors from gaining access to specific buildings or locations, or interferes at inspection sites (4).
4. Inspectors do not find evidence that Iraq has chemical, biological, or nuclear weapons, but the Bush Administration says its intelligence reports indicate that Iraq does have such weapons (3).
5. (Not) give Saddam Hussein another opportunity to comply with UN resolutions and allow weapon inspection teams into the country (3).

6. Inspectors do not find weapons of mass destruction in Iraq but they find that Iraq has the ability to make these weapons (2).

7. Diplomacy does not work with Iraq and it's about time for the U.S. to stop talking (2).

8. as part of the war on terrorism (2).

9. If President (George W.) Bush decides that it is necessary to use military force (1).

10. President Bush has delayed too long (1).

11. Bush administration now has enough international support from our allies, the Arab nations, and other countries to go ahead (1).

12. UN inspectors recently issued a report saying that although the Iraqis have been cooperating, [] inspectors have not been able to account for large amounts of poison gas and anthrax. Inspectors have not, however, uncovered any direct evidence of Iraqi violations (1).

13. Inspectors do not find a weapons program, but the Iraqi government can't prove they do not have such a program (1).

14. Inspectors do not find a weapons program, but they can give no assurance that Iraq is not hiding one (1).

15. Inspectors find evidence of weapons of mass destruction, but find no weapons (1).

16. Inspectors do find evidence that Iraq has failed to dispose of its weapons of mass destruction (1).

17. Inspectors find that Iraq is hiding nuclear, biological or chemical weapons (1).

18. UN finds weapons of mass destruction in Iraq, but does not support immediate ... (1).

19. If Iraq fails to meet the December 8, 2002, deadline (1).

20. U.S. were able to present evidence that convinced you that Iraq has biological or chemical weapons (1).

21. U.S. were able to present evidence that convinced you that Iraq has facilities to create weapons of mass destruction, but does not have any weapons at this time (1).

22. U.S. were able to present evidence that convinced you that Iraq has nuclear weapons (1).

23. U.S. were able to present evidence that convinced you that Iraq is obstructing the United Nations weapons inspectors (1).

24. U.S. were able to present evidence that convinced you that Iraq has ties to Osama bin Laden's terrorist organization, known as al Qaeda (1).

25. To disarm Iraq and ensure it cannot threaten other countries with nuclear, chemical, or biological weapons (1).

26. Because Iraq has had enough time to disarm (1).

Mentions of Saddam Hussein

The next category, mentions of Saddam Hussein provide the most straight-forward test of wording effects. These can construed as reasons but form their own category because these six items bear the closest resemblance to traditional split-half manipulations. For example, phrase 27 "to remove Saddam Hussein from power" is identical to phrase 30 save for the inclusion of "try and" In addition, these items appear the most frequently, an average of 16.5 times. None of them goes into Saddam Hussein's history of transgressions; instead they focus narrowly on his tenure in office and seem closely comparable in substance:

27. To remove Saddam Hussein from power (24).
28. To end Saddam Hussein's rule (21).
29. To force Saddam Hussein from power (16).
30. To try and remove Saddam Hussein from power (15).
31. and Saddam Hussein (13).
32. To disarm Iraq and remove Iraqi president Saddam Hussein (10).

Diplomatic Situation

The third category covers phrases related to the United States' allies, the United Nations, and others international actors who might support or oppose an Iraq invasion. These 23 phrases capture diplomatic contingencies such as the United States and one or two of its major allies' attacking Iraq without UN support (phrase 33):

33. U.S. and one or two of its major allies attacked Iraq, without the support of the United Nations (5).
34. The United States joined together with its major allies to attack, with the full support of the United Nations Security Council (5).
35. U.S. acted alone in attacking Iraq, without the support of the United Nations (4).
36. Only with the support of the UN (3).
37. Great Britain is willing ... but some countries, like France and Russia, oppose (2).
38. Only if our major allies agree to join us (2).
39. UN Security Council votes against (2).
40. Should the U.S. first get a UN resolution to use force (2)?
41. Support of the international community (2).
42. U.S. should ... even if no allies are willing to take part in the military action (1).

43. US should ... (not) if our allies are willing to take part but the United Nations is not (1).
44. under no circumstances, only if sanctioned by the United Nations, or unilaterally by America and its allies (1).
45. UN Security Council does not approve ... but the U.S. has the support of some allies, such as Great Britain (1).
46. Essential for the U.S. to get a fresh mandate from the UN before (1).
47. U.S. efforts to win international support ... have taken too much time (1).
48. The U.S., Great Britain, and Spain may offer a new resolution on Iraq in the UN Security Council. The new resolution would set specific conditions for Iraq to disarm its weapons of mass destruction, and could permit military action against Iraq if it does not meet those conditions ... the U.S. offers the resolution and the UN approves (1).
49. even if we cannot obtain full support of the UN Security Council. (1).
50. If UN does not take another vote (1).
51. even if the UN opposes that action (1).
52. (U.S., Great Britain, and Spain may offer a new resolution on Iraq in the UN Security Council. The new resolution would set specific conditions for Iraq to disarm its weapons of mass destruction, and could permit military action against Iraq if it does not meet those conditions) ... U.S. offers the resolution and the UN rejects (1).
53. If other countries refused to support (1).
54. Only if ... support of the UN Security Council (1).
55. (U.S., Great Britain, and Spain may offer a new resolution on Iraq in the UN Security Council. The new resolution would set specific conditions for Iraq to disarm its weapons of mass destruction, and could permit military action against Iraq if it does not meet those conditions) ... U.S. decides not to offer the resolution and says it will proceed ... without any new vote in the UN (1).

Timing

The fourth category encompasses eight phrases on the timing of military action. All these phrases mention a specific time frame, such as phrase 56, "fairly soon/(not) wait and give the United Nations and weapons inspectors more time." (The slash and the not stands for a negation in the nonsubstantive material.) The wording of all these phrases incorporate the idea of taking military action sooner rather than later.

56. Fairly soon/(not) wait and give the United Nations and weapons inspectors more time (9).

57. Bush administration has presented enough evidence to show … is necessary right now (5).
58. Move forward quickly/only way to effectively deal with Iraq (5).
59. In the next month or so, even if many of our allies continue to oppose … to not give Saddam more time to prepare (4).
60. Iraq's development of weapons is a threat to the U.S. that requires … right now (4).
61. Suppose Iraq does not comply with the UN resolution (requiring Iraq to cooperate with UN inspectors who are looking for Iraqi weapons of mass destruction), should … begin immediately and not go back to the UN for authorization (1).
62. Should we take military action now, if Iraq does not allow the inspections to continue (1)?
63. In the next 2–3 weeks (1).

Methods and Tactics

The fifth category, with four phrases, covers methods and tactics associated with military action, such as phrase 65 "using air strikes against Iraq without troops on the ground." Phrase 64, "ground troops," applies to all questions in which those words specify the use of land forces as part of the military action:

64. … ground troops (17).
65. Using air strikes against Iraq without troops on the ground (8).
66. Sending in commandos or Special Forces to capture Saddam Hussein or work with local anti-Saddam forces (8).
67. Organizing an international force/take control of the country (5).

Costs

The final category covers the costs of a potential war, like "U.S. would be involved in a war there for months or even years" (phrase 68). Eight phrases fall here:

68. U.S. would be involved in a war there for months or even years (8).
69. Sending in large numbers of U.S. ground troops to ensure control of the country (8).
70. Suppose … would result in substantial U.S. casualties (8).
71. If it means committing as many as 200,000 American troops (5).
72. Suppose … would result in substantial Iraqi civilian casualties (5).

73. Even if it meant that U.S. forces might suffer thousands of casualties (5).
74. Keeping U.S. military forces in Iraq for five years after the fighting stops to help maintain order and establish a new government (3).
75. At the same time it is fighting a war in Afghanistan (1).

One final phrase, number 76, "and finally, after thinking about different aspects of a possible war," fit the interchangeability criterion though it may not have substantive meaning. It was included to complete the analysis, and to perhaps shed light on pollsters' addendums, although the regression revealed it is not associated with a systematic effect.

RESULTS: (EACH PHRASE'S ESTIMATED IMPACT ON ATTITUDES TOWARD MILITARY ACTION)

A single multivariate OLS regression provides all the information on the phrases' effects detailed below. Each regression coefficient estimates the effect of having that one phrase in the question because they coded as "dummy variables." This common regression wrinkle, also called a dichotomous or binary (two-way) measure, means that if the phrase is present, the independent variable takes on a value of one, but if the phase is absent, a value of zero. Given this construction, each regression coefficient can be quickly interpreted as the change in aggregate support relative to the constant for taking military in Iraq when that phrase is in the question.

Before going into the coefficient estimates, we need to look over the adjusted R-squared value and the all important constant. Overall, the regression fits the data quite well; it obtains an adjusted R squared value of 0.9. We discussed the importance of this value above; it literally attests to the fact that these 76 predictors, which only stem from changes in wording, account for 90 percent of the changes in the dependent variable—aggregate support. For purists, the analogous overall F statistic with 173 degrees of freedom is 30.9. The constant is central to interpretation; it describes support for the war after accounting for all the wording variations. This value is 61 percent, indicating an overall majority support for the war in line with our trend analysis in Figure 5.1. The different picture surfaces from examining the estimated impact of the phrase mix, showing support for taking military ebbs and flows to match the conditions laid out in the question. By looking at these carefully, we can gain real insight into what the public wanted at that time.

Though the impacts of all 76 phrases were estimated simultaneously— the proper procedure—I broke them into categories for discussion. When reviewing the coefficients, we will also discuss their statistical significance.

As mentioned, significance testing involves forming a ratio between the size of the effect (measured by the coefficient itself) and the standard error. The larger this ratio, the more likely the effect is statistically significant (read: nonzero). Statisticians have cutoffs that convey this likelihood, and use asterisks to denote the level a coefficient reaches. In these results, one star represents the 0.1 level, meaning that the effect is likely to be due to chance only 1 time in 10. Two stars stand for the 0.05 level, or 1 in 20, and three stars stand for the 0.01 level, or 1 in 100. In addition, we—respecting tradition—will postpone discussion and interpretation until we go over all the coefficients. I will present each category's results in order of magnitude, detailing the ones that associate with increased support first, and decreased support last.

Let's go over the first coefficient estimate in detail as all of the interpretations follow this pattern. Take a look at Figure 5.2a. Given how I arranged

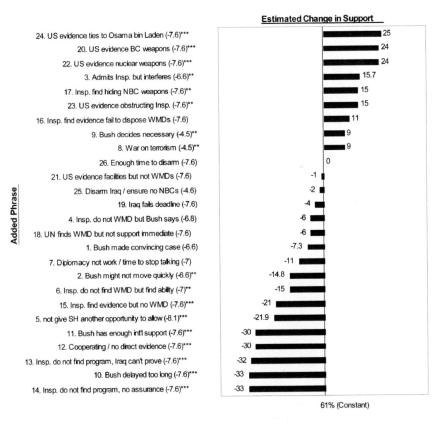

Figure 5.2a   Question Wording's Effect on Military Action Support (Rationales)

things, the first phrase—phrase 24, "U.S. evidence ties to Osama bin Laden" has the largest coefficient, 25 percent. Thus, when that phrase appears in a question, support increases by an average of 25 percent relative to the "average" question. In combination with the 61 percent constant, the predicted support for that phrase item (and the "taking military action" in every all question) would be an overwhelming 86 percent. Further, this question has three stars, so it is significant at the 0.01 level. Therefore, the chance that the estimate stems from error in the data is less then one in a hundred. Equivalently, the chances that the true value of the effect from including that phrase equals zero is less then one in a hundred.

The average change in estimated support decreases as we move down the panel. Two other reasons attain roughly the same increase in percent support, phrase 20 "U.S. evidence biological or chemical weapons," and phrase 22 "U.S. evidence nuclear weapons." Another three estimates register around 15 percent increases—phrase 3 "admits inspectors but interferes," phrase 17 "inspectors find hiding nuclear, biological or chemical weapons," and phrase 23 "U.S. evidence obstructing inspectors." The next three yield 10 percent increases in average support, though one is not statistically significant— phrase 16 "inspectors find evidence fail to dispose WMDs," phrase 9 "Bush decides necessary," and phrase 8 "war on terrorism."

The next eight coefficients (moving down) are not statistically significant, so we cannot distinguish whatever effect they have from zero—which translates to saying they have no effect past the base (61 percent) support. As we scan, we also see negative signs, indicating that the phrase's presence reduces average aggregate support for military action. The first two phrases that reach statistical significance are associated with roughly 15 percent drops, phrase 2 "Bush might not move quickly" and phrase 6 "inspectors do not find WMD but find ability to produce." Thus, when either phrase appears in a question, predicted support drops below the baseline by 15 percent, to roughly 46 percent.

The next two coefficients, with phrase 1 "inspectors find evidence but no WMD" and phrase 5 "not give Saddam Hussein another opportunity to allow inspectors," associate with statistically significant and steeper 20 percent declines. At the bottom, five phases prompt 30 percentage point drops; added to the constant, they indicate a clear lack of majority support (predicted to be roughly 30 percent); they are phrase 1 "Bush has enough international support" (implying that respondents think he does not have that support), phrase 12 "cooperating/no direct evidence," phrase 13 "inspectors do not find program, Iraq can't prove," phrase 10 "Bush delayed too long," and phrase 14 "inspectors do not find program, no assurance."

Figure 5.2b details the estimated effects of six phrases explicitly mentioning Saddam Hussein in the poll questions. As stated, these are among the

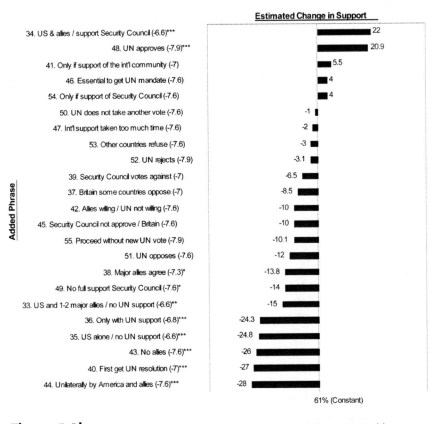

Figure 5.2b Question Wording's Effect on Military Action Support (Saddam)

most frequently used phrases in the question set. None of the six coefficient estimates is statistically significant. There is a small chance that two, phrase 32 "disarm Iraq/remove Iraqi President Saddam Hussein" and phrase 30 "try to remove Saddam Hussein from power," could be substantively important with coefficients around 7 percent, but the rest, phrase 29 "force Saddam Hussein from power," phrase 31 "and Saddam Hussein," phrase 28 "end Saddam Hussein's rule," and phrase 27 "remove Saddam Hussein from power," have no average substantive or statistical impact whatsoever.

Figure 5.2c lists the phrases concerning diplomatic support for military action in Iraq. Here, the pattern matches that of Table 2.1—namely, it shows that some phrases dramatically increase aggregate support while others have the opposite effect; however, fewer of the phrases reach a statistically significant status. Around 20 percent more support associates with phrase 34 "U.S. and allies/support Security Council" and phrase 48 "UN approves." The next

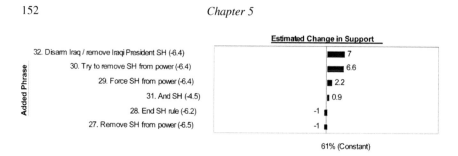

Figure 5.2c   Question Wording's Effect on Military Action Support (Diplomacy)

13 estimates are not statistically significant. The bottom eight phrases link to decreases in aggregate support, except for one, phrase 38 "major allies agree, relate to opposition from allies or the United Stations"; that one is this analysis's sole odd finding. The next two phrases, 49 "no full support Security Council" and phrase 33 "U.S. and one to two major allies/no UN support" have statistically significant decreases of approximately 15 percent while the last five, phrase 36 "only with UN support," phrase 35 "U.S. alone/ no UN support," phrase 43 "no allies," phrase 40 "first get UN resolution," and phrase 44 "unilaterally by America and allies," see average decreases of roughly 25 percent.

Figure 5.2d inventories the effects of the rest of the phrases, starting with specific mentions of the timing of the any military action at the top. The estimates of the impact of these eight items are all negative, with seven surpassing conventional levels of statistical significance, suggesting the public was not in a hurry to go to war. The one nonsignificant estimate, with the phrase 57 "necessary right now / Bush evidence," reaches a magnitude of 10 percent. The next attains almost negative 15 percent, phrase 60 "right now/development weapons threat"; 20 percent, phrase 59 "next month/allies oppose/not time"; 25 percent, phrase 58 "move forward quickly/effectively deal"; and phrase 56 "fairly soon/not wait on inspectors"; almost 30 percent, phrase 63 "next two to three weeks" and phrase 6 "Iraq not comply/ immediately/not UN." The final phrase, the singleton phrase 62 "Iraq not allow inspections/now," correlates with a 40 percent drop, meaning predicted aggregate support for military action in a question with this phrase would be around 20 percent.

Lower in Figure 5.2d, we see the relatively sparse phrases tied to military tactics and the potential costs of war in Iraq. Among the four phrases dealing with the method of military action, aggregate support increases by about 10 percent with phrase 66 "commandos, local anti-Saddam forces" and phrase 67 "organize international force/control country." In contrast, defining military action with phrase 65 "air strikes, no ground troops" has no statistically

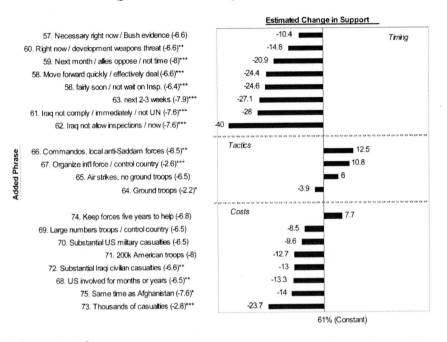

Figure 5.2d   Question Wording's Effect on Military Action Support (Time, Tactics, Costs)

significant effect while mentions of "ground troops" (phrase 64) depress aggregate support by 4 percent, which is statistically significant but not substantively large. All except one of the eight phrases isolated concerning costs depress aggregate support. Of these, four reach statistical significance. Phrase 74 "keep forces five years to help" has a positive coefficient. Three statically significant negative items are all associated with near a 15 percent drop: phrase 72 "substantial Iraqi civilian casualties," phrase 68 "U.S. involved for months or years," and phrase 75 "same time as Afghanistan." Finally, phrase 73 "thousands of casualties" ties to almost a 25 percent drop.

TEMPORAL DYNAMICS?

With the question wording effects in hand, we can look more closely for any trends in the survey data. Such a trend would indicate that support was moving toward or away from war during the course of the year the questions were asked. One great way to do this is to run a second regression on the residuals from the first regression. In statistical lingo, a *residual* is the difference

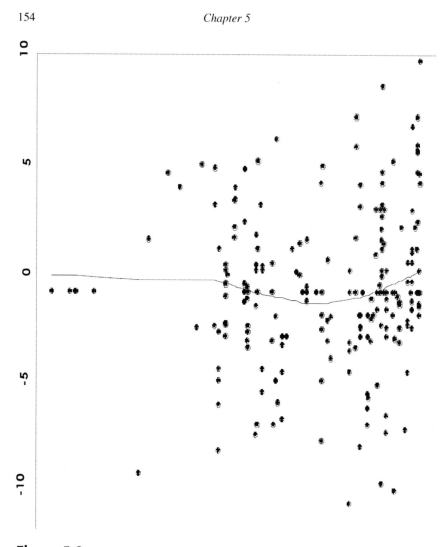

Figure 5.3 Regression Residuals over Time 3/15/2002-3/15-2003

(Black line represents LOWESS—robust locally weighted regression—fit)

between the predicted value generated by the regression and the true (actual) value. For instance, if predicted support for a question was 40 percent and actual support was 43 percent, the residual value would be 3. There are 250 questions, so there are 250 residuals.

Figure 5.3 plots the residuals from the primary regression against the end date for each question; in this "scatterplot" 250 marks chart the residuals across time. I added a line to Figure 5.3 that was produced by another, auxiliary, regression. This line stems from an advanced regression technique, known as Cleveland's (1979) LOWESS. Technically, this procedure super-imposes a smoothed line from points specified by a robust locally weighted regression. This line captures systematic change in the dependent variable by moving through the plot point by point. Practically, all it demands is asking the computer to draw that type of line.

A meticulous look at Figure 5.3 requires taking in the scale of the y axis (vertical on the left hand side); it runs from $+10$ to -10. None of the residuals are all that large, which is to be expected with such a good fit. Within this range, the LOWESS line in this case stays nearly flat, having the slightest uptick at the end. Moreover, no movement goes past the 3 percent (roughly equal to sampling error) interval. This secondary analysis strongly suggests that the timing of poll questions exerts little impact on aggregate support for military action in Iraq.

CONCLUSIONS (WITH A DISCUSSION OF REGRESSION RESULTS)

The first thing to take away from this study is that structuring a regression around the wording changes in poll questions accounts for almost all the changes in aggregate support in a great fit, statistically explaining 90 percent of the variation in responses concerning taking military action in Iraq. The bulk of the individual regression coefficients are highly statistically significant despite having relatively few cases and instances of each case. Of the 76 phrases, 37 surpass conventional significance levels and another 10 are marginally significant. Meanwhile, none of the six variants focusing on Saddam Hussein exerted discernable effects. Evidently, the public that these samples represent responds to substantive changes in wording but remains insensitive to minor alterations. This pattern of results seems quite desirable from the standpoint of public competence and democratic theory.

Interpretation of the coefficients themselves must be more circumspect due to the fact that no one can be certain of the truth—the best course to take with regard to Iraq. Is it better, for instance, for us to ignore our allies, or to wait for their support? In place of absolute truth, we can look to the public's ability to author government action. Here, the categories of addendums set out clear mandates regarding what the public does and does not want, and to what degrees. First, in the methods and tactics category: though few would expect the public to fully understand the war's technicalities, respondents seem to array the alternatives forms of military action by the intensity of commitment. The findings show some willingness to send in special or international forces, ambivalence toward airstrikes, and less enthusiasm for ground troops.

Similarly, opposition in the costs category seems to increase with the size of the price, doubling from less than 10 to more than 20 percent. More support, for example, accrues to "keeping troops for five years to help" (phrase 74) than "sending in large numbers of ground troops to control the country" (phrase 69), while substantial opposition attends phrase 73 "thousands of casualties." These changes suffice to move aggregate response decisively below majority support.

The category covering international assistance is the only area with a counterintuitive estimate, where the agreement of major allies associates with reduced support. Some note of ambivalence toward the UN is identifiable, as well, which may be reasonable. The rest of these estimates seem entirely reasonable; the findings suggest that citizens preferred aid, either from allies or the United Nations—not wanting to take on the burden of military action alone.

More striking findings come from the timing category and uncover the public's willingness to wait to take action. While seemingly underplayed in accounts of the war's start, these results indicate that the public was not rushing to war. Though some items are confounded—for instance, the appearance of "Bush administration has presented enough evidence to show" is perfectly correlated with the presence of "necessary right now" in questions—the more strident the timing phrase's wording, the stronger the opposition. "In the next month" and "move forward quickly" see less opposition than "fairly soon" and "next two to three weeks," while the inclusion of "immediately" with "Iraq does not comply with the UN resolution and not go back to the UN for authorization" comes with a 30 percent drop in support, meaning that predicted support is below the 50 percent mark.

Overall, this approach creates precise insights into the public's judgment. The first category—rationales for war—best exemplifies the technique's strength and also acknowledges pollsters' efforts to come to grips with the public will prior to invasion. The 26 interchangeable phrases span the range of justifications for taking military action. Some see clear and overwhelming approval even as others are wholly rejected. It would be hard to put all these items in a single poll, let alone a single question, so this method grants a unique holistic look at sample survey results.

The regression coefficients disclose some skepticism regarding the administration's case (phrase 1) and abandoning diplomacy (phrase 7). More notably, majority support for taking military action evaporates under several scenarios related to weapons inspections, such as phrase 6 "inspectors do not find WMDs but find the ability to make them." Under other assumptions, the public opposes military action—even if "inspectors find evidence of weapons of mass destruction, but find no weapons" (phrase 15) and "inspectors do not find a weapons program, but they can give no assurance that Iraq is not hiding one" (phrase 14). Far from the overwhelming and unconditional support for an invasion of Iraq that many accounts perceive, the only situations where such support appears cover convincing evidence of Iraqi possession of WMDs and ties to terrorism or interfering with inspections: phrases 24, 20, 22, 3, 17, 23, and 16, in order of decreasing magnitude.

Instead of blaming an unsophisticated public, this study suggests that we must look elsewhere for those responsible for war. Pollsters are another group we should not fault; for one, they asked enough questions to allow this examination. Though organizational rivalry may have introduced too much inconsequential wording variation and precluded looking at other pollsters' questions with enough depth, the body of results available at the time uncovers significant contingencies within public support. In addition, the residual analysis into temporal stability shows that the presumed propagandistic campaign did not work in the conventional way. One would expect propaganda to generate increasing support until the demand for taking military action is insatiable. Quite the opposite actually occurred: beyond changes initiated by alterations in questions, public support remained stable.

In a sense, the argument for war took the form of a syllogism, the logical consequence of two premises: an "if" statement, such as *if terrorism, then war*, and a statement of the condition's truth, like Iraq-supported Osama. Here, this data analysis permits no more than speculation. It does seem that the Bush administration's message lined up perfectly with the few aspects of public opinion that coincided with their agenda. Perhaps with the help of private polls and focus groups, the Bush administration correctly guessed that public support depended on Iraqi ties to al Qaeda, weapons of mass destruction, minimal international opposition, and few costs. So the administration focused on establishing these points in the public mind.

While proximal blame may rest with the administration, other office holders and the rest of the political system share some responsibility. We can suspect that the rest of the political system either did not understand the nuances of public opinion or was unwilling to look for them. In the event a better mechanism for bringing the public's will to bear on government policy, perhaps via the better use of polls with methods akin to the one presented here, may enhance future democracy. There is also the question of truth and propaganda, which we shall take up in the next chapter.

Chapter 6

Debunking Manipulation Myths, Featuring the Infamous Harry and Louise

THE MYSTERY OF AMERICANS' POLITICAL REACTIONS

The last chapter strongly suggests that the overlap between the Bush administration's message and the dynamics found within poll results created a perception of widespread public support that propelled the Iraq War. This point emphasizes that polling can be misused. In the Iraq case, it seems pundits' presumptions had as much to do with this perception as the results themselves. To benefit democracy and maximize the good polls produce, we need more than uncontroversial interpretation. We need to discuss polling's part in the political system. This sketch, which will continue in the next—and last—chapter, completes the theory laid out at the beginning: loosely, that polls convey the judgments citizens render over issues put before them by the media and politicians. This chapter centers on the concept of public reason. To clarify, the Iraq analysis showed the public was reasonable, that its support for war ebbed and flowed sensibly in response to the questions. Public reason enlarges this idea, requiring that the public put sensible thinking together with good information to produce sound judgments.

The point that citizens can be as good, or better, than experts at making judgments brings us directly into conflict with Walter Lippmann. Like John Dewey, however, we must recognize that the public makes mistakes. The immediate cause of these mistakes is bad information. Thus, in addition to clear interpretation, proper application of public judgment demands spelling out the right informational conditions. This duty requires knowledge from a different social scientific arena, the study of Habermas's unforced force: persuasion. We already know persuasion holds the key to legitimate

159

governance—humanity progresses as states win noncoercive and noncorrupt compliance. Yet, the Bush administration's Iraq message generally meets this standard. Certainly, it does not meet ordinary definitions of coercion (direct force) or bribery.

Our study of persuasion will draw a line between good persuasion and bad, which we call *propaganda*. This separation will enable us to divide good public judgments from bad, which are based on propaganda. Put bluntly, we will develop a criterion for disqualifying certain public judgments because of flaws in the educational process that preceded them. This step requires answering two tough questions. First, given all the messages flying around, how can we determine which are propaganda? This issue is as much philosophical as empirical. Respecting the right to free speech, I will argue that no message is inherently bad; rather, propaganda acquires improper power when it dominates the flow of information concerning that topic. At heart, propaganda is not evil because it advances disagreeable ideas, but because it represents a failure in the marketplace of ideas. This definition prepares the foundation for the mass informed consent standard.

The second question is how we can trust public judgment given the messages people receive. Social science's relative immaturity makes any viable answer to this question complex. Consider the fact that nobody knows exactly what makes messages persuasive. Summon our definition back; successful persuasion entails getting people to think or do what they otherwise would not. While science has some clue as to what will fail, it offers a thin foundation for forecasting message success. Marketers cite retail pioneer John Wanamaker: "[H]alf the money I spend on advertising is wasted; the trouble is, I don't know which half." Likewise, nobody can guarantee a hit movie. Some combinations of script, cast and production are more likely to produce winners, but studios' best efforts, involving famous actors and huge budgets, regularly flop. Why? Success depends on an unpredictable audience's decisions, just like public judgment.

This uncertainty about persuasion's effect extends to survey responses. Poll questions, like all messages, arrive in a persuasive context that gives rise to a wealth of mental states and processes, which bear on the answer. Roger Tourangeau, Lance J. Rips, and Kenneth Rasinski's fine book *The Psychology of Survey Response* exhaustively details this list. To spotlight one aspect, when someone asks how you are doing, many factors may induce you to respond "fine." Perhaps you are in a hurry or do not know the person well. Alternatively, you may know them very well but want to hide your troubles; finally, we cannot discount the prospect that you really are fine. The same verbal response stands in for any number of possibilities. In this way, a host of psychological, sociological, linguistic, economic, and communication research may illuminate response as it winds through citizens' eyes and ears to the brain, and then to the mouth.

Unpredictability, however, is not the same as capriciousness or fickleness. I will argue that this unpredictability has value; indeed, it can be a sign of reason—or, at least, honest appraisal. Retrieving our public judgment meta-phor explains that in theory, there ought to be no way to know a jury trial's outcome in advance. If we do, we suspect prejudice or tampering. We can only guess who will win in an honest world, so settlements normally proceed uncertainly. We must go through the proceedings to know the outcome with complete confidence. During these, the judge monitors each side as they argue—this monitoring gives each side an equal chance and guards against propaganda. At the end, the jury rules in favor of the more persuasive. Any procedural blemish reduces our esteem. For example, if the accused loses because the courtroom is too hot, we would not think the jury reasonable. This metaphor foreshadows a reasonable description of reason—the residue of judgment after we discount other unreasonable factors.

After we discuss social scientific research on persuasion and propaganda, a famous case in recent political persuasion forms this chapter's empirical study. You may recollect that Bill Clinton came to office in 1992 with plans to reform health care. Despite initial public support and massive effort, nothing really happened. Many observers attribute this failure to propaganda—specifically, a television campaign paid for by the Heath Insurance Association of America that starred Harry and Louise, fictional characters who derided the Clinton plan. This message (not coincidentally) meets our definition of propaganda. Thus, many offer this case as proof of well-designed propaganda's ability to manipulate the public into holding nearly any opinion, or endorsing detrimen-tal points of view.

Our study will look carefully at public opinion, and the media's coverage of poll results, at the time. Luckily, the analysis will require no new statisti-cal techniques; our new approach to interpreting poll results will show that the public's attitudes never changed. Besides replicating the Iraq findings, this evidence contradicts the manipulation claim. We will trace the appar-ent movement in public opinion portrayed by the media and trumpeted by pundits to a change in the wording of poll questions. The ironic fact is that in this case, the notion of public manipulability seems to be self-fulfilling. Stepping back, we will be happy the Harry and Louise campaign failed, because it indicates that the public was immune to that propaganda, and so more reasonable than pundits think. At the same time, it will motivate our ultimate discussion of political and media reforms that can help increase the chances that future propaganda will fail, and that poll results will convey wise public decisions.

DEFINING PROPAGANDA

Such a negative overtone surrounds the propaganda concept that we have to spend some time on its categorization. A Latinate word, *propaganda* roughly translates as "that which spreads"; it evokes the idea of disease, which many still associate with propaganda's effects. The term appeared in the name of the *Congregatio de Propaganda*, which Pope Gregory XV formed in 1622 to preach Catholic doctrine in opposition to the Protestant Reformation. That group still works today, though tellingly, John Paul II renamed it in 1982. This word resurfaced during World War I to label messages sent by belligerents, as well as the rival sides in the Russian Revolution. In the first chapter, we met George Creel, who proudly described the way he propagandized Americans into joining the war. Since then, the term's negative cast has grown larger, associated with evil regimes, particularly Nazis or Communists. Today, no one graciously accepts the charge of propaganda.

This negativity demands a clear definition. When we hear of propaganda, it triggers images of persuasion taken to a coercive extreme, like mind control or brain washing. This connotation turns the word into an insult, ready to be used on any message we disagree with: *my speech is persuasive, but theirs is just propaganda*. Richard Petty and John Cacioppo, two leading psychologists whom we will discuss shortly, avoid the term completely. Still, the word aptly describes bad persuasion, so I will use it—trusting that careful definition will keep the word from being abused. To start, we must acknowledge that propaganda is a proper subset of all persuasive messages, meaning that all propaganda is persuasive, but not all persuasion is propaganda. (Many attempts to classify propaganda fail to separate it from the rest of persuasion.)

Here are two prevailing definitions of propaganda: Jowett and O'Donnell say that propaganda is "the deliberate, systematic attempt to shape perceptions, manipulate cognitions, and direct behavior to achieve a response" (from *Propaganda and Persuasion*, 2006). Pratkanis and Aronson call it "mass suggestion or influence through the manipulation of symbols and the psychology of the individual" (from *Age of Propaganda*, 2001). Aside from alluding to the mechanics, these definitions adhere too closely to the common definition of persuasion—once again, communicative attempts to get people to think or do what they would not otherwise. Hence, they do not isolate what makes propaganda bad. In addition, some reflection shows that propaganda can be put to good ends. For example, attempts to persuade people to buckle their seatbelts in cars, or to exercise regularly are propaganda in some sense, though they espouse worthwhile causes.

In common use, the charge of propaganda implies that the message is full of lies or distortions. That may be true; however, basing a definition on this characteristic is futile and will never lead to the insight necessary to reform the provision of political education. To illustrate, consider the book *What Happened?* In it Scott McClellan, White House press secretary at the Iraq War's start, offers an insider's account of the Bush administration's attempt to use faulty intelligence to sell the war. One look at the White House's vindictiveness says that it hit close to home, truthful or not. However, the book ends with some ludicrous recommendations for avoiding future governmental stumbles. McClellan argues that increased candor on the part of our leaders and a tougher media will prevent any misdeeds. In this way, he concentrates on reshuffling propaganda to make it more truthful.

McClellan correctly observes that the administration (probably instructed by focus groups) seized upon questionable claims to win popular support for a war, as our Iraq public opinion analysis showed. Yet this view also makes McClellan's call for candor seem laughable. He expects the same kinds of people, elected leaders with well-defined agendas, who misled the public, to refrain from doing so again. Asking for a more skeptical White House press is similarly hollow. Could journalists repeating endless versions of the question "Is that true?" to White House officials have changed the administration's stance, or counteracted the supposed effects of the administration's propagandistic campaign? It is doubtful. We know how carefully politicians manage reporters, going so far as to "punish" tough questioners by denying them access. In sum, begging for more truth is unlikely to succeed, and a definition of propaganda that stresses truth is a dead end.

The solution to separating propaganda from the rest of persuasion lies outside message content—be it "eat your vegetables" or "invade Poland." Propaganda points to a lack of freedom in the circumstances surrounding message delivery. Consider popular imagery of brainwashing, propaganda's cousin. In the movie *A Clockwork Orange*, to take one searing scene, a victim of brainwashing is belted to a chair and his eyes forced open. This portrayal cautions that the power of brainwashing resides in force; if the target can walk away, it does not work. To take a less heinous example, we propagandize kids when telling them to brush their teeth, repeating it until our innocent victims comply. These observations lead to insight. Should the intended victim have some freedom, whether to leave or to listen to other messages, then propaganda ceases to be a threat. If, for instance, one parent points out the bad aspects of toothbrushing (though, having been indoctrinated, none come to my mind) as the other preaches brushing's virtue, the choice is more voluntary, and not a consequence of propaganda.

Propaganda, then, is an unchallenged message. Any persuasive message that the audience sees or hears in isolation counts as propaganda. This does not mean that rebuttal messages have to convince; rather, it means that the audience hears one side as well as counterbalancing information, so they have the necessary background to make up their own mind. Propaganda, in this definition, is a matter of degree. Paradoxically, screaming that a message is propaganda makes it less likely that the message fits the definition. In the same way, suppressing that scream fulfills the definition. We will develop this notion of countervailing messages as an antidote to propaganda and fair competition in public speech—what philosophers call the "Protagorean" ideal. For the moment, this way of thinking pushes us away from blaming the propagandist, who after all is just exercising his or her right to persuade (insofar as he or she shuns coercion). This view encourages us to examine the audience's environment and ultimately will highlight the route toward better public decisions and the idea of mass informed consent.

POLITICAL PROPAGANDA IN ACTION

Along with seeing propaganda as a negative, we want to think that we are immune to its effects. Conceivably, others get bamboozled by slick sales people—but not us! Taken to an extreme, few empathize with suicide bombers or can remotely imagine doing something similar. Thus, we happily concede that they are propaganda's victims. Some *Matrix*-like conspiracy rests on the coin's other side. A fringe believes that big business or government uses propaganda to control our lives. What's more, the control is so meticulous that we do not know it exists (beyond their ineffectual warnings). In reality, as our characterization clarifies, propaganda is a common phenomenon that influences all the people, all the time.

Persuasive magic can lead humans to do all sorts of things, because good sales pitches really are irresistible. Moreover, selling of itself is not inherently evil; if an advertisement brings opportunity knocking, why not smile and say yes? The shrewd even reward opportunity's messenger. In governance, persuasion is a necessity—as we know. Successful democracy manifests in constant persuasion. Propaganda's improper power—its evil—stems from the elimination of competing messages. In an environment devoid of other influences, for example, certain training produces humans who sacrifice their lives (for instance, suicide bombers, as well as the unfortunate Japanese soldiers in the film *Letters from Iwo Jima,* who killed themselves rather than surrender). The definition applies only because their regimes ruthlessly eliminated competing messages, murdering dissenters. Had they been exposed to sufficient countervailing messages, they may have laughed at suicidal calls. Though not in the same league, these judgments analogize to survey responses; both originate in the totality of mental states and processes.

Congressional incumbents epitomize propaganda in American politics. A first-rate wonk will never bet against one running for reelection; they win well over 90 percent of their contests. Why? An answer comes from political communication research. As Cain, Ferejohn, and Fiorina explain in *The Personal Vote* (1987), representatives offer constituents services and take advantage of franking—the free mail privilege. On its face this power seems desirable; why not help citizens and provide information? Nevertheless, the members orchestrate these contacts, and they are, unsurprisingly, upbeat. Sitting representatives use their resources to bombard the public with favorable messages. Every residence in the district receives "look what I've done" postcards. When the election comes, the representatives redeem the reputation they built.

Why is this practice propaganda? Not because Congress ties people down and forces them to listen or lies; not even because the messages come from incumbents. It is propaganda because when deciding who to vote for, the other side has no presence in the voter's mind. In fact, the challenger is rarely heard. Before the election, opposition barely exists, so citizens get help or receive reports in an informational vacuum. Incumbents also raise more money; in their campaign they routinely outspend the opponents' by ratios of up to 20 to 1. The overwhelming relative volume of incumbents' messages dims challengers' prospects. Essentially, knowing only the incumbent deprives the voter of free choice—the definition of propaganda. Countless observers argue that this state of affairs harms democracy. At minimum, it reduces the quality of competition for a large category of important political offices.

Propaganda's relationship to some of America's wars is equally serious. Chapter 1 lists six wars whose starts conceivably involved propaganda; we have already discussed World War I, Viet Nam, and Iraq. The other three, 1812, the Mexican-American War, and the Spanish-American War, fit this pattern, too. Of these, the press played the most astonishing role of all in the Spanish-American War of 1898. This era saw the rise of "yellow" journalism. Named after a cartoon that catered to baser instincts, yellow journalism is distinguished by sensationalism, like Upton Sinclair's book *The Jungle*—a gory exposé of meat packing, chock full of gruesome descriptions. Yellow journalism sought to attract readers, and we still see it in today's coverage of celebrities and politics. Around the turn of the century Joseph Pulitzer (yes, the one with the prize) and William Randolph Hearst relied on yellow journalism in their competition to sell newspapers. In one scheme, Hearst sent an artist to Cuba—the last of Spain's colonies—to sketch rebels trying to overthrow Spanish control. His alleged instruction was telling: "You furnish the pictures, and I'll furnish the war."

The artist arrived and began transmitting pictures of Cuban suffering to Hearst using an early form of fax machine. Consequent public outrage prompted President William McKinley to send the battleship *Maine* to Havana, Cuba's capitol. The *Maine* was intended to remind Spain of the United States' interest in Cuba; tragically, she exploded and sank just after arrival. This disaster created pandemonium in the United States. Though no one thinks Hearst bombed the ship, he and the rest of the media noisily blamed Spain and inflamed public anger. They cried "Remember the *Maine*," and the United States declared war. Later investigation revealed the explosion was an accident, instigated by *Maine's* coal engine (*How the Battleship Maine Was Destroyed*, 1976). As a scientist, consider a counterfactual: what if the headlines had read "*Maine* had bad engine!" Had the media had not blamed Spain, would there have been war? Any answer is speculative, but *no* seems to be a good guess. Moreover, it takes no guesswork to qualify the unanswered accusation, as well as other reports of atrocities, as propaganda, as the public never heard Spain's side.

Propagandists' current instrument of choice is framing. Framing, as portrayed in chapter 3, is more subtle persuasion that attempts to change attitudes through the manipulation of language, particularly the referents in descriptions. We saw an instance of framing in the label "partial birth abortion." The media's near-exclusive use of that label as well as the word *baby* establishes it as propaganda. Had the media used the terms "fetus" or "dilation and extraction" instead, our analysis provides a basis to suspect that abortion opponents would have had a harder task. In general, framing effects imply that communicators possess substantial persuasive power. Think back to the optical illusion: a slight push and viewers perceive a vase, while a tap in the opposite direction lets them see two faces. Likewise, we all have a nagging urge to use euphemisms. Our loved ones never die, they *pass away*. No wonder political consultants seize on framing as central to their craft.

Consultants' claims regarding the "death" tax supply one formidable display of framing. The facts are clear. As told by Graetz and Shapiro's (2005) *Death by a Thousand Cuts*, the federal government taxed the wealthiest 2 percent of Americans' inheritances since 1916. In 2001 a bipartisan Congressional coalition repealed this estate tax. The reason for the abrupt shift in policy is murkier. One narrative attributes the victory to the label "death" tax. This story has a few rich folks hiring savvy consultants to target what they saw as an onerous tax. The mercenary wizards refined their genius with some focus grouping to construct an irresistible message. By reframing the estate tax affecting only the ultrarich into a death tax that jeopardized family farms and small businesses, they won enough support to prevail. Beyond explaining a political outcome, this tale and others like it affirms the worth, if not the necessity, of hiring political consultants.

POLITICAL WIZARDS AND PERCEPTIONS OF RAMPANT STUPIDITY

Recent years have seen political consulting expand into an industry. One off-shoot has been a revival of rhetoric, a time-honored name for the persuasive arts. A series of books have appeared claiming to disclose political persuasion's secrets. If they held such knowledge, they would be indisputable treasures. Truth be told, they do not; the idea that anyone can ensure persuasion is fantasy. Worse, this fantasy incorporates and spreads a belief in public stupidity. That word, *stupidity*, is harsh. I use it both to get your attention—a prerequisite of persuasion—and because it loosely fits. Think back to the Kahneman framing experiment: a slight change in wording produces a huge shift in responses. We cannot help but question the public intellect, though economists use a nicer term, merely calling them *irrational*. Digging through popular works on political communication repeatedly uncovers this hidden premise.

George Lakoff may be the leader of the political manipulation fan club. A distinguished academic and evidently smart guy, he has published at least six best sellers on persuasion's secrets in the past 10 years. His first book, 2000's *Moral Politics: What Conservatives Know That Liberals Don't* reveals his theory most clearly. If you read this work, you will discover that Lakoff offers a version of framing; furthermore, he argues that one frame dominates popular politics. According to one blurb, "what conservatives know that liberals don't is that American politics is about family values." Specifically, conservatives and liberals "gravitate" toward opposing metaphors for the "ideal family." Conservatives cling to the image of a "Strict Father," where a patriarchal structure fosters responsibility, while liberals employ the "Nurturant Parent," revolving around caring familial interaction. Lakoff concludes that the conservative movement's successes, for example Ronald Reagan's 1980 victory and Newt Gingrich's 1994 congressional takeover, resulted from having developed language that taps this metaphor. In contrast, liberals fail because they use bad language. To succeed, Lakoff recommends liberals "get over their view that all thought is literal and that straightforward rational literal debate on an issue is always possible."

Two points emerge from this overview. First, we should see that Lakoff's metaphorical language counts as propaganda whenever one metaphor dominates the message space. And second, if we substitute the word stereotype for metaphor, his theory of public judgment parallels Lippmann's. The underlying idea is that style beats substance when it comes to dealing with less than sagacious citizens.

Another academic, Drew Westin, offers a high-tech persuasive alchemy. His 2007 book *The Political Brain: The Role of Emotion in Deciding the Fate of the Nation* argues that "we vote with our hearts, not our minds." Paraphrasing, Westin's view depends on some brain biology that has psychological consequences. He spotlights the amygdala, the brain part shown to processes emotion. He goes over amygdala studies that employ functional magnetic resonance imaging (fMRI) to observe the flow blood in the brain, showing that fear and other emotions correlate with amygdala activity. Westin extrapolates to conclude that successful messages hit the amygdala, which (not to discourage poets) is the location of the figurative human heart; thus, citizens, again, are somewhat less than rational. Can you guess who Westin resembles? If you thought of Le Bon (from chapter 2), you're right!

Finally, I want to hold up a lesser-known tale told by respected political scientists. The book is *Politicians Don't Pander: Political Manipulation and the Loss of Democratic Responsiveness*, published in 2000 by Lawrence Jacobs and Robert Shapiro. Their work also revolves around the premise that the right construction (read: frame) guarantees the success of almost any political message. In their view, polling (and its focus group cousin) allows politicians to figure out what language will make the public support their programs, so it does not convey public judgments. Thus, akin to Ginsberg (chapter 2), polling has become the propagandist's scalpel, slicing through the public's beliefs "to identify the language, symbols, and arguments to win public support for their policy objectives." In short, the public lies at the propagandists' mercy.

Two case studies form the bulk of Jacobs and Shapiro's book. Like Lakoff, they discuss Newt Gingrich's "Contract with America," the Republicans' sales pitch of ethical reforms and substantive proposals deployed during their victorious 1994 campaign. The second tale covers the failure of health care reform during the Clinton administration, which we will enjoy at chapter's end. In both, political consultants used public opinion research to craft messages that compelled the pubic to adopt a particular view. Because these messages were disseminated without much confrontation, both are propaganda. The question we must ask, which applies to Lakoff and Westin, too, is *do these messages truly work, and*—crucially—*if so, why?*

THE REALITY OF PROPAGANDA'S FAILURES

Initially, we need the scientific idea of overdetermination to respond to the wizards and their acolytes. A phenomenon that is overdetermined, like persuasion or the 1994 Republican victory, has multiple causes. When something is overdetermined, which often happens in complexity of politics, we can list many factors that could account for the effect. Typically, responsibility lies with one or more of these potential causes. Voting presents a prototypically overdetermined action. We know the two most important variables behind voting—partisanship and the state of the economy—but other things affect the vote as well. We may really like one candidate or hate the other—regardless of partisanship. These impulses have various sources, as well: character, substantive positions, or hair color, to name a few. The lesson is that all these factors play some part—but that we should be wary of anyone who claims that a particular factor was decisive.

The possibility of overdetermination casts doubt on wizardly explanations for the 1994 Republican congressional takeover. Let's consider just three. First, we have that of Lakoff, as well as Jacobs and Shapiro, all of whom attribute the victory to propaganda. Second, I offer the fatigue hypothesis—after 40 years of Democratic control of the House, the public got tired and voted for change. Third, we can guess that the Republicans kept launching new messages in their 40 minority years until they discovered an effective one. Any one, all, or some combination could explain the outcome. Without examining all three, we will never know the truth—the real reason for the triumph. Further, to sort things out, we must laboriously observe all the factors in concert to see which best accounts for the vote. Putting the magical language hypothesis in this context reveals that it is correlated with victory but may not be causal. In terms of the Republican contract, believers may have seized a mirage and ignored other factors. It turns out that our new regression tool is ideal for addressing overdetermination, provided each potential cause and the outcome can be systematically observed.

Turning to propaganda itself, the social science case for its effectiveness is not so persuasive. More advertising campaigns fail, then succeed (though the inclination to highlight success and hide failure obscures this point). The same holds for political consultants. Every memorable presidential election features a fresh media guru. Ronald Reagan had Roger Ailes, Bill Clinton had James Carville and George Bush had Karl Rove—omnipotent Svengalis whose genius brought about an all but inevitable outcome. These legends generally overlook the less than omniscient gurus working for the losers—and presidential elections have at least one loser for every winner. They also overlook external factors (again, the state of the economy) that make a guru's job far easier or nearly impossible. We will see that failure is the most likely result when we review systematic research into propaganda. More significantly, an overview of this research helps to identify ways to curtail the circumstances associated with propaganda's wins.

Contemporary propaganda ties to the invention of broadcasting, and research into propaganda and persuasion began soon after. The yellow journalism we discussed foreshadowed a new communication era characterized by massive audiences and few speakers. When radio appeared in the 1920s, with Lippmann and Dewey, it locked in the distinction between listener and broadcaster. We still live in the broadcasting age, though we will discuss the changes the Internet may bring in next chapter. Thus, the story of radio is our story, and the early social science research into propaganda sets the tone for understanding modern political communication.

The most heated communication research took place after World War II, prompted by a search for the war's cause. The obvious culprits were the totalitarian dictators—Italy's Mussolini, Japan's Tojo, and Germany's Hitler—so social scientists wanted to find out how they seized power, mainly to prevent any recurrence. Simple comparison eliminated the harsh Versailles Treaty as an explanation. Yes, it punished the Germans, but dictators also took over Italy and Japan, who had been on the winning side in World War I. Another explanatory candidate was the Great Depression—yet dictators did not seize control of other countries it affected, such as Britain and the United States. After dismissing these unsatisfactory accounts, research turned to propaganda and radio.

Here, researchers were familiar with the argument over propaganda and World War I. They had also seen the Russian Revolution's posters and films, like the *Battleship Potemkin*. The newfangled radio seemed tailor-made to increase propaganda's power. To whip up enthusiasm, Creel employed "four minute men," who preached Germany's evils to small groups in movie theaters and other public places. How much more potent would a radio message be that reached everyone simultaneously in their own homes? The images we remember also support the propaganda hypothesis: the *Hindenburg* painted with gigantic swastikas, crazed extremists preaching to mesmerized crowds, millions cheering. Thus, the most plausible proximate cause of the worst war in human history was radio-enabled propaganda.

The emergence of new technology and a new enemy heightened the climate of fear. The researchers believed that if radio was dangerous, television would be worse. Television is still regulated as a version of radio, having sound plus pictures. In addition, the Soviet Union, our war ally, abruptly transformed into a communist monster that threatened the United States. Finally, on top of television and communism, the atomic bomb loomed. Money poured into propaganda research, spawning the field typically known as communication studies. That period's most talented social scientists led these programs, which abandoned the traditional topics of sociology, psychology, and economics to study persuasion. They believed that studying persuasion might save humanity. Study after study searched for persuasion's key. The largest and most significant research was conducted by the same scholars from Columbia we met in chapter 4.

Paul Lazarsfeld and his colleagues sought American politics' Holy Grail—the secrets behind voting. As we saw, they settled on a demographic answer, but only after their first hypothesis, concerning propaganda, failed. In 1940 and 1948, they ran intense studies of Erie County, Ohio, and Elmira, New York, respectively. The latter study tracks a sample of 1,267 households through interviews in June, August, October, and November. Lazarsfeld uses this data to trace his respondents' reactions to the presidential campaign. The working hypothesis was that the candidate with the best message would prevail. Nothing of the sort happened. In both studies, the mass media had little impact on the vote. In 1954's *Voting*, Berelson, Lazarsfeld, and McPhee concludes that campaign media, including advertising, merely reinforced existing views instead of changing minds. They offer the idea of selective exposure, the principle that people only pay attention to ideas they already believe, to explain this result.

These and similar studies let everyone breathe a sigh of relief—no need to worry about propaganda. By 1960, Joseph Klapper, a Lazarsfeld student, coined the "Law of Minimal Effects," which good political communication courses still teach. He states that the effects of any message are so contingent on a variety of factors that its net effect is negligible. According to this law, propaganda doesn't work. The failure of this flurry of studies had another consequence; from 1960 to around 1980 serious scientists stopped studying political communication. When political communication research resumed, people realized that the initial conclusions, while correct, had been overstated. After all, we have listed several examples of successful propaganda.

Contingency is the critical element in Klapper's law. To some, the law centers on the Hypodermic or Silver Bullet Model: the idea that broadcasting can inject or shoot messages into the audience at will, each with profound consequences. Accordingly, media effects are not contingent, because they do not depend on other variables. In reality, the law states that the complexity of audiences' responses generally prevents any one message from having dramatic effects. The chief contingencies in presidential campaigns illustrate the real point. As we know, most voters strongly favor one party long before the candidates' selection. This obstacle alone prevents the lopsided outcomes that the Hypodermic Model predicts. Second, as one candidate does their best to persuade, the other candidate tries to push them the other way. This combination of strong dispositions and countervailing messages generally limits concrete campaign achievements. In short, the message is decisive only in rare circumstances.

However, *rare* does not equal *never*. This research also suggests that when the contingencies align—that is, when other factors permit—messages can have spectacular effects. To create successful political messages, you need to understand these contingencies. Our definition of propaganda captures the foremost contingency—the lack of competing messages. Throughout history, the propagandists' first task is to squelch the opposition. In reviewing American politics, we see that suppression may not be overt. Congressional incumbents, for example, do not jail their opponents; instead the political system showers resources on those in power and swamps the opposition. We see the same phenomenon in the march toward war. Instead of having a roughly even debate between those in favor and those opposed, the pro-war side bulldozes the opposition. However, even without competing messages, propaganda does not always succeed. Looking into psychological research on persuasion highlights two other factors: processing and counterarguing.

SOME PERSUASIVE PSYCHOLOGY

The study of psychology naturally bears on public opinion research, and we have already covered several psychological concepts. When talking about Lippmann, we discussed stereotypes—what psychologists call *generalizations based on category membership*. Converse and his colleagues were fundamentally psychologists, interested in attitude dynamics. Zaller's notion of filtering also comes from psychology. This section put these pieces together and fills in some gaps regarding the psychology of persuasion. No one—to reiterate—knows exactly what makes a message persuasive. In fact, the only proven route to persuasion involves taking chances, sending a lot of messages to see which work. The best that current psychology offers comes in the form of models that identify several correlates of message success. Despite this lack of completeness, this vast literature offers valuable information to anyone interested in politics.

At this time, we can only dip into a few relevant highlights, leaving more to pursue. We will not go over some intriguing findings such as the halo effect, whereby people's positive evaluations on one dimension spread to others. (For example, research shows that more attractive people are perceived as smarter, though intelligence and appearance are actually uncorrelated.) Similarly, there is the idea of projection: we tend to think that people we like share our beliefs. Both ideas have potential political import, but not enough to sway my overall evaluation of public opinion. I would group these effects with other fallacious reasoning that polling's opponents raise—pitfalls to be conscious of, and to minimize where possible. We will also skip much of the burgeoning field of emotional research; suffice it to say that current psychology rejects the classical separation of emotion from reason, holding that emotion motivates the use of reason, as detailed below.

The central thread in persuasion research started in a Yale lab. Mainly associated with psychologist Carl Hovland, this work systematically examines the factors surrounding successful persuasion. Like all first steps, it seems elementary in hindsight; it also relies exclusively on experimental designs. Neither detail invalidates the studies. The most interesting angle attends the focus on externalities as opposed to message content. While rhetorical traditionalists tend to focus on the art of message construction, Hovland's experiments systematically manipulate external factors, holding the message constant. For instance, he demonstrates that certain types of communicators always do better than others, confirming the idea of source credibility. By 1960, he had studied dozens of factors regarding the source and the audience, although the results say precious little about messages themselves.

This research also covers the audience. Hovland's colleague, William McGuire, applies the idea of inoculation to persuasion, showing that persuasion fails when the audience can respond with prepared counterarguments. In fact, the failure to counterargue, which McGuire calls *yielding*, is the single best predictor of persuasion available. Zaller's notion of filtering, for instance, stems from this idea. Recall—Republicans immediately discount or reject messages tagged as Democratic, and vice versa. McGuire teaches that inducing counterarguing, through forewarning or rebuttals, builds resistance to propaganda. This is how voters' dispositions frustrated propaganda in the Elmira study and prevented large swings to one candidate. This fruitful idea also extends to framing effects; many think that what separates effective frames from the rest is their ability to slip past filters. If these points sound speculative, they are; while existing research supplies important clues regarding persuasion, no one has built a definitive model.

Most psychologists credit Richard Petty and John Cacioppo's Elaboration Likelihood Model (ELM) as the best holistic work on persuasion. Their 1981 *Attitudes and Persuasion: Classic and Contemporary Approaches* is a must-read. At heart, the ELM holds that an incoming message takes one of two paths, depending on the audience's motivation. With less motivation, processing follows a peripheral route. Here, attitude change is a function of externalities, not message content. So, if my wife says, "Let's have fish for dinner," I agree without thinking, just because I am hungry. This more automatic path corresponds to the use of heuristics we discussed earlier; when a bad economy causes people to vote for the challenger, they may not have processed anything the challenger says.

With more motivation, in part due to emotion, messages take the central route; people put on thinking caps and study the content. Factors like comprehension and relevance come to the fore while external factors fade. Petty and Cacioppo literally ask experimental subjects to list the thoughts and feelings messages generate. Messages that produce more positive responses—what are called cognitive elaborations—are much more likely to be persuasive. Taken as a whole, the ELM orders the obstacles that would-be propagandists face. The audience must have the motivation as well as the ability (read: time and intelligence) to process, and a message must elicit favorable responses, which occurs only when the recipient lacks countervailing information and finds the argument compelling.

In line with earlier comments, the ELM does not say a lot about what is compelling. Petty and Cacioppo's designs nearly always contrast strong arguments with weak ones, showing that both kinds pass muster under peripheral processing but only strong ones persuade under central processing. Indeed, the weak arguments in their stimuli are almost laughable, effectively demonstrating that peripheral processing ignores content. On the other side, they pretest the strong arguments to guarantee success under central processing, so we know they are persuasive without knowing precisely why. This research, in concert with the rest of the persuasion work, does show that processing depends on sufficient motivation—and most important, in these instances, the outcome is plainly thoughtful.

In sum, three contingences stand in the way of any propagandistic campaign: the audience's motivation to process, dispositions or background information, and competing messages. Thus, we should expect political persuasion to fail if

- Citizens counter argue due to pre-established dispositions
- Citizens hear effective rebuttals
- Citizens process a message and find it wanting

These points are not new, and I would venture to say that even the narrators of propagandists' tales would agree. The question, first, is of emphasis. I expect propaganda to fail; they do not. The second question is what to do. Lakoff, like others, suggests liberals fight fire with fire and focus on creating superior linguistic manipulation. I believe that answer is shortsighted.

The ancient Greeks, the first masters of persuasion, came up with a better idea—the "Protagorean" ideal. Protagoras was a sophist, a teacher or practitioner of the persuasive arts. That title comes from their word for wisdom, as in philo*soph*er (wisdom lover). This linkage of persuasion to wisdom seems intentional. Protagoras thinks good decisions arise only when both sides are heard. Not to overly romanticize, a random sample of citizens—selected by lot—made many Greek political decisions. This random sample of citizens met in an amphitheater. Ideally, when an issue came up one or more sophists would speak with all their persuasive skill, and then others responded, trying to shred the argument. Like jury trials today, the rebuttal is part of due process. They voted after all were heard. The Fairness Doctrine, an old Federal Communication Commission rule requiring broadcasters to give equal time to opposing views, also descends from Protagoras' view.

Many will recognize that John Stuart Mill had similar notions, enshrined as the "marketplace of ideas" in Justice Oliver Wendell Holmes' opinion in the Supreme Court case *Abrams v. United States*. The marketplace notion holds that the best public decisions occur when everyone is free to speak their minds. I examined this idea in my first book, *The Winning Message*. There, I found that our two-party system often causes this marketplace to fail. For example, if the president stirringly asks for a declaration of war, broadcasters typically have a member of the opposition party respond. This Fairness Doctrine remnant is fine, but it gives no assurance that the responder will oppose the president. A rebuttal could run: "We agree with the president but would like to wait a week." Somewhat strangely, the lukewarm response traces to public opinion; both speakers seek the same public's support and the opposition is rarely willing to risk challenging the president. As we shall discuss, our politics might be better if someone publicly rebutted presidential initiatives point by point.

As Dewey argues, faulting the provision of political information spares the public. And, as I argue, psychological research suggests that propaganda is more likely to fail. Thus, even in the absence of a strong rebuttal, persuasive attempts may not move public opinion. Let us reexamine the Harry and Louse story, one of political consultants' favorite yarns, to substantiate these points.

STUDY NUMERO CINCO: DISPELLING HARRY AND LOUISE

Without doubt, the Health Insurance Association of America's Harry and Louise characters have become a fixture of contemporary political legends. Leaving aside the parodies, these characters reappeared in 2002, starring in a CuresNow ad for therapeutic cloning, an event that prompted an unprecedented lawsuit over their ownership. More recently, Barack Obama, as candidate for the 2008 Democratic nomination, said he would "get on television and say Harry and Louise are lying," should lobbyists attempt to block his plans for health care reform. The characters returned for a final encore during the 2008 presidential election, in a similar commercial that urged both candidates reform health care. This time an umbrella organization of special interests sponsored the ad, having hired the characters from their owner, advertising agency Goddard Claussen (and making them change their original position). Finally, the ad may have given politicians an erroneous impression of the insurance industry's power in the 2010 health care debate. Harry and Louise's status derives from the credit they received for fatally undermining the 1992 Clinton health care reform plan. Yet the case for their success is entirely circumstantial. Our investigation will show that these ads had little discernable impact on the public's attitudes toward health care reform.

In addition to debunking this myth; our investigation identifies pollsters and the media as the consultants' accomplices in the legend's creation—and, perhaps, in the failure of Clinton's proposal. Specifically, our examination shows that pollsters shifted the phrasing of the questions they used to assess attitudes toward coverage as the debate progressed. This change, from relatively positive to more negative wordings, occurred just as the ads aired. Using the technique developed in the last chapter, this analysis shows that the public's attitude toward the expansion of healthcare remained remarkably stable before, during, and after the Harry and Louise campaign. Further, the media's selective reporting of the results from biased questions supported the inaccurate perception that the public had turned against reform. In sum, consultants capitalized on media coverage of a shift in public attitudes that never happened.

THE HARRY AND LOUISE TALE

In the 1992 presidential election, health insurance (or the lack thereof) was a major issue. In his campaign, Bill Clinton vowed to "take on the health care profiteers and make health care affordable for every family." Upon taking office he established the Task Force on National Health Care Reform under Hillary Clinton. The task force sought to turn political support for expanding healthcare into a legislative proposal. In September of 1993, Congress began hearings on the Clinton plan, formally the Health Security Act, which was introduced on November 20. This bill's main goal was to provide health care to all Americans via employer-financed managed care organizations monitored by the federal government. Among others, Richard Perloff (in his 1998 book *Political Communication*) states that the public supported the plan despite not knowing its specifics; for instance, in the fall of 1993, 6 out of 10 Americans supported the Clinton plan.

Nearly everyone believes that public support for the Clinton plan started dropping sometime after its introduction; thus by the spring of 1994 majority public support had dissipated. For instance, in the *Journal of the American Medical Association* Robert Blendon states "initial public support, in the range of 56% to 59%, for President Clinton's health care plan has declined over time. As of late February and March 1994, public support stood at 42% to 44% . . . . Although the Clinton plan contains several elements that have previously been shown to have considerable public support, Americans have a more negative view of the plan as a whole." Thus, the health care euphoria turned sour, the legislation was never brought to a vote, and scholars were left asking why.

Here, nearly everyone perceives that the plan's opponents played a central role in changing the public's mind. The most vocal adversary, the Health Insurance Association of America (HIAA), began lobbying against the Health Security Act in 1993. Among its messages, the Harry and Louise ads became famous. In fall of 1993, the HIAA spent roughly 17 million dollars (a minuscule amount in TV terms) on television advertisements that displayed a middle-class, middle-aged couple named Harry and Louise sitting at a table casually criticizing the proposal. Here is the text of one 30-second spot:

LOUISE: But this was covered under our old plan.
HARRY: Oh, yeah. That was a good one, wasn't it?
NARRATOR: *Things are changing, and not all for the better. The government may force us to pick from a few health care plans designed by government bureaucrats.*
LOUISE: Having choices we don't like is no choice at all.
HARRY: They choose.
LOUISE: We lose.
NARRATOR: *For reforms that protect what we have, call toll-free. Know the facts. If we let the government choose, we lose.*

The obvious goal of these ads was to turn public opinion against Clinton's plan, which in turn would weaken Congressional support. Most researchers see the HIAA's campaign as an enormous success. Raymond Goldsteen and his colleagues summarize their study by saying the Harry and Louise campaign "captured public opinion when support . . . was increasing and turned public opinion back to pre-campaign levels," in *Journal of Health Politics, Policy and Law* (*JHPPL*). Richard Perloff proposes that the ads linked the Clinton plan with government managed health care, resulting in a change in public opinion. Lawrence Jacobs (also in *JHPPL*) argues that "the HIAA's well funded Harry and Louise advertising campaign played a part in changing public opinion," turning "public opinion against President Clinton's health care plan." He attributes the ads' success to three factors: the ads' direct effect on public support for health care reform, the indirect effect stemming from the perception that the plan was controversial, and the repetition of the ads' content by the media.

A few scholars, writing (somewhat oddly) earlier, present a dissenting view. Kathleen Jamieson straightforwardly suggests in a 1994 Annenberg Public Policy Center press release that the ads had a "negligible impact" because they were not memorable and aired infrequently. Darrell West and his colleagues come closer to voicing my suspicion, attributing the ad's success to a change in elite perceptions of public opinion rather than a substantive change in the public's attitudes (again *JHPPL*, this time from 1996). On balance, the conventional wisdom about the ads ignores dissenting opinions and holds that the Harry and Louise campaign was a singularly effective piece of political communication—one that we can define as propaganda because the Clinton side never systematically responded to the HIAA's message. We shall investigate an alternative hypothesis: namely, changes in question wording made citizens appear to change their minds regarding expanding health insurance coverage. Thus, media reports of a shift in attitudes tied to perception rather then verifiable fact.

DATA

The first half of the data we need to examine public support for expanding health insurance during the Clinton era comes once again from iPOLL from the Roper Center for Public Opinion Research at the University of Connecticut. You can turn back to the last chapter to review the details of their operation. This time we searched for questions containing the words the words "health" and "plan," "coverage" or "insurance" between 1990 and 2000, retrieving roughly 8,000 questions! Following the rules in chapter 5, a team of undergraduates went over each to determine its suitably for analysis. Ultimately, we found a total of 128 standalone (not referring to earlier items) attitudinal questions with appropriate responses. These were the only questions that specifically targeted attitudes toward the issue of health care coverage expansion. That number may not seem like a lot of questions, particularly given the 8,000-item starting point, but it is more questions than most, if not all, public opinion studies of a discrete episode use.

In a second analysis Neil Chheda and I gathered data on media coverage to examine their reportage and discussion of public opinion before, during, and after the Harry and Louise campaign. These observations came from an exceedingly valuable media database, *Lexis-Nexis*, which archives the full text of articles from numerous sources around the world. We chose to look at the *Washington Post* for two reasons; first, they have a reputable organic polling unit and, second, their geographic exposure ensures that their readers will contain a high number of political professionals. Here, we searched for every article mentioning the words "health" and "plan," "coverage" or "insurance" and "coverage" as well as one word from the set "poll, public, American, percent" recovered from LexisNexis.

ANALYSIS

Again we start with a trend analysis, the common polling technique described in the last chapter. With a smaller number of questions it is hard to find a good candidate wording—one that is highly consistent. The more questions, the better, so to produce a chart I used the most-asked question: "Do you favor a national heath plan, financed by tax money?" and graphed the 10 responses between 1990 and 2001 in Figure 6.1. As you can see, the figure also adds five question variants, for a total of 15 more questions. These items add and subtract components to the base phrase "Do you favor a national heath plan" as the legend details.

Overall, the irregularity of polling stands out; fulfilling our expectations from chapter 2, pollsters ask more questions during debate; afterward, polling tails off. The black line traces responses to the 10 askings from the most

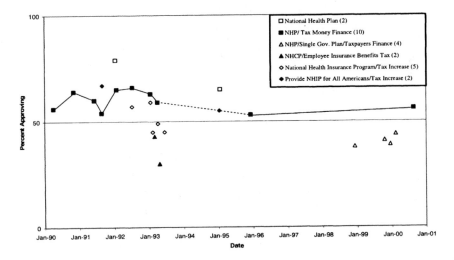

Figure 6.1. Variations and Trends in 25 More Consistent National Health Questions

(NHP = "Nation Health Plan")

frequent variant over the decade's course. Here, two apparent dips—one in the middle of 1991 and the other beginning in 1993 (right after the Harry and Louise ads aired)—are noticeable. Perhaps the ads did change the public's attitudes? On the other hand, the first dip is lower than the second. The main series ends abruptly in the middle of the second dip and does not resume until 1996, years later. It seems realistic to observe that there are too few questions to produce a definitive answer. The question variations seem to explain part of this irregularity; pollsters asking about national health plans seem to have frequently changed wordings.

Within this chart's 25 items, pollsters tried six different combinations, which again cluster during the time of the debate. We can also perceive that these wording changes affect response. The two black triangles signify questions that substitute the phrase "financed by a tax on employee insurance benefits" for "financed by tax money"; these two garner dramatically less support, moving below the 50 percent threshold. Likewise, the four clear triangles, which add "single government plan," also move below this threshold (though they were not asked until 1999). In contrast, the two questions, symbolized by clear squares, that ask about a national health plan in isolation and do not allude to financing do markedly better. You could spend some time examining this chart; I want to mention one more puzzle. The black diamonds, which represent an addition of "for all Americans" and a substitution of "financed by a tax increase," indicate a similarity with the 10 main variations in 1995, falling along the dashed line, yet show more support in 1991 when compared to the main variant.

In a sense, the irregularities frustrate our ability to discern a trend, not to mention the impact of the Harry and Louise campaign. Though those who value question consistency over everything else might focus on the black line, this approach provides a dubious answer. More important, it dismisses the bulk of the polling data. It seems likely that 128 questions are better than 10. The trend chart's variants also appear to suggest that adding, subtracting, or substituting phrases systematically affects the public's response. To test this hypothesis, we turn to our new ally, multivariate regression. Following the recipe from last chapter, the dependent variable in this analysis is the percent of the public that supports expanding health insurance. To standardize across questions, this measure contains a number of synonyms such as *approve* or *favor*, as well as combinations of scales, such as the sum of *strongly support* and *support*.

Once more, the independent variables in this analysis come from the phrases that appear in the questions. The architecture of regression allows us to isolate the impact of each component on aggregate public support. To illustrate, the variants in Figure 6.1 that feature concepts such as "national health plan," "financed by tax money," "financed by a tax on employee insurance benefits," "single government plan," and "for all Americans" form the building blocks of the 25 questions. We can think of them as bricks (regular or Lego) that pollsters put together to build questions.

To recover the components in the 128-question dataset an undergraduate team first identified the 72 unique questions (meaning, the average question was asked less than twice). These coders again trimmed fluff phrases such as "would you favor or oppose." Finally, they listed all the remaining phrases. In this analysis, however, they sorted the phrases to group synonyms— phrases that conveyed the same substantive idea. This criterion is less conservative then the interchangeability principle used last time; it eliminates minor variations (which had no effect in the Iraq study) to reduce the number of concepts and to clarify the results. Verbs seemed to be the main synonym indicator, so "increase in taxes" and "additional taxes" are combined into one root phrase but "payroll tax" and "income tax" were not.

In all, 28 phrases exhaust all the meanings within the 128 questions in the dataset. In other words, all the questions can be reconstructed by combining some of these 28 parts. Here they are sorted by frequency in each category; the number in parentheses represents the number appearances in all the questions. (The abbreviation HI stands for health insurance.)

Expanding Coverage

National health plan (42)
Provide HI to all Americans (21)
Guarantee all Americans have access to HI (10)
Guarantee every American private HI
Never be taken away (4)
Clinton health care plan (9)
Guaranteed health care coverage for every American (9)
Increase the number of Americans who have HI (9)
HI for Americans (5)
Universal health coverage for all Americans (5)
Americans have HI that covers medically necessary care (3)
Basic health care coverage (3)
Assure HI for all Americans (2)

Financing

Increase in taxes (34)
Financed by tax money (12)

Tax on cigarettes or alcohol (12)
National sales tax (7)
Pay more either in higher HI premiums or higher taxes (8)
Pay additional taxes (7)
Tax on (7)
Increase in income tax (3)
Payroll tax increase (2)
Tax on employees HI benefits (3)
Tax on guns (3)

Specific Groups

Uninsured/do not have (13)
Low-income Americans (2)

Drawbacks

Major new costs for many small businesses (2)
Services would be limited (2)
Would not pay for terminally ill (2)

These items then serve as the independent variable in a multivariate regression analysis that estimates their effect on aggregate approval. Each of these is dichotomous—recall that means one if the phrase is present within a question and zero if not; a statistician would call these "dummy" variables. Figure 6.2 presents the estimates in a bar graph; this chart includes the standard errors in parentheses next to each concept, as well as asterisks that indicate the level of statistical significance for each regression estimate, where more asterisks mean a more statistically significant coefficient estimate.

These regression estimates come with an adjusted R-squared of roughly 62 percent, indicating that the variation in question components accounts for almost two-thirds of the changes in public support for expansion in these 128 questions. The constant, the predicted reaction to an equation with no components, is high—around 65 percent. This number approximates support at an abstract level, after taking away the effects of any specific wording. Let us go through each item to see how its presence affects public support. In this discussion, negative coefficients move the bar to the left, indicating a reduction in public support, whereas positive estimates point to the right, showing an increase. The farther the bar moves, the greater the effect. Finally, keep in mind that we examine each coefficient estimate relative to the 65 percent baseline and its standard error; only estimates that are multiples of the

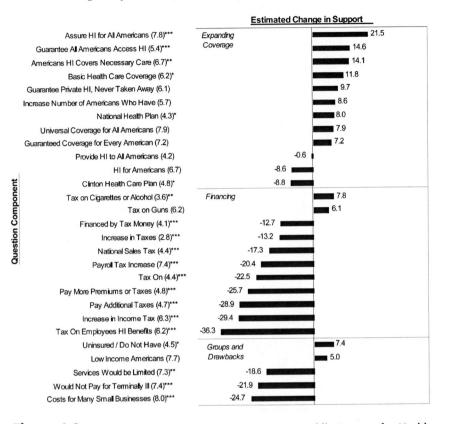

Figure 6.2. The Effect of Survey Question Phrases on Public Support for Health Coverage Expansion

standard error (at least twice as big) are statistically significant; the asterisks next to the label helpfully highlight these.

The topmost portion presents the results for 12 components connected with expanding health insurance; at least one of these appears in every question. Looking at all of them, reaction is generally positive; nine have coefficients greater than zero, while three are negative. The larger effects, which I have put at the top, accompany "assure health insurance to all Americans," "guarantee all Americans access," and "covers necessary care." Support increases (beyond 65 percent) by 20.4, 13.4, and 13 percent, respectively, when poll questions include one of these items. Put another way, controlling for the presence of the other components, we would expect any of these items to generate overwhelming support (the constant plus the coefficient) of roughly 80 percent!

The next six items correlate with smaller positive gains. Thus, we would expect questions containing "basic health care coverage," "guarantee every

American private health insurance that can never be taken away," "increase the number of Americans who have health insurance," "national health plan," "providing universal health coverage for all Americans," and "guaranteed health care coverage for every American" to return between 75 and 71 percent approval. Notice that public support is fairly consistent across these nine items without regard to the exact wording.

Of the next three expansion items, "provide health insurance to all Americans" has a coefficient close to zero, signifying that it does not systematically affect base support. "Clinton health care plan," in contrast, comes with a 10 percent drop, meaning that the nine questions with that phrase (that number comes from the frequencies listed above) receive an average support of 55 percent (the constant plus the negative coefficient), controlling for other items. The last item, "health insurance for Americans," also has a 10 percent drop, though this coefficient is not statically significant (that is, separable from zero), because the SE is so high (probably because it only appeared twice).

Moving down to the next panel, estimates associated with the components embodying financing proposals, unsurprisingly, reveal drops in support. The only expected increase in approval that attains the conventional level of statistical significance stems from "sin" taxes on cigarettes or alcohol. The increase for a gun tax reaches a similar size but is not significant, again probably because it had few cases. I have ranked the remaining nine items by the size of their drop. Less specific allusions to taxes, "financed by tax money" and "increase in taxes," prompt a roughly 10 percent decrease, whereas the decrease in support associated with "national sales tax," "payroll tax increase," and "tax on" hovers around 20 percent. At the extreme, "higher premiums or taxes," "increase in income tax," "additional taxes," and "taxes on employee health insurance benefits" see 30 percent drops in expected support.

In the next panel down, neither group that pollsters mentioned exerts a systematic effect on response. Hence, the presence of "uninsured/do not have" or "low-income Americans" in a question would not change our expectations of public support. Finally, in the lowest panel, the three drawbacks "services would be limited," "would not pay for terminally ill," and "major new costs for many small businesses" all evince statistically significant drops of roughly 20 percent. Going through all the information the regression produces is not easy, but this one is less involved than the Iraq study. Also, keep in mind all the work that went into collecting the data and putting it into the right format. If you want, stare at the chart some more and reread this section to appreciate the findings.

How should we interpret these results? Initially, we replicate the Iraq finding that substantive changes in the questions systematically affect the public's attitudes toward expansion. Furthermore, they provide a clear sense of the public's will with regard to health insurance reform. Overall, the support is high; 65 percent is more than a majority, and is far past the sampling error the questions contain. Yet when pollsters mention financing or drawbacks, support goes down—sometimes substantially. Remember that constructing an expected outcome requires summing the coefficients of included items with the constant, given that each question must have one expansion item. Thus, despite negative components' pushing support down, support typically remains well above the 50 percent mark. Naturally, throwing in favored financing mechanisms such as sin taxes increases support. On the other hand, when pollsters pile on negative components, the results strongly suggest that support falls.

Now we turn to the Harry and Louise hypothesis: namely, that support fell dramatically in the fall of 1993 (regardless of question wording). We will use the LOWESS method, which analyzes the residuals from all 128 questions with a more sophisticated form of regression. Recall that residuals are the leftovers in the dependent variable after accounting for the independent variables, and remember also that the adjusted R-squared pinpoints the amount of explained variance, so at 100 percent there are no residuals (read: nothing left to explain). Our regression has an R-squared that indicates that roughly a third of the variance is left over. This third may contain the Harry and Louis ads' impact. If so, we should see a drop in the residuals at the time the ads aired when we plot them by time.

Figure 6.3 plots the residuals from the right hand regression against the question's date. We used the same type of graph—the scatterplot—in the last chapter; it allows us to look at the relationship between two variables; here we look at the residuals (public support after subtracting the effects of question wording) by time. The plot features the same LOWESS line, using a smoothed local regression to highlight the average effect of time as we progress through the data. Pay close attention to the scale of the y axis, and I trust you will spot two things. First, the effect never exceeds 3 percent, the sampling error in a poll question; and second, the gentle decline during the Harry and Louise period starts before the ads aired in 1993 and extends almost until 1995.

QUESTION BIAS AND MEDIA COVERAGE DURING THE CLINTON DEBATE

Our analyses seems to show that public opinion regarding expanding health insurance remained remarkably stable—the first step toward demonstrating that the Harry and Louise story is a myth. The second step deals with the

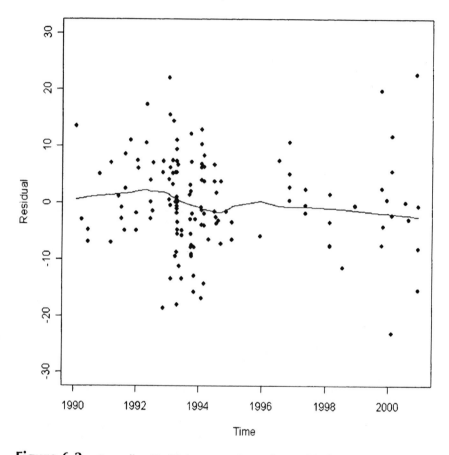

Figure 6.3. Expanding Health Insurance Regression Residuals 1990 – 2000

question of source: how did the myth arise? A look at media coverage of polling can supply the answer. We have seen that wording changes systematically affect response, so we may suspect that a relationship between question wording and time would create the perception that underlying attitudes changed. To check this guess, we need to examine wording and time together. The idea is to see how the mix of positive and negative components changed over time. If that balance remains constant, then public opinion should be stable, if it does not, then we might expect reported poll results to rise and fall despite no change in public opinion.

The regression estimates allow us to develop this measure by identifying the effect of each component. After discarding components with no systematic effects, I put the remaining components into four categories organized by the

Time		Impact					Bias	
	Half	*+25*	*+10*	*−10*	*−25*	*Total*	*Net*	*Average*
1990	1st	0	2	3	0	5	−10	−2
	2nd	0	1	1	0	2	0	0
1991	1st	2	1	2	0	5	40	8
	2nd	0	4	5	0	9	−10	−1.1
1992	1st	0	6	6	0	12	0	0
	2nd	0	5	2	3	10	−45	−4.5
1993	1st	0	29	22	6	57	−80	−1.4
	2nd	0	9	13	3	25	−115	−4.6
1994	1st	0	16	10	7	33	−115	−3.5
	2nd	0	7	0	2	9	20	2.2
1995	1st	0	2	1	0	3	10	3.3
	2nd	0	1	1	0	2	0	0

size of the coefficient: very positive phrases, "assure health insurance for all American," for instance, which associate with about a 25 percent rise; positives ones, such as "basic health care coverage," that attend a 10 percent increase; negative ones, like "financed by tax money," see a 10 percent fall; and very negative components, like "increase in income tax," roughly have 25 percent drops. Then I cross-tabulated the components' frequency by the six-month period in which they appeared (until 1996, after the debate ended):

This crosstab adds three more columns on the right. The first, "total," is self-explanatory, being the sum of the component frequencies. The "net" column comes next; it combines the frequency of poll question components with a rough estimate of their impact, giving a measure of question bias for each period. Not to be pejorative, bias (from our discussion in chapter 2) can be defined as the overall positive or negative thrust of the questions given stable underlying attitudes. We see no bias in the second half of 1990, and positive biases in the first half of 1991, as well as starting in the second half of 1994, for instance. The final column divides the net bias by the volume of components producing a measure of average question bias.

On the whole, the average bias measure reveals a pattern that may explain some of the Harry and Louise myth. Compared to the public's stable and strong support for expanding health care (as the regression analysis reveals), the questions had a positive bias: 8 percent in the first half of 1991. After this peak, the bias shifted becoming negative in the second half of 1992, reaching nadirs of around –4.5 percent in the second half of 1992 and the second half of 1993. After this period, bias decreased and turned positive as the number of survey questions diminished. While it may be coincidental, the peak in bias corresponds with the beginning of the so-called health coverage crisis, while the valleys occur during election and the airing of the Harry and Louise ads.

The reshaping of the Harry and Louise story requires one last piece that centers on media coverage of public opinion during this debate. This half of the study concentrates on the *Washington Post*. The intuition for this study hinges on the idea of gatekeeping, or, to use Herbert Gans' title, *Deciding What's News*. This idea, detailed in the last chapter, rests on the premise that the media has a limited amount of space, like the 30 minutes in a news broadcast, so the media's gatekeepers have to select what to cover. In terms of public opinion there are probably more poll questions asked than reported, and in addition, public opinion articles may reach broader conclusions after discussing questions.

From the full text of the *Post* articles the search retrieved, two measures developed using content analysis. To construct the first, "Post reported questions," undergraduates cut every poll result related to health care coverage expansion mentioned in the text, also observing each's date. The second media measure, "Post support claims," comes from an extraction of all the sentences containing the search words. After recording the date, each of 964 sentences was coded at random by three undergraduates who (after discarding false hits) were instructed to identify the level of public support for expanding coverage on a scale of 0 to 100 to the nearest 10 points, where 100 is total support; their scores were then averaged for each time period.

Figure 6.4 charts the frequencies, as well as the ebb and flow, of these two measures for each six-month period from 1990 through 1995. The top panel shows the number of times the measures appeared as well as, for comparison, the number of actual poll questions (out of the 128) asked at that time. Inspecting this panel shows something unexpected, even though the number of questions asked varies substantially—ranging from none to a peak of 34 in the first half of 1993—the number of claims the *Washington Post* makes about public opinion remains steady, around 30 (about one a week) through the entire period. Also, the number of poll questions the *Post* discusses is low, meaning that examples of specific results rarely accompany broader claims about public opinion.

Figure 6.4's lower panel shows the average level of support for both measures—the reported questions and claims—expressed in the six periods. For comparison, I added the average poll question bias (the squares with the line) from the crosstab above. Somewhat oddly, the questions the *Post* chose to report (seen as triangles) seem higher during the debate than the claims (the circles),

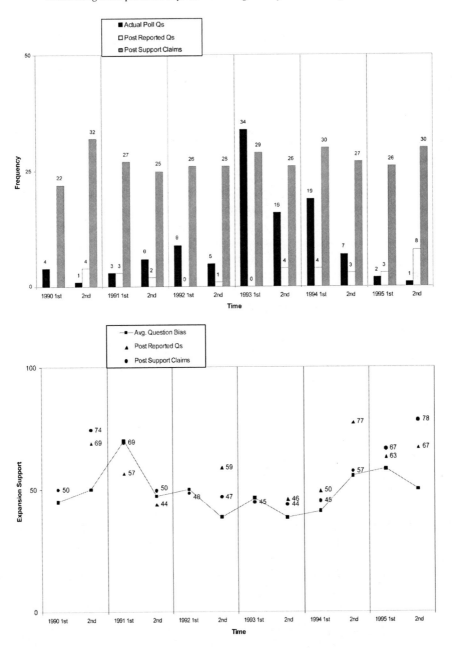

Figure 6.4. Media Coverage of Health Insurance Public Opinion 1990-1995

but before and after the debate, this pattern reverses. Of course, this pattern may be due to chance. Overall it seems the points follow similar paths, peaking in the first half of 1992, then falling and staying low until the debate ended.

CONCLUSIONS

Regarding the Harry and Louise myth, I believe our analyses reveal the truth that overturns its circumstantial case. Our very sensitive LOWESS regression analysis detects little, if any, significant change in the public's attitudes toward expanding health care during the Clinton debate, after controlling for wording changes. Second, our regression suggests that pollsters' mention or exclusion of substantive components, such as financing mechanisms, in questions can dramatically affect response. Third, the changes in components coincided with the Harry and Louise campaign, so that poll questions had positive biases before and after the debate but a strong negative bias during. For example, referring to average question bias in the lower panel of Figure 6.4, we see that question bias associates with a 12-point drop between 1991 and 1993.

In the media coverage of public opinion during the Clinton health care debate, we see, fourth, that the *Washington Post* regularly commented on public opinion without tying these remarks to actual public findings. Perhaps this practice exacerbates the effect of question bias. Fifth, and finally, this media coverage seems to affirm the perceptions generated by the bias in poll questions. On balance, it seems that believers in the Harry and Louise ads' impact are mistaken, which suggests propaganda's relative impotency. Further, this episode replicates our Iraq study: larger alterations in questions' wordings affects response, but smaller ones do not.

Returning to the central question of public competence, the resiliency of the public in response to propaganda suggests that polling has the potential to be a reasonable guide for policy. Throughout this health care debate, the public maintained its support for government action to expand health insurance coverage. We can see this as a sound decision made on the basis of individual dispositions, informed perhaps by personal experience or background information. Likewise, we should not believe that public judgment responds to wizardry or other manipulation. Instead, our review of research into persuasion—not to mention the Harry and Louise investigation—suggests that citizens typically ignore propaganda. Sufficiently motivated citizens, ideally having heard both sides of an argument, make up their own minds. The final chapter takes up the question of how to ensure that both sides are heard.

Chapter 7

Political Reforms and Thoughts on Media Old and New

Your reading should have made my faith in the United States and democracy clear. At the same time, patriotism cannot blind us to the problems this nation faces. People of all stripes could agree to a list that would certainly include the astonishing number of people incarcerated in America. In 2007, 7.5 people of every 1,000 Americans were incarcerated. The comparable number for developing Brazil is 2.2, whereas for developed Germany it is 0.8 (*New York Times*, April 22, 2008). This disparity translates into a staggering opportunity cost in terms of maintenance and foregone effort. And our dependence on foreign energy sources also commands increasing attention. The Department of Energy estimates that we pay some fairly unattractive regimes $105 billion a year for oil. Finally, I am particularly sensitive to the national debt, which the U.S. Treasury reports is $9.5 trillion (a 1 followed by 12 zeroes!), or more than $30,000 for every man, woman, and child in the United States.

This chapter uses our theory of public judgment to show how polling and improved public education can help meet these challenges. However, instead of dealing with them piecemeal and talking about each issue's specifics, we concentrate on systemic reforms. In large part, this upgrade involves using polls to combat special interests and to offset swings of the political pendulum caused by political competition. Here, we will spell out why politicians and lobbyists resist accepting the public judgments that polling presents. The last section discusses the media—old and new—with respect to the standard of mass informed consent. After detailing some half-truths that have stymied media reform, we will cover the nature of broadcasting and new communication technology. This history will allow us to identify some paths that citizens' use of new media can take that would increase the chances for good public education.

This discussion transports us from science to speculation. No stark line separates truth from conjecture. We learned how the term *generalization* covers the move from concrete findings to the wider world. Any reformer must go further, must apply what is known to the system as a whole. We will extrapolate from what we have understood to an ideal public education. I would hope to test these ideas experimentally—to randomly assign political changes and measure their impact. Sadly, this hardly ever happens on a grand stage. Correlational study is nearly as difficult, because reforms occur in an overwhelmingly complex system—and often only once. This situation forces us to speculate. Nevertheless, our findings about polls and public opinion, observations of past trends (especially in the technology, regulation, and content of political communication), and a vision—expressed as mass informed consent—point the way. The recommendations presented below are grounded in the best available knowledge, including our theory and evidence. This point also underlines the need for constant monitoring and evaluation, to improve understanding and prepare for more change.

POLITICAL CHANGE

In 2008, the United States was in the midst of another tremendous political shift. The Republican ascendancy that began in 1980 with Ronald Reagan's election, that won congressional control in 1994, and that peaked in the aftermath of the 9/11 terrorist attacks had ended. In 2006 voters gave Congress back to the Democrats were ready to elect a reformist president in 2008. Candidates Barack Obama and John McCain pledged themselves to change, leaving it up to the electorate to decide the type of change they wanted. Conservative Republicans, caught short by Iraq, Hurricane Katrina, economics and other policies, were in retreat as Democrats celebrated their newfound power no matter who wins the oval office.

Scientists appreciated this reversal at a deeper level, seeing another swing of the political pendulum that would bring a new agenda to the fore. American politics regularly features such swings, each heralded by calls for change and, sometimes, a new set of officeholders. Presidents from Thomas Jefferson to George W. Bush take office with the intention of undoing some of their predecessor's works. If the 2008 election was surprising, it was only because both candidates promised change—perhaps because this was the first national campaign without an incumbent, whether president or vice president, since 1952. This point is not cynical; indeed, change is part and parcel of the political process. We do, however, need to come to grips with this dynamic and its relationship to public opinion.

Democratic politics, if you recall, lives in continuous persuasion. At the national level, this process pits the majority, who are generally happy with the status quo and the power it grants, against a disgruntled minority. The minority wants nothing more than to win power back, just as the majority tries to stop them. We already know the minority tries to split off majority support or attract new blood to the system, and that they succeed when the numbers shift enough to "throw the bums out." This dynamic, in case you are wondering, accommodates more than two parties, only requiring majority rule. Every political party—past, present, and future—under that rule respects the pattern. Thus, while differences in style and program are important, they do not affect the underlying structure. In this way, the Republican takeover in 1994 exactly matches that of the Democrats in 2006.

While political upheavals are necessary and often great, failure to recognize the basic blueprint leads smart people to believe stupid things. Consider the attempt to link political parties to recent developments in political communication technology. Pundits repeatedly compare the Republicans' success with talk radio to the Democrats' superiority at blogging. Having mastered the obvious, they feel entitled to guess at the cause. Republicans, they say, are more authoritarian and therefore suited to a broadcast medium. Likewise, the more democratic Democrats thrive on internet blogs. These pundits naively fall into the classic statistical trap, confusing correlation with causation. Their observation that party performance relates to medium fails to account for the effects of time.

A more thoughtful analysis must admit that communication technology evolves constantly—more quickly in recent years then most. The advent of talk radio preceded blogging; less clearly, the rise of talk radio occurred in a period of Republican dominance. By the same token, the explosion of blogging happened as the Democrats developed a winning message. The unwary may confuse technical change with some sort of fundamental party personality, without bothering to look for systemic evidence. My alternative hypothesis—the rising party rules new communication conduits—is certainly plausible. Though I also have offered little evidence, my view does not encourage unwarranted speculation into the metaphysical properties of various media. In fact, I would guess blogs and talk radio have much in common. Radio personalities may require larger audiences (on average) to succeed, but they share the prospect of increased feedback relative to "traditional" media. Our speculation will be more careful insofar it is grounded in an analysis of the past and present.

WHY ELITES DON'T LIKE POLLS

The Making of Elites

Given our discussions, particularly the response to polling's critics and public opinion's ties to democracy (detailed in our theory of public judgment), the first question we must ask is why elites resist using polls. The answering conjecture grows out of a precise definition of *elite*. My use tracks that of Lippmann: the elite are those who head the fight for power—the governors, as opposed to the governed. The saving grace of the American system is that the border between these two groups is permeable. One saying goes, "Anyone can run for president"—yet elitehood (or *elitedness*, if you prefer) goes past this right. When members of the elite declare their intention to run, people take note, ignoring or making fun of the rest. To be precise, any elite announcement attracts media coverage; non-elite messages do not. Thus, elite membership guarantees the ability to be heard, where the volume of expected coverage indicates one's status.

Let's refine this classification with some famous names. Britney Spears definitely gets attention, but not in the political sense of being able to send a message. She is a celebrity, not a political elite. What about someone who hoists a Free Tibet banner at the Olympics? They may heighten awareness, yet this success is too haphazard. A speaker for the Free Tibet movement, however, has more standing. Ralph Nader supplies a middle case. He routinely receives coverage, so he falls into the elite category. But as he appears to attract less notice over time, we can also see his status eroding. What about Ross Perot, or his more recent incarnation, T. Boone Pickens? These tycoons send messages, so they count as elites. Their use of personal wealth to buy advertising also underlines money's weight in politics. Last, consider unpaid bloggers, who churn out messages with whatever intention. Their eliteness rises and falls with their readership and the attention they attract.

Establishing this rough border between the elites and the masses uncovers some provocative aspects of our political system. First, admitting that anyone can rise to political prominence does not mean that this achievement is easy or common. Richard Ben Cramer makes this point in his excellent book *What It Takes: the Way to the White House* (1993). He suggests that every kid inevitably dreams of being president, and that many take baby steps—running for student office, and the like. With age, if not wisdom, increasing numbers drop out, waving on the ambitious diehards as they climb to the next level. At the top of this pyramid stands the most ambitious of all, the president of the United States—not by accident does the president command the lion's share of American attention. And the rest of politics works similarly. A community organizer, business owner, or intellectual builds a following that offers a readymade slice of attention. At some point, she or he mutates into a higher political species—not in the same league as the president, yet more "newsworthy" than the average Joe.

This winnowing has consequences. At a broad level, the struggles reverberate though the system and affect the provision of political information. Among individuals, the same struggle shapes the character of those who succeed. We can clarify these tendencies of those at or near the top to show how their training, selection, and reward nurture a resistance to polling. The essential fact comes from Phil Converse's study in chapter 4. Elites, operationalized (we know that word!) by congressional candidates, are ideological in a way that "normal" people are not. Ideology, again, equates to an "ism" (as in capitalism). Joiners gain a set of preferences, known as an *agenda*. Agendas center on an acute vision of the way things should be—what Habermas calls a "totalizing worldview." Our stereotypes of the parties reflect these inner visions; we know Democrats want *x*, *y*, and *z*, while Republicans prefer *a*, *b*, and *c*. To be sure, partisan agendas in the United States are not the straightjacket of traditional Communism, yet believers still qualitatively differ from the norm.

As an elite-in-training rises through the ranks, an assortment of forces combine to reinforce their native affinity. Elites self-select; they care enough to act. On average, parties lose as much as they win, so it takes motivation to stick with a political program. Losing streaks can last years; from 1964 to 1980 conservatives had little success, for instance. Only the extraordinarily dedicated resist dropping out in the fallow period. Other selections augment self-selection—peer pressure, for one. We want to be "cool"—everyone strains toward a subcultural ideal. If your peers are young Democrats, you may well aspire to fit the mold. At higher ranks, selection is more formal. Only the best partisans, committed, orthodox and the like, win the contest to lead, head groups, or run for office.

The same forces apply to experts, even so-called "nonpartisans." Following Lippmann's notion, experts are the ultimate *ins*. Extreme focus characterizes their highly specialized education (in school and out), because reward only comes to those who literally *know* better than anyone else. The cost takes the form of forgone knowledge; by definition, experts are not generalists. Rather than going for knowledge a mile wide and an inch deep, experts take a mile deep and an inch wide. A final rung removes true experts (and elites)—the top 1 percent of 1 percent—from the more common: the ability to earn a living in politics. It is one thing to volunteer—amateurs set their hours and mostly control their actions. To have a career, to get paid, means acceding to the boss's wishes. Almost all Americans face this trade-off; the journalists featured below, for example, accommodate themselves to a distinct notion of professionalism.

Elites and Special Interests

Now we come to the critical—maybe shocking, maybe obvious—revelation: professional (read: paid) elites and experts are beholden to special interest paymasters. With few exceptions, politicians and experts answer to their constituency (possibly a lobby) as well as to fellow experts. It may seem odd to think that an expert has a constituency, yet expertise requires a fundamental consensus about what an expert should know. There is the old claim that four out five dentists prefer sugarless gum (for their patients who chew gum); analogous are the similar beliefs of economists, or the way nearly every psychotherapist seems to dress. These uniformities originate in the training that produces similarity across graduates. Further, the trappings of expertise, such as diplomas, signify internalizing certain modes of thought. If a radical challenge a field's dogma, his or her credentials, meaning expertise, draw the first attacks.

Constituencies hire trained experts (or elect politicians) in light of their reputation, which telegraphs their agendas. Think tanks are the most prominent organizations for expert care and feeding, and each approaches the world with a relatively unambiguous point of view. The American Enterprise Institute's website proclaims its devotion to "limited government, private enterprise, individual liberty and responsibility, vigilant and effective defense and foreign policies, political accountability, and open debate." The Brookings Institution, in comparison, seeks to "strengthen American democracy, foster the economic and social welfare, security and opportunity of all Americans and secure a more open, safe, prosperous and cooperative international system." A between the lines reading confirms their ideological thrust, AEI to the political right and Brookings to the left. Employees by and large follow suit. Politicians also hold office at the pleasure of their constituents; thus we can expect an ideological correspondence between experts and politicians, on one hand, and their constituent-patrons, on the other.

Notice that this is far from a Marxian critique. Yes—politicians and experts have a deep interest in maintaining the status quo, if only because it ensures their livelihood. This outline also treats elites as a class as well, though not in the same way as Marx does. But my disagreement lies in the assumed nature of the elite class; I see them as heterogeneous (read: diverse) and conflicting. Citizens, by way of contrast, are much more homogeneous, or similar. Thus, while Marxists see a class struggle between elites and masses, politics in the present United States is actually a battle between competing elites in line with our theory of public judgment. The situation would be far different if a stronger barrier kept citizens from rising to an elite level or from gaining elite representation. Under our definition, that would mean that the media (in whatever form) refused to pay attention to the public's needs. Though some argue this point, it is false for the most part.

Interest Group Politics

Public satisfaction, in this sense, goes hand in hand with constituency-seeking. Some elites are happy to serve existing constituencies, whereas others are driven, by need or principle, to create a new following. Research calls both types *political entrepreneurs*. Just like others in business, they define a target audience, make a pitch, and use the proceeds to advance their agenda. The more successful earn a living. This task, again, is not undemanding; nevertheless certain websites testify to the successes of past years—entrepreneurs who hit the jackpot! Take, for instance, the AARP, formerly the American Association of Retired Persons, "a membership organization leading positive social change and delivering value to people age 50 and over through information, advocacy and service," or the National Rifle Association, "America's foremost defender of Second Amendment rights . . . the premier firearms education organization in the world." Although this kind of representation slants toward the rich and the powerful; at equilibrium, this lively market—aided now by the Internet—exhausts the possibilities, lobbying on behalf of groups of all stripes and sizes.

This consumerist version of political agency has both advantages and disadvantages. As discussed in chapter 2, interest groups breathe some life into the First Amendment by turning numbers (and money) into effective speech. They also assist in fulfilling the democratic need for initiative, giving citizens opportunities to be heard. Donating money to the right interest group, or starting your own, can be the best way to express an intensely held preference. In short, these organizations sort out the voices in our society, doing a decent job. A closer look at interest group politics, however, exposes the need for polling to counteract their ill effects.

The extremity of the active participants relative to the average American citizen may be the most remarkable facet of American politics. The ideology crosstab in chapter 3 confirms that roughly 5 percent of a national sample placed themselves in one of the extreme categories. In contrast, few (if any) honest activists would put themselves anywhere but the scale's ends. Extremity, dogmatism and fervor psychologically accompany elites as they go about their day. In sum, it inspires their actions, spawning the hustle necessary to propel them through the winnowing process. Second, it ensures success in the numerous selection rounds. Instead of competing on musical talent, contestants must prove their commitment and purity. This makes sense to those in organizations. If you were entrusted to choose the next AARP president, would you select someone who "cares about the elderly," or someone who is fanatically devoted to the cause? By the same token, would you rather donate money to a group that "will make things better," or to one that promises to "change the world?" Third, interest groups, like the NRA and AARP, and to a lesser extent the AEI and Brookings, live and die according to the passion of their members' commitments.

The overall effect of these specialized passions is murky. We can detect that activists face an odd incentive structure. To illustrate, in the hours after Supreme Court Justice Sandra Day O'Connor announced her retirement, the group NARAL Pro-Choice America (described in chapter 4) collected a huge influx of donations (*Washington Post*, July 5, 2005). Thus, a bona fide setback for the cause—Justice O'Connor largely supported abortion rights—recharged the organization. This relationship between defeat and payoff seems perverse. Epidemiology provides a more intuitive model. When a disease is crushed, we expect doctors will rejoice and turn to a new ill. In politics, narrow focus and intense loyalty prevent radical changes in direction. These factors also prevent compromise, if only because compromising elites see constituency-patron rebellions in favor of less flexible leadership. Democratic politics left to issue groups is an issue by issue arms race of mobilization and counter-mobilization. So, although we cannot forget that politics is inherently conflictual, the interest group menagerie aggravates this propensity.

A more insidious threat comes from co-option; specifically, interest group politics is more vulnerable than polling to money's influence. Jurgen Habermas gives an almost mystical angle to the biggest threat to democracy. His 1975 book *Legitimation Crisis* divides the political universe into "system" and "lifeworld," roughly matching our distinction between formal and informal politics. Understanding his point requires some background that refers to chapter 1. Habermas argues that legitimacy—the unforced acceptance of government authority—originates in the lifeworld, where authentic action weaves us into a communal net that sustains society. The system consists of routine and typically inauthentic transactions, such as buying and selling. Harmonious existence requires that the system serve the lifeworld. Picture a happy village, where economic activity sustains a vibrant commons. Unfortunately, Habermas observes that the system tends to "colonize" the lifeworld, despite their interdependence. Bureaucracy and commerce, for instance, "co-opt" the lifeworld's authentic expressions. Habermas could well have used Darth Vader's evil empire (read: monolithic faceless power), relentlessly crushing hope and freedom (Luke, Han, and Leia). Colonization prompts a "legitimation crisis" if left unchecked. Citizens lose confidence in government and supporting institutions, resulting in a range of troubles from disenchantment to rebellion.

Let me illustrate and apply Habermas's thought to interest groups. A traditional interest group tactic had members flood congressional offices with letters before key votes. Their goal was to pressure each member into voting their way (where more letters meant more pressure). Wise representatives paid heed to these genuine expressions of public opinion, often tallying the number of letters for and against. Habermas suggests that this system is ripe for abuse. Seeing that impact increases with the number of letters, smart interest groups make sending easier. For example, they send supporters pre-addressed and pre-stamped post cards that can be dropped in the mail. Smarter representatives react by discounting the messages presented in the less authentic medium. The better financed groups then step up and write the letters, replacing authentic communication with an indistinguishable substitute. This same process has been repeated with different communication technologies, from telegrams to phone calls to website reviews.

This specter of inauthenticity constantly challenges interest group politics. To take another example, entrepreneurs try to maximize their apparent strength. The AARP, for instance, claims roughly 38 million members, more than 10 percent of the nation's population! Closer inspection reveals this number includes anyone 50 or over who joins AARP for $12.50 a year. While nearly a half a billion dollars of annual dues is respectable money, their pitch dilutes the political expression. Their website details four categories of membership benefits: travel discounts, health products and services, financial and legal advice, and lower insurance rates. I only pick on AARP as one case among many; the point being that the modern interest group has strayed from the prototype of likeminded people coalescing to send a clear message. Many think the Internet has revolutionized authentic expression, yet it can be argued that it fosters co-option. The same technology that permits a flash mob to protest also enables free T-shirt panics. In general, money hollows out mechanisms for demonstrating grassroots support, transforming channels for effective political speech into Astroturf.

Polls v. Interest Groups: **Take Two**

These forces conspire within individuals to produce grand rationalizations; in other words, elites and their fans (Walter Lippmann) naturally think they know best, and everyone should listen. The trouble with listening is that their agenda often takes precedence over other considerations, like the truth. We saw this happen in the 2000 Bush–Gore election. Without taking sides, we can agree that partisanship rather than principle drove nearly every elite message. Part of the controversy concerned "hanging chads." If you remember, a chad is the paper punched out of some kinds of computer ballots. Sometimes chads stick. The issue in this case was: *should we count these less successful ballots, or not?* Not knowing the right answer, we can agree that virtually no one in the country knew about chads in October, though of course every partisan knew whether he or she supported George Bush or Al Gore. A few weeks later, however, any number of experts could bloviate on chad and, conveniently enough, argue vehemently for counting the ballots or throwing them away way. The other clear fact is that their positions exactly matched their partisan loyalties. These opinions, though correlation is not causation, seem impressively opportune. We generally dismiss reasoning when it moves backward from the desired conclusion instead of an open-minded deliberation on the case's facts.

More often, there is no "right" answer in politics; put another way, politics concerns values, our deep and unverifiable beliefs about the best world. Economists speak of values conflicts as distributional questions, which cover policies that are economically efficient yet that benefit different groups. Inflation is an archetypal distributional issue. Everyone admits that inflation hurts lenders and helps borrowers. If I borrow 100 dollars in an economy inflating at 5 percent annually, I only pay back 95 real dollars to zero out the principal the next year. With zero inflation, I owe all 100. Hence, while no one can pinpoint the right rate, it has substantial (and conflicting) consequences. Lenders, like banks, want the Federal Reserve to fight inflation. Borrowers, most businesses and the workers they hire, don't mind it so much. Naturally, their elite representatives happily and noisily argue the point.

Who should the government favor: borrowers, or lenders? The Fed, as it stands, compromises when making this decision, reputedly targeting inflation at 2 percent. This approach may or may not be satisfactory. On the whole, however, the government acts on any number of distributional issues, such as agricultural subsidies, energy policy, and the income tax rate. The absence of an optimal (read: obviously best) policy creates a vacuum that experts and special interests fill with their biased, extreme, and sometimes corrupt arguments. The result is a politics of compromise, which could be good, but that may have little to do with what the public wants—which is definitely bad.

My last word on special interests and experts concerns their ambivalence toward polling. We have detailed how elites, experts, or politicians represent a slice of the public. Even the president's representation of the country does not equal speaking for the whole. Like all politicos, presidents have conflicting loyalties—to donors, to supporters, and above all to their own agenda, that make messages regarding public welfare challengeable. Activists happily accept polls aligned with their goals; they can use these in the struggle. Then again, when polling finds opposition to a scheme, they are more likely to belittle results than abandon their plans. Their scorn repeats the criticisms we have fought throughout the book—the public is fickle or stupid. They often believe some version of "if they knew what I knew, they would agree with me." At bottom, public opinion interferes with the work of special interests, and we suspect that many secretly wish it would go away. More sophisticated interests try to shape public opinion, which is the way things should be. The question then: will they respect the publics' judgment once rendered?

EDUCATION: GETTING THE MOST FROM PUBLIC OPINION

Our philosophy and evidence compels us to respect polling; yet we also want to take public opinion at its best. Enter the standard of mass informed consent, which establishes a benchmark for public education. To recap, informed consent requires: competence, freedom, and education. We have addressed the first two items. The evidence we have collected or reviewed shows that the public responds sensibly to poll questions. The circumstances surrounding the interview also seem to secure sufficient freedom. At the other end, our regression approach can solve many problems associated with the interpretation of results (chapter 5). Here, our thoughts turn to the education that precedes the decision. We should know the importance of education by now; some kinds of education validate poll results and lend public judgment legitimacy. Without sufficient education, or with a misleading education, we cannot trust sample survey results, no matter how they were conducted or interpreted.

Let me relist the issues. First, just as value questions do not have right answers, there can be no perfect education—one that everybody agrees covers all the necessary information (and that might inextricably lead to consensus regarding the best choice). Second, we can expect competitive ideas in education delivery. This fact implies that the public will hear conflicting analyses, if not facts, as well as some falsehoods. Heated competitors will draw attention to each other's biases and, rightly or wrongly, call each other liars. Third, the media may come between the public and necessary information. Thorny issues all, but perhaps more easily resolved than it appears. Resolution turns on the definition of *necessary information*. We will discover that dissent is the key to proper education. In short, promoting effective dissent is the best way to ensure the public receives the proper education on any political topic.

I want to organize this closing section around a thought experiment; its setting matches the one commonly used in polling with one exception. Before we question a respondent and record the results we warn them about an upcoming poll. Today's polling has a peculiar obsession with the pop quiz. Too many (if not all) polls intentionally surprise respondents, calling them while they may be relaxing or working on something else to ask them about matters far from their immediate situation. This change, a manipulation if you will, gives the respondent a chance to research and consider a specified topic, transforming the pop quiz into a less unusual interview or exam.

Many political theorists—Ben Barber, Jim Fishkin, Amy Gutmann and Jane Mansbridge, to name a few—claim that politics would be better if citizens put more thought, what they call *deliberation*, into their opinions. A typical sample's adults, long past most schooling, probably put little thought into polls, if only because they have little time. Although it would be great to study actually forewarned respondents, this section is normative. This setup allows us to talk about what we expect from citizens and systemic reforms that can help them reach that potential. After Asimov (chapter 2), we will name our imaginary respondent Norma. To be concrete, we will tell Norma that she will be asked her opinions on health care coverage, for instance, in the next day or two, perhaps stressing there are no right or wrong answers and given a sample question, such as "Do you favor or oppose a national heath plan, financed by tax money?" Now we can ask what Norma should do, and how we (read: the system) can help her maximize the payoff from the time spent.

BACKGROUND SKILLS, RESOURCE ACCESS, AND PRUDENT REFORMS

Resources come first. For example, we might want to pay Norma's wages or child care costs to carve out time she can devote to the public. Unsurprisingly, many deliberation theorists propose similar subsidies, and this tiny expenditure qualifies as a no-brainer; really, Norma is working for all of us in that time. Next, the first of *education*'s twin meanings deals with the skills and general knowledge she needs. This preliminary is not tricky, due to the fact that we should not demand too much. We do not want experts; Norma does not need a law degree or specific technical training. But since we've selected her at random, we will not exclude her if she has these credentials, either. The need for competence does mandate a basic intelligence, especially language fundamentals—listening, reading, and speaking. This competency gives the ability to comprehend and incorporate new information. The language does not have to be English, polls can be in any language; but to avoid the risk of poor translations and inadequate information, a command of English would be nice.

What about political knowledge? We would prefer that Norma graduated from a high school that taught the general workings of American governance. I would modernize the traditional three branches curriculum by emphasizing definitions of democracy, majority rule, and the like. The relevant section from the first chapter, naturally, provides my outline. We would not disapprove if Norma followed the news to keep this background up to date. On the other hand, knowing trivia would not help her judge issues like expanding health care or invading Iraq. The most important information for our purposes is an understanding of polling's representative value. Initially, these facts would highlight Norma's duty to speak for the American people and motivate her deliberation. More broadly, this awareness would encourage widespread respect for public opinion and instill resistance to baseless criticism of polling results.

Norma also needs basic computer skills. Once warned, she could head to the library and page through books and magazines; most strongly believe that a few webbed hours would be dramatically more efficient. Looking to the future, we assume she has a networked computer with the ability to retrieve information. Some people may never acquire this kind of equipment and skill; we all have relatives who are mystified by PCs and smart phones. The truth is that the prime correlate of digital skill is age; thus, we will eventually realize the dream of a ubiquitous and friendly information appliance.

The essence of polling marks the path toward satisfying this minimal list. Norma, part of randomly selected sample, literally corresponds to the average American. Thus, saying she should have these capacities means we want to see them in every American. The compulsory school system must be their primary provider. This is not the place to evaluate contemporary education; suffice it to say that literacy is a prerequisite of democratic citizenship. I would also have all high schools mandate a course in government (many already do). These courses should spend a week on polling and public opinion. A more elaborate advanced placement syllabus would discuss political behavior basics, particularly the median voter model (chapter 3) and a study of framing/question wording effects (chapter 5).

Some may not believe that high school students or even average citizens can grasp these concepts. I respond that education standards continuously increase. Subjects like trigonometry and calculus were once reserved for math majors; now we expect every college graduate to be familiar with these methods. In the same way, I expect future democratic generations to know the fundamentals of polling, such as random sampling, by heart. I suggest that

Thomas Jefferson and Abraham Lincoln—not to mention James Bryce and George Gallup—would rather have students learn about the dynamics of public opinion than memorize the Declaration of Independence or the Gettysburg Address. It would also be wise to send Norma a pamphlet on polling that summarizes key points.

On the technical side, successful democratic politics requires universal access to high-speed networks and computing. The nearest analogue is indoor plumbing. Well over 90 percent of American households have this former luxury. Stipulating to the hurdles and expenses, I refuse to believe that such machines will not be in place in the near future. With a high-school diploma, time access, and maybe her polling pamphlet, Norma is ready to go! Thus, we come to the second meaning of education: the immediate knowledge necessary to meet the informed consent standard.

DISSENT AS THE INDICATOR OF SUFFICIENT POLITICAL INFORMATION

What do we want networked Norma to learn in the time before a poll? One promising ideal is not so different from the Wolverines' vision from chapter 4. Facing an investigative poll on a singular topic or national problem, she should be able to summarize the status quo, identify competing proposals, and know something of each's pros and cons (adjustments can be made for other types of polls). To gather this information in today's milieu, Norma goes online; we find her sitting in front of a computer, staring at Google's homepage. In all probability, she will enter the pollster-provided subject to begin her search. What next?

Protagoras (described in the previous chapter) would have Norma hear arguments that forcefully present each side in the debate. This simple formula distills generations of political theory on freedom and information. Still, it is not precisely applicable. The problem is one of structure; loosely translated, *exactly what action* (read: government policy) *is at stake?* Specifying a topic itself poses problems, and the pollster should not have to detail a policy as well. We hope that the 30-minute poll would contain a mix of questions in which the aim is left relatively vague—on the order of "should the government expand health care?" This is the easiest way to counter framing effects and capture the contingencies of Norma's judgment. The final stage of politics does reduce to passing legislation, issuing an order or not; hence, all decisions are ultimately yes-or-no binaries. Reaching that end, of course, is a vital—some say decisive—part of the process. Forcing Norma to make this choice prematurely defeats the purpose of forewarning. A less leading question, such as "we are going to ask about the government's role in health care coverage" would better preface our instructions.

Worries about premature two-sidedness also reflect Robert Lane's warning (chapter 4). Pollsters need to avoid building elite ideological consistency into their questions. To define certain points of view as liberal or conservative may seem necessary to the deeply engaged, but may hinder Norma. In a related vein, we may also want to quash partisan cues. Though empirical research on heuristics shows that loyal Republicans and Democrats often let partisanship decide their answers, we could encourage deeper thinking by leaving out indications of party as well as particular political personalities. To loyal partisans, drawing attention to the parties' positions suggests there is a right answer. Of course, Norma is free to choose partisan sources of information, which brings us to the core concern.

The logic behind deliberation's presumed benefits builds directly on John Stuart Mill's pioneering exploration of political expression, which Oliver Wendell Holmes labeled the "marketplace of ideas." Mill justified free speech rights by arguing that societies made better collective decisions when everyone spoke their mind. His formulation flows through the traditional end of a marriage ceremony; "if any person objects, let them speak now or forever hold their peace." Silence means everyone concurs that the match is good. Likewise, according to Mill, if no one challenges a civic claim, it must be true. Free speech has other justifications—it vents anger and promotes communal solidarity, for instance. Leaving aside some metaphysics, however, it was Mill's harnessing of truth that led to the First Amendment. This notion also had us add free speech to the three democratic basics of chapter 1.

Challenge is the engine of Mill's, as well as Protagoras's, good decision machine. The absence of challenge, for instance, blesses the wedding. In the same way, failed challenges make us more likely to accept a claim's truth due to the success of its armor. This mechanism's governor is almost wholly psychological, relying on the judgment of individual audience members. Once again, we know little about successful persuasion; but we do know that challenge prompts a more energetic consideration. Significantly, this energy comes from supporters in addition to opponents; both sides in a lively public sphere have to think harder to win the persuasion battle. Furthermore, even if the challenge fades, proponents benefit from the extra thought. Our recent Iraq policies supply good and bad examples of challenge at work. The reticence of the media and the opposition, along with national security strictures, prevented a significant challenge to the initial invasion plans. One likely consequence was the plan's failure to achieve its immediate objectives. In contrast, when the administration proposed a "surge," sending an additional troops to Iraq, strong critiques immediately appeared. While some may attribute the surge's achievements to stubbornly staying the course, I suggest that the added thought put into the surge plan to meet challenges helped its execution.

Effective free speech necessarily takes the form of dissent. By dissent, I do not mean screeching or violence, but rather communicative confrontations of accepted claims. This metamorphosis grows out of two palpable realities. Elites, principally politicians, think carefully before uttering an unpopular opinion. (I do not mean that they only say accepted things; such a rule would devastate any chance for a successful idea marketplace. Rather, they make careful calculations about the benefits of taking unpopular stances.) We know that the fashionable position is not necessarily true. For instance, let's look at Christopher Columbus and his travels. His journey was risky; most people believed he would fail. He challenged conventional wisdom, calculating the risk's worth. His success, and whatever acclamation he received, stemmed from his disproof of prevailing knowledge. Of course, the crowd could have been right—and would have been, had he disappeared. To take another illustration, we know authoritarian regimes rigorously suppress dissenters; here, force takes the place of popularity. All in all, maintaining the proper level of dissent is critical to the success of the marketplace of ideas.

At the individual level, sufficient dissent ensures an informed decision. The worst educational circumstance fits the "man in a bubble" stereotype—a decisionmaker cut off from dissenters by a coterie of "yes" people. This scenario leads to decisions made without the benefit of productive thought, and particularly without a good estimate of risk. The thick bubbles enclosing totalitarian regimes often induce them to do wildly stupid things. Imperial Japan, for instance, risked a galling attack on a substantially bigger country in World War II. Historians believe that the Japanese convinced themselves that the United States lacked the will to mobilize its own resources. In the end, the bubble popped, and with a devastating price.

Despite the dangers, social science research suggests that people like bubbles. Many researchers suggest humans avoid conflict to maintain communal harmony. In this vein, Diana Mutz tracked exposure to political dissent—and her 2006 book *Hearing the Other Side* indicates that citizens do not receive enough. Nearly all of us choose friends and neighborhoods that match our likes and dislikes. This sameness impedes hearing dissenting views. Correspondingly, few listen to disagreeable elites in the media; it is less stressful to change the channel. At work, the preeminent spot to encounter disparate views, the need to get along squelches dissent's last chance. She essentially concludes that despite citizen's pretensions to open-mindedness, dissent is the endangered specie of political messaging.

For these reasons, our primary educational goal entails exposing Norma to information laden with a helping of dissent; we want to open her bubble and provoke some thought. In addition, we want her to understand the risks attending any decision. Because we cannot rely on her friends and associates, we have to count on the media, either in its older form or, increasingly, within the results of her Google search. Sadly, at this moment the media's ability to fulfill this duty is questionable. Part of the reason lay in the aforementioned ability to filter, change channels or point web browsers in a different direction—Lazarsfeld's idea of selective exposure (chapter 5). The other part resides in the structure of media, old and new.

OLD MEDIA'S CLUES

Comparing new media to the older still existing use of "mainstream" media illuminates the delivery of political information. While much has changed, a lot has remained the same. Our formal political system is the most visible constant. Some see the continuous campaign, where the next election's priorities influence all government activity, as the harbinger of a new era. Though true, the rise of permanent campaigning predates so-called new media. Similarly, the omnipresence of candidate websites indicates some type of shift, but my informal impression suggests that these sites' messages closely parallel the ones spread through less novel media. Finally, the electoral cycle follows the same pattern: every two years for Congress, every four years for president. In contrast, the news cycle has clearly changed. Other potential changes relate to government regulation and the financing of content.

News, in a broad sense, serves as the wellspring of political information and changes in its structure require careful consideration. The story of radio (as I said) is our story in that the bulk of current information passes through traditional channels. Far less than 10 percent of the money spent on advertising, such as on presidential campaigns, goes to new media; the lion's share of the rest heads to television. We look forward to this proportion's change, but the timing is cloudy. The shift to a "24 hour," or instant, news cycle is also less drastic than it appears, if only because the rest of the political system has not kept pace. So although someone can post a salacious tidbit at any time of day; barring resignation or impeachment, we have to wait for the next election before we can take action. Similarly, many cases of political self-destruction can be traced to new media (George Allen comes to mind), but we still need to acknowledge the pivotal role played by old media in circulating the faux pas. Many fantastic scholarly works depict the mainstream media's key features. As it stands, we know less about new media, so my strategy extrapolates from old to new to identify potential sources of dissent.

Government Regulation

Everyone can agree that the new media has not coalesced into a final form; this situation means that efforts inside and outside of government can affect the outcome. A review of old regulatory frameworks brings in the thematic and practical factors driving media policy. I specifically want to contrast competing regulatory approaches—the "hands-off" path, based on free market principles and more interventionist notions prompted by scarcity. I hope to justify regulation that can improve the quality of information and ease Norma's task.

At one end, many extremist experts malign government interference in media matters as free speech violations. As one might guess, certain corporations finance these experts. Leaving aside any bias, fanatical free-marketers generally proceed from erroneous interpretations of law and history. The First Amendment, in Alexander Meiklejohn's eyes for instance, does not prevent the government from taking measures to encourage speech. On the reverse side, hands-off approaches have led to chaos. Paul Starr's book, *The Creation of the Media: Political Origins of Modern Communications*, illustrates this point with a scholarly account of early broadcasting. In brief, technological advances made radio possible around the turn of the century. The United States Navy froze development during World War I, exposing a classic chicken and egg problem when they relinquished control. This story foreshadows new media development.

No one wanted to buy a radio without programs, and no one would create content until people had radios. Manufacturers, like General Electric and Westinghouse, paid for the first stations to juice sales. According to Starr, the crucial change came when a department store station announced linens would go on sale the next day. Hundreds, instead of the usual dozen, customers showed up. Broadcasters found a treasure—their audience—which they could sell to advertisers. Keep in mind the fact that radio programming was pretty dull before advertising. Buying a transmitter—a minimal investment—put you in the broadcasting business. Early broadcasters struggled to fill airtime with shows that featured athletic events, concerts, and church sermons. These spectacles went on whether or not anyone tuned in, so they required no funds beyond running a microphone wire. A new source of finance changed the ballgame; advertising improved content and made stations profitable. Then, everyone wanted a transmitter; too many transmitters created interference. Nature, read the spectrum, limits the number of radio stations in one area.

In radio's case, the invisible hand led to an oversupply of broadcasters and destroyed the resource—the ability to send and receive content.

Broadcasters demanded governments intervene to regulate transmission. Some countries responded by nationalizing radio. In Great Britain the British Broadcasting Corporation (or BBC, known to Monty Python and Doctor Who fans) monopolized practically all programming. Taxes, in the form of receiver permits, paid for the BBC. This solution may seem alien to the American experience. On the other hand, some of today's best news comes from PBS and NPR, broadcasters consciously modeled on the BBC. On the other hand, many Britons complained about the BBC's menu, and in the ensuing years a large amount of British content was privatized. In the end, who would only want to watch PBS? The United States Congress debated regulation and came up with "licensing"; 1927's Radio Act awarded frequencies in a "media market" to private groups. The original licensees were judged on technical criteria; essentially the applicants who could transmit the clearest signals won. Nascent media networks were built on these licenses, and these same companies led the move to television. In 1934 Congress changed the name of the Federal Radio Commission to the Federal Communications Commission (FCC), establishing licensing throughout our present broadcast system.

Licensing melds private and public ownership. On one side, private corporations control advertising-supported content. On the other, the public holds legal title to the broadcast spectrum. Yet, in this scheme the public has little practical power. The law does mandate that licensees operate in the public "interest, convenience, and necessity." Notice that when the first licenses were awarded, the public interest was defined as receiving a clear signal. Related interpretations implicate ratings, as in more viewers equals more interest. Contrasting definitions require changes in content (that may not attract viewers). Emergency broadcasting, for instance, fulfills the public interest obligation in by warnings of impeding disasters. Over the years, many have sued the FCC, forcing the courts to interpret this phrase. *Red Lion Broadcasting* (1969) is the most significant Supreme Court case. In a nutshell, *Red Lion* balances the interest of licensees (who do not like meddling that reduces profitable airtime) against that of the public, some of whom want to meddle. The court acknowledged that only so many radio stations could operate in a given market, ruling that scarcity justified government intervention.

Justice Byron White also affirmed a content-based view of public interest in *Red Lion's* majority opinion:

> The people as a whole retain their interest in free speech by radio and their collective right to have the medium function consistently with ends and purposes of the First Amendment. It is the rights of listeners and viewers, not the right

of broadcasters, which is paramount . . . . Congress need not stand idly by and
permit those with licenses to ignore the problems which beset the people.

This law found expression in requirements for equal time, such as the Fairness Doctrine. The FCC once required that broadcast news be balanced by
providing the same amount of coverage to both political parties. Stations also
had to give community spokespeople a chance to respond when they offered
editorial opinions. Each of these mandates (in combination with the limited
number of available channels) increased the chances that citizens would
hear dissent. Paradoxically, some argue that the Fairness Doctrine eventually reduced the political information flow, including dissent. Knowing that
they would have to give free time to adversaries, most broadcast news outlets
stopped doing editorials.

The story of media regulation gets even more convoluted. The equal
time rules, for instance, never applied to publishing, because the spectrum
argument excluded newspapers and magazines. The idea was that anyone
could start a paper, whereas nature limited the number of broadcast outlets.
Changing technology has obviously altered the landscape, yet new regulatory
debates continue to bring up scarcity. In one battle, cable television won less
regulation than broadcast, because it offered more channels. Accordingly,
censors must censor dirty cable words before cable shows they reach the public airwaves. Today, many argue that technological advancement has eliminated scarcity, so the government should completely deregulate all media. At
the same time, many media companies argue for another kind of government
interference: namely, the protection of intellectual property, particularly
copyrights. We need not spend time on their efforts to enlist the government's
help in stamping out piracy, but we should see how this kind of contradiction
reinforces skepticism of interest group politics.

More broadly, we can conclude that scarcity still limits media distribution.
When cable first came to American households, for example, companies had
to dig up the streets to make connections. Much like no one wanted too many
transmitters, communities licensed local operators to curtail the trenching.
Scarcity of channels morphed into being stuck with one cable provider. In
exchange for the monopoly, the operators agreed to reserve some channels
for "public access," shows produced by local interests. My channel covers
local council meetings. The ultimate impact of public access is unclear, but
it is a legacy of that bargain. The cable story exposes another kind of scarcity, as well. When cable began, it competed with television broadcasting,
which offered—at most—seven channels. Thirty cable channels seemed like
a huge windfall. In retrospect, 30 channels is not so much; today many systems offer up to 500 and will probably go higher. Yet cable channels are still

scarce. Notwithstanding networks that cater to video gamers (G4), gardeners (HGTV), and infants (BabyTV), not everyone will ever have their own cable channel.

Ironically, now newspapers are the scarcest of all media. Over time, economies of scale in publishing meant cities could support only one profitable newspaper. The government actually tried to save weaker papers from bankruptcy by authorizing "joint operating agreements." This law lets two papers, like the *Seattle Post* and the *Seattle Times*, share production costs and revenues while producing different news sections. The FCC still prevents anyone from owning both a station and a newspaper. These regulations seek to encourage dissent, or at least to discourage one outlet from controlling the information flow. The decline of second newspapers continues; now very few cities have more than one major paper. That is not the last word; technology has made the concept of even one major paper economically untenable. These former giants will move onto the web and compete in a new space, or disappear in the long run. In this history scarcity has run its full course: from the overabundance of *anyone can start a newspaper* to extinction (though the reason is economic as well as technical). When it comes to new media, everyone acknowledges the government's encouragement, from DARPA research through browser development to grants provided to Google's founders for their studies.

Scarcity also stems from sociology and psychology as well as from technology and economics. The phrase *anyone can start a newspaper* has currently been replaced by *anyone can start a website*. There still can never be enough channels, because humans—in commerce or as part of the lifeworld—have an ability to exhaust any bandwidth. As fast as networks develop to carry media into Americans' lives, expansion of content means competition to send messages, whether on television, computer screens, or cell phones. The largest supernetwork may carry every media some day, along with political information, into every mind, but some ultimate scarcity comes from the limits of human attention. *We* can only consume so much. In sum, government will always play a role in political communication. Laws facilitate or block certain technologies (broadcasting cable, and now wireless) and in so doing can privilege certain corporations (licensees and copyright holders) and interests (advertisers and producers) at others' expense. It is a mistake to think that increasing the spectrum (read: bandwidth) can ever alter this fundamental idea.

Content Financing

Another factor weaves through the chronicle of political information—the relationship between content and finance. We have already touched on advertising, the primary source of American media funding. Too many reformers rail against advertising without considering its import. Someone must pick up the tab for content, either with money or time. At the same time, we must recognize the current political calculus that equates money and effective speech. This discussion will list some systemic consequences imposed by the dependence on ad revenue. The phenomenon's critical aspect concerns "authoritative" news. Many would-be reformers want people to consume more news, supposing that the public will gain more information. Research, in the form of content analysis, demonstrates that more news does not equal better news. There is some irony in the fact that news seems to be a finite product. To make this point we need to talk about the economics and sociology of news production. Yet authoritative news has benefits. Driven by the need to be seen as fair as well as by ever-increasing criticism, much authoritative reportage contains a helping of dissent that may not relocate to new media.

Old media news is a byproduct of advertising. If, for instance, you call a station and ask to speak to customer service, they will direct you to the people who sell commercial time. Why? The station's customers, generally, are marketing agencies. Content, shows, and programming (loose synonyms) have no purpose other than to attract viewers to ads. In other words, media builds audiences to sell; content can be considered bait, designed to lure the product. You can see this reality in ratings; more people tuning in means airtime is worth more. Hence, commercials on daytime shows cost more than nighttime commercials, and commercials run during the Super Bowl cost more than commercials run during *Law and Order* reruns. And ad revenue is only the half the story; media companies have a fiduciary duty to increase shareholder profit, which equals revenue minus cost. The media business constantly tries to maximize the take and minimize costs. Networks came about because producing every show locally is not cost-effective; that imperative created the present system whereby New York and Hollywood manage production. New programs are also expensive, so producers air them so long as enough people watch. In the extreme, this calculus allows programs with no content—the infomercial. Before despising this format, we should remember that Ross Perot built his campaign (which probably led to Bill Clinton's election and a balanced federal budget in the 1990s), on these 30-minute ads.

News fits into this rubric, and Lance Bennett's book *News: The Politics of Illusion*, supplies the best treatment of the subject. To summarize his work, there is a demand for news that programs satisfy, letting them sell audiences to earn money. Objectors may bring up PBS, supposedly advertising-free news; but I would point out that they care almost as much about ratings and have advertising-like corporate sponsorship. I, for one, get irritated when

Chuck E. Cheese ads appear in my kids' Mr. Rogers. In addition, Bennett discusses the way sociological factors turn news into routine. This may seem odd; news should be exciting, right? *Dog bites man*, boring, *man bites dog*, news! In truth, the news serving we get each day is highly predictable. This "news" comes from a funneling process researchers call *gatekeeping*. To use Herbert Gans's title *Deciding What's News*, editors separate the newsworthy wheat from the chaff in a process that crams everything going on in the world (if not the universe) into the "newshole." The size and configuration of the newshole varies by media; one radio station promises, "You give us 22 minutes; we'll give you the world." Newspapers and magazines set aside a number of content pages. The newshole can expand for big events, such as war and hurricanes; pointedly, programmers subject these expansions to the same profit calculus. Is it worth cutting into other programming or printing more pages?

This routine starkly homogenizes content across news outlets. For example, content analyses regularly show that major broadcast and cable outlets (as well as newspapers) feature the same stories, in roughly the same order. You can confirm this by flipping through some cable channels. As a result, reading one daily newspaper will leave Norma with roughly the same political knowledge as reading 10. This correlation across outlets is generally attributed to editors' use of the same gatekeeping criteria. Cost enters the decision as well, in the form of allocating resources to cover various stories. In politics, the news coverage of the president, to the point of ignoring nearly everyone and everything else, caps this pattern. From a budgetary standpoint, no one commands the same allocation. The president has at least one reporter—worth over $100,000 a year—from each news organization, 24 hours a day. Compare that to Congress, where a different reporter covers 535 people. Other beats scramble for attention; a part-timer may cover the Supreme Court, for instance. This allocation may be justifiable; the powerful president may be the most newsworthy person. Nevertheless, this arrangement allows the president to dominate traditional flows of political information. One study, reported in Daniel Hallin's *The Presidency, the Press and the People*, maintains that 40 percent of all political news stories originate in the White House, and that the president is mentioned in another 40 percent. Skillful presidents can use this asset to bring their message close to propaganda; as a regular news viewer, Norma could be bombarded with the presidential point of view.

A more subtle aspect of financing concerns the nature of news. Turning again to Starr's work, until the 1890s most media was sponsored by political parties. Some living newspaper names, such as the *Albany Democrat-Herald* and the *Arizona Republic*, formerly the *Republican*, reflect their partisan heritage. However, publishers realized that a partisan approach repelled roughly half their prospective audience, so nonpartisan news was born. In theory, the nonpartisan paper would provide better news, being fair and balanced. Even today, media leaders take umbrage at the charge of bias, and claims of nonpartisanship, or unbiased, news feature in many news outlets' slogans. In practice, the quest for profit removed papers from the political fray. This gives rise to authoritative journalism where news anchors and colleagues tell you all you need to know; the *New York Times* features "all the news fit to print."

The concept of "horserace" coverage demonstrates how authoritative news shapes political campaign coverage. As the name implies, this template emphasizes the strategic part of the campaign, such as a candidate who is ahead or behind, and who may be rising fast or fading. Likewise, when a candidate tries to talk about an issue, nonpartisan news adds a horserace frame. For example, candidate x talked about issue y to win the support of group z. Some scholars intuit that this tendency is the reason for widespread political cynicism. In addition to not offending readers and appearing more objective, many think horserace coverage is cheaper. In my work on Senate campaigns, over 50 percent of all newspaper coverage qualified as horseraces. Because the newshole's capacity is largely fixed, this coverage crowds out more substantive journalism.

NEW MEDIA'S PROMISES AND PITFALLS

I do not want to take this mainstream media criticism too far. Were Norma to regularly follow the news, particularly my favorites, the *Washington Post*, *New York Times*, and *Wall Street Journal*, as well as the *NewsHour with Jim Lehrer*, she would be well prepared for any poll. The same can probably be said if she follows less "prestigious" media, like *USA Today* or her local stations. Two points follow from my complacency: First, information is available to citizens who want it. This suggests that problems with political information have as much to do with demand as supply. Chapter 3 pointed out that most Americans are not political junkies because they lack the time that only a few can lavish on affairs of state. However, this demand shortage is not constant, because second, when the world intrudes, the public generally pays attention. News consumption for big events multiplies. During elections, for example, news viewership persistently swells; moreover, the closer the election, the more coverage. At the level of specificity broader questions require, this small exposure goes a long way. Typical issues and events do not involve political knowledge staples, such as name a Supreme Court Justice. Instances like Hurricane Katrina and the Iraq invasion motivate citizens to examine what is going on and study the issues raised by the media. In a traditional media paradigm, our forewarned poll may simply encourage this existing tendency.

When thinking about new communication technology, the word *unprecedented* repeatedly materializes. It is spot-on. We live in the midst of a messaging revolution the likes of which humans rarely see. Many spectators compare new media, the web or Internet (whatever you call it) to the printing press, a machine-wrought transformational tidal wave. The Protestant Reformation and democracy were two little things encouraged by the widespread literacy that printing spawned. This view ranks broadcasting (read: radio or television), downward, another medium for the few to reach the many. The implication here is that the revolutionary part of the Internet lay in its ability to connect the many to the many. Yet I say again, other aspects of political communication have not changed, and those that do may change for the worse. Indeed, few can predict the future, especially with regard to recent communication technology, and this concluding section is the most tentative of all.

We touched on one key claim: *anyone can start a website* (or blog). For citizens, this route may be the only way to air deeply held convictions freely without annoying their friends and neighbors. This opportunity does not exist in any other media. Philosophically, we would like effective speech, which involves citizens' efforts to link to an audience. On top of that, the audience should rise and fall with the merit of their ideas, so better messages should reach more citizens. This utopian ideal is difficult to achieve. The new path to prominence involves the same kinds of compromises that hound all elites. For example, Alexa's most viewed news websites are owned by the same companies that run traditional media. Less mainstream web news sources, such as Google, Yahoo, and Drudge, chiefly aggregate traditional political news. One look at them confirms that they produce little, if any, original political news content, drawing instead on standard sources—particularly wire services. Blogs themselves have been reviled as an "echo chamber," Key's term (chapter 4) for content that does not add value. In all cases, new media's news depends on existing supply.

Commerce also pressures new avenues of expression. Banks and retailers—old (Target and Walmart) and new (Amazon and eBay)—own popular websites, and that's not even bringing up other pornographic sites. Tools, like search engines, and opportunities for self expression, such as Facebook and MySpace, are advertising-based. The threat of co-option also menaces formerly open endeavors. Internet users have witnessed price comparison engines mutate into entities that only list their sponsors, for instance. Public input can be a marketing gimmick, following the path set by television's *American Idol*. Should sites offer unlimited feedback opportunities and not censor reports, public input can still be yoked to moving merchandise. While this avenue increases economic efficiency, its political impact is unknown. We do know that more politically relevant producers often screen the input they re-send. Perhaps these efforts promote better discussion; perhaps not. Beyond biased screening, traditional media efforts (like radio call-in shows and citizen news panels), or the braver experiments (embodied in ReelzChannel's *Movie Mob* and G4's and CNBC's webcam commentators) only allow so many "average" speakers. Past that, this type of political speech may commit the citizen to principles they do not endorse. The presence of moderate punching bags on ideologically extreme websites, for example, lends the site legitimacy.

FINANCING?

It has become clear that advertising will not disappear; the alternatives are too impoverished. Books, video games, and movies survive with little direct advertising support. Product placements add to their bottom line, but never exceed a small part of the take. I have trouble imagining how this model would translate to extensive information provision beyond a few quasi-political hits. *Consumer Reports* (web and print) exemplifies a subscription-based ad-free success; they offer a service that people willingly pay for on an extended basis. Certain news organizations, notably Bloomberg, take the same course, regularly supplying information to paid users. The web has also seen hybrid models that divide free from paid offerings to lure subscribers. This technique reaches its peak when producers inundate lookie-loos with ads, and offer to eliminate them for a fee. Beyond lascivious pictures, separating out premium political content is too tough. Donated content, in contrast, merits more interest.

The financing problem is not unique to the web; on the other hand, some Internet models are more promising; not only are they ad-free, but they also encourage balance. Wikipedia—the best—relies on contributions, largely of many individuals' time, and adheres to mainstream news principles. This ethic properly puts it front and center in new media studies. It seems that its setup realizes many characteristics espoused in classic idea marketplace thought, tasking many eyes with scrutinizing content and openly resolving editorial issues. Furthermore, these features produce reasonably high-quality information (see *Nature* 2005) and, more important, offer these details to everyone with access, without charge. So far, its design also has inhibited co-cooptive threats, and maintains an unusually high ratio of producers to consumers. Similar services are taking on more newslike duties, although this approach has not intimidated existing providers in the same way, and its upper bounds are unknown. As it stands, Norma would do well to include this extraordinary Internet resource in her effort insofar as possible.

All financing methods, advertising, pay-once, subscription, and donation, share a politically dangerous potential of specialization. Niche marketing, micro-targeting, and personally tailored marketing all describe the same audience segmentation technique; the idea builds on persuasion research—the lesson that the less diverse the audience is, the easier it is to design appealing messages. Recent reductions in scale have made segmentation a central aspect of all media. Before cable, according to Russell Neuman's 1991 *The Future of the Mass Audience*, ABC, NBC, and CBS aired similar national news shows every night, and roughly a third of the nation's population watched. This mass audience did not splinter randomly; new channels took very specific bites. CNN, the first, appealed to news junkies, and garnered expanding viewership during crises. More specialization followed; the Weather Channel and Financial News Network (now CNBC) accommodate quite specific tastes. Fox News, of course, is the classic segmentation success. Not all that different from CNN, it built a loyal viewership around news with a conservative bent. The Internet promises to shrink the size of profitable pieces further.

Segmentation hits dissent head-on. Changing editorial standards evince segmentation's first impact. Formerly, gatekeepers agreed that certain issues and events qualified as newsworthy, so Norma would receive roughly the same news across channels. New media has transformed editorship, if not eliminating it completely. Just as time-shifting with DVR recording devices makes you a programmer, selecting from an Internet news menu makes you an editor. True, you do not control production, but your "personal" news can vary widely from Norma's. Segmentation effectively means groups pick their own editor. The job remains the same—editors supposedly find out everything to decide what you should see. However, changing standards mean that this filter accommodates individual desires instead of a communal standard. Homogenization also builds in the requirement to cater to these ever-smaller groups. Authoritative television, newspaper, and radio editors once enforced balance, whereas new ones may be rewarded for glossing over less appealing facts. Again, this problem affects media regardless of financing.

In contrast, relying on other search engines (read: Google) may prove to be equally hazardous. A 2005 *Pew Internet and American Life* study found that 62 percent of respondents could not distinguish content from ads, 91 percent had "full confidence" in online searches, and 71 percent thought all web information was "unbiased." Our budding inner scientist would encourage us to examine the internal and externally validity of these results; they should at least make us cautious. First, to the extent that site rankings depend on popularity, they may push users away from dissenting sources (see Jean-Noel Jeanneney's 2006 *Google and the Myth of Universal Knowledge*). The mechanism of searches may also foster those who prey on misplaced trust. Norma may satisfy her informational needs with the supersegmented sources. The worst of these would capitalize on a person's perception that they were delivering the whole story.

A less obvious problem relates to searches themselves. This Achilles' heel parallels content analysis, as both stem from categorizing content. Although web providers compete to rank high on Google's results, Norma's search may not hit the best sites unless her search term is dead-on. To take an example from chapter 4, imagine the difference in results if Norma entered the search terms "partial birth abortion" as opposed to "dilation and extraction" for an Internet search. Yet again, extant studies are insufficient to determine the extent of this problem

A LAST WORD ON WHAT CAN BE DONE

In my optimism, I think beneficial reform needs to focus on three areas. The first involves renewing everyone's commitment to the rules of the democratic game. Here, game theory teaches us not to rely on elite actors' good behavior, but on altering the incentive structure they face. Democratic politics will always require reaching the masses, and the masses can use this leverage. Put bluntly, I would like to see anyone who proudly argues against public opinion loudly booed until the potential usurper can clarify their challenge to the people's will. At least this kind of resistance would reveal the emptiness of some leadership claims. In contrast, I would suggest that for once, we vote en masse for someone who promises to honor sample survey results and to follow public opinion. Deeper political reform would encourage citizens and elites to acknowledge the common end point of building majority coalitions. Because ideologies, parties and special interests will never disappear, this also addresses the audience, who should respect such coalitions and enforce this reverence with calls for fair play and condemnation of sore losers. The audience must also know enough to separate communal regard and bipartisanship from empty rhetoric.

In particular, second, to limit the influence of experts and special interests, every citizen ought to know how polls and their segmented opposition work. I believe this book covers the basics. High schools should teach random sampling and representation in government courses. It would also be enlightening for students to poll their fellow students or other citizens on substantive local issues, and might provide a lesson in democracy whether leaders follow or ignore the results. On a larger scale, polling organizations can and should do more to publicize the reason for their existence. Why not at least explain to respondents how they were selected, and the process that aggregates their judgment? For a slight extra expense they can email respondents the results. Not only would this encourage everyone to respect polls, but it would also make it easier for them to recruit respondents. Old and new media should increase and deepen their public opinion coverage, and live up to their obligation to provide more expansive information on poll results. In other words, existing and future media need to use better methods to uncover the nuances in public opinion by examining all the available questions instead of those produced only by their organization, or none at all.

Third, in this time of change citizens, parties and other interests need to examine the provision of political information. The Internet brings the opportunity to revolutionize politics for good (by making organization and information delivery cheaper) and for bad (via co-option and segmentation). I believe that a sliver of the money flooding into new media should be devoted to increasing the supply of news content, and I applaud Wikipedia and similar efforts. The most promising locus for change lies in heightening public demand and awareness. Though I suspect future Internet users will be less trusting, the Pew results cited above give cause for alarm. Besides basic education, the best way stimulate demand for different viewpoints would be to make "get a second opinion" the new motto for web research. Public campaigns should persuade citizens that they need to view two or more web sites before concluding any search. In this vein, the government should expand political advertising disclosure laws to all media. This small step would make Norma's job easier and enhance the overall quality of information.

Bibliography

Allport, Gordon. (1935) Attitudes in *A Handbook of Social Psychology* Worchester, MA: Clark University Press.

Almond, Gabriel (1950) *The American People and Foreign Policy* New York: Harcourt Brace.

American Psychiatric Association (2000) *Diagnostic and Statistical Manual of Mental Disorders* New York: American Psychiatric Publishing, Inc.

Aristotle (1998) *Politics* Translated by C.D.C Reeve Indianapolis, Indiana: Hackett Publishing Company.

Asimov, Isaac (1955) Franchise, *If: Worlds of Science Fiction* August 1955.

Bagdikianm Ben (2000) *Media Monopoly* Boston, MA: Beacon Press.

Beard, Charles (1933) *The Rise of American Civilization* New York: The Macmillan Company.

Ben Cramer, Richard (1993) *What It Takes* New York: Vintage Press.

Bennett, Lance (2008) *News: The Politics of Illusion* New York: Longman Press.

Berelson, Bernard Paul Lazarsfeld, William McPhee and Hazel Gaudet (1948) *The People's Choice* New York: Colombia University Press.

Berelson, Bernard, Paul Lazarsfeld and Willim McPhee (1954) *Voting* Chicago, IL: University of Chicago Press.

Bishop, George F.; Robert W. Oldendick; Alfred J. Tuchfarber; Stephen E. Ben (1980) Pseudo-Opinions on Public Affairs, *The Public Opinion Quarterly* 44, 198-209.

Blum, John Morton (1985) *Public Philosopher: Selected Letters of Walter Lippmann* New York: Houghton, Mifflin, and Company.

Blumler, Herbert (1948) Public opinion and public opinion polling *American Sociological Review* 13, 542-549.

Bryce, Jame (1903) *The American Commonwealth* New York: The Macmillan Company.

Burke Edmund (1790) *Reflections on the Revolution in France.* London. UK: J. Dodsley.

221

Cain, Bruce, John Ferejohn and Morris Fiorina (1987) *The Personal Vote* Cambridge, MA: Harvard University Press.

Campbell, Angus, Philip E. Converse, Warren E. Miller and Donald E. Stokes (1960) *The American Voter* New York: John Wiley and Sons.

Caplan, Brian (2007) *The Myth of the Rational Voter* Princeton, NJ: Princeton University Press.

Caraley Demetrios (2004) *American Hegemony: Preventive War, Iraq, and Imposing Democracy* New York: The Academy of Political Science.

Chomsky, Noam and Edward S Herman (1988) *Manufacturing Consent*. New York: Pantheon Press.

Clark, Wesley (2003) *Winning Modern Wars: Iraq, Terrorism, and the American Empire* New York: Public Affairs.

Converse, Philip, Aage Clausen, and Warren Miller (1965) Electoral Myth and Reality *American Political Scince Review* 59 352-257.

Converse, Phillip (1964) The nature of belief systems in mass publics In D. E. Apter (Ed.), *Ideology and discontent*, 206-261, London, Free Press of Glencoe. 107-112

Crespi, Irving (1990) *Public Opinion, Polls, and Democracy* Nashville, TN: Westview Press.

De Tocqueville, Alexis (1863*) Democracy in America* Cambridge, MA: Sever and Francis.

Delli Carpini, Michael X. and Scott Keeter (1990) *What Americans Know about Politics* New Haven, CT: Yale University Press.

Demasio, Antonio (1995) *Descartesí Error* New York: Harper Perennial.

Dewey, John (1927) *The Public and its Problems* New York: Henry Holt and Company.

Erickson, Robert and Kent Tedin (2006) *American Public Opinion* New York: Longman.

Fiorina, Morris (1981) *Retrospective Voting in American National Elections* New Haven: Yale University Press.

Gallup, George (1976) *The Sophisticated Poll Watcher's Guide* Princeton NJ: Princeton Opinion Press.

Gallup, George and Saul Rae (1940) *The Pulse of Democracy* New York: Simon and Schuster.

Gans, Herbert (1980) *Deciding What's News* New York: Vintage Press.

Geer, John (1996) *From Tea Leaves to Opinion Polls* New York: Colombia University Press.

Ginsberg, Benjamin (1988) *The Captive Public* New York: Basic Books.

Goffman, Erving (1974) *Frame Analysis* New York: Harper and Row Press.

Goldsteen, Raymond L., Karen Goldsteen, James Swan,. and Wendy Clemenä, (2001) Harry & Louise & Health Care Reform: Romancing Public Opinion. *Journal of Health Politics, Policy and Law* 26 1325-1352.

Graetz, Michael and Ian Shapiro (2005) *Death by a Thousand Cuts* Princeton, NJ: Princeton University Press.

Habermas, Jurgen (1996) *Between Facts and Norms* Cambridge, MA: The MIT Press.

Hayward James (2004) *Myths and Legends of the First World War* Gloucestershire, UK: Sutton Publishing.

Heider, F. (1946). Attitudes and Cognitive Organization *Journal of Psychology* 21.

Held, David (2006) *Models of Democracy* Cambridge, UK: Polity Press.

Herbst, Susan (1995) *Numbered Voices* Chicago, IL: Universtiy of Chicago Press.

Jacobs, Lawrence (2001) Manipulators and Manipulation: Public Opinion in a Representative Democracy *Journal of Health Politics, Policy and Law* 26 1361-1374.

Jacobs, Lawrence and Robert Shapiro (2000) *Politicians Don't Pander* Chicago, IL: University of Chicago Press.

Jennings, Kent and Richard Niemi (1981) *Generations and Politics* Princeton, NJ: Princeton University Press.

Jowett, Garth and Victoria O'Donnell (2006) *Propaganda and Persuasion* Newbury Park, CA: Sage Publications.

Kahneman, Daniel, Amos Tversky and Paul Slovic (1982) *Judgment under Uncertainty* Cambridge, UK: Cambridge University Press.

Key, V. O. (1961) *Public Opinion and American Democracy* New York: John Wiley.

Key, V. O. (1966) *The Responsible Electorate* Cambridge, MA: The Belknap Press.

Lakoff, George (1997) *Moral Politics* Chicago, IL: University of Chicago Press.

Lane, Robert (1952) *Political Ideology* New York: Free Press of Glencoe.

Le Bon, Gustav (1896) *The Crowd* London, UK: Unwin

Lippmann, Walter (1922) *Public Opinion* New York: Harcourt Brace and Company.

Lippman, Walter (1927) *The Phantom Public* New York: The Macmillan Company.

Lustick, Ian (2006) *Trapped in the War on Terror* Philadelphia, PA: University of Pennsylvania Press.

McClellan, Scott (2008) *What Happened?* New York: Public Affairs.

Oskamp, Stuart and P. Wesley Schultz (2005) *Attitudes and Opinions* Mahwah, NJ: Lawrence Erlbaum and Associates.

Page, Benjamin and Robert Shapiro (1992) *The Rational Public* Chicago, IL: University of Chicago Press.

Perloff, Richard (1998) *Political Communication* Mahwah, NJ: Lawrence Erlbaum Assocaites.

Petty, Richard and John Cacioppo (1981) *Attitudes and Persuasion* Boulder, CO: Westview Press.

Phillips, Keven (2004) *American Dynasty* New York: Viking Press.

Pinker, Steven (1997) *How the Mind Works* New York: W. W. Norton and Company.

Plato (1992) *The Republic* Translated by G.M.A. Grube, Revised by C.D.C Reeve Indianapolis, Indiana: Hackett Publishing Company.

Popper, Karl (1971) *The Open Society and Its Enemies* Princeton NJ: Princeton University Press.

Pratkanis, Anthony and Eliot Aronson (2001) *The Age of Propaganda* New York: W. H. Freeman.

Rickover, Hyman (1976) *How the Battleship Maine Was Destroyed* Annapolis, MD: Naval Institute Press.

Ricks, Thomas (2007) *Fiasco* New York: Penguin Publishing.

Rogers, Lindsey (1949) *The Pollsters* New York: Alfred A. Knopf.

Ross, Stewart (2009) *Propaganda for War* Joshua Tree, CA: Progressive Press.

Schuman, Howard and Stanley Presser (1996) *Questions and Answers in Attitude Surveys* Newbury Park, CA: Sage Publications.

Simon, Adam and Jennifer Jerit (2007) Toward a theory relating political discourse, media and public opinion, *Journal of Communication* 57, 254-271.

Steven Kull, Clay Ramsey and Evan Lewis (2003) Misperceptions, the Media, and the Iraq War" *Political Science Quarterly,* 118, 569-598.

Sullivan, John, James Piereson and George Marcus (1978) Ideological Constraint in the Mass Public *American Journal of Political Science* 22, 233-249.

Webb, Eugene, Donald Campbell, Richard Schwartz and Lee Sechrest (1966) *Unobtrusive Measures* Newbury Park, CA: Sage Publications.

West, Darrell, Diane Heith, and Chris Goodwin (1996) Harry and Louise Go to-Washington: Political Advertising and Health Care Reform *Journal of Health Politics, Policy and Law* 21, 35-68.

Westen, Drew (1997) *The Political Brain* New York: Public Affairs.

Young, Michael (1990) *The Classics of Polling* Metuchen, NJ The Scarecrow Press.

Zaller, John (1992) *The Nature and Origins of Mass Opinion* Cambridge, UK: Cambridge University Press.

Index

About the Author

Adam F. Simon is a senior researcher at the Frameworks institute. He received a Political Science Ph.D. in 1997 from UCLA where, among other awards, he was a National Science Foundation Graduate Fellow. He has taught at Yale University and the University of Washington. His first book—*The Winning Message: Candidate Behavior, Campaign Discourse and Democracy*—broke new ground in investigating candidate behavior in American electoral campaigns. His current research focuses on how media interacts with political elites to create and disseminate information affecting citizens' attitudes and actions. This research also emphasizes the role of polls and pollsters. His work has also appeared in the *American Political Science Review* and the *Journal of Communication* as well as other scholarly journals. He is a member of the American Political Science Association and the International Communication Association.